Perspectives on the History of Global Development

Yearbook for the History of Global Development

Perspectives on the History of Global Development

Volume 1

Perspectives on the History of Global Development

Edited by
Corinna R. Unger, Nicholas Ferns, Jack Loveridge, and
Iris Borowy

DE GRUYTER OLDENBOURG

The Yearbook for the History of Global Development is supported by the Center for the History of Global Development, Shanghai University.

ISBN 978-3-11-073516-1
e-ISBN (PDF) 978-3-11-073023-4
e-ISBN (EPUB) 978-3-11-073029-6
ISSN 2702-1327
DOI https://doi.org/10.1515/9783110730234

Library of Congress Control Number: 2022939969

Bibliographic information published by the Deutsche Nationalbibliothek
The Deutsche Nationalbibliothek lists this publication in the Deutsche Nationalbibliografie; detailed bibliographic data are available on the internet at http://dnb.dnb.de.

This book is published with open access at www.degruyter.com.
Cover image: Gettyimages / ipopba
Printing and binding: CPI books GmbH, Leck

www.degruyter.com

Table of Contents

Iris Borowy, Nicholas Ferns, Jack Loveridge, Corinna R. Unger
Introduction — 1

I Development and History (ed. Corinna R. Unger and Nicholas Ferns)

Margherita Zanasi
Globalizing Development: A View from Late Imperial China — 17

Eric Helleiner
Where Did the Idea of International Development Come From? Looking Beyond the Industrialized Core — 37

Dena Freeman
Entangled Histories of "Development," "development," and "Christian development" — 59

Frederick Cooper
Development, Modernization, and the Remaking of an Imperial World Order — 81

Ruth Rempel
Which Speeches Matter? Reflections on the Invention of Development — 103

II Measuring Development (ed. Corinna R. Unger and Jack Loveridge)

Stephen Macekura
The Historiography of Measuring Development — 133

Artemy M. Kalinovsky
Numbers in Space: Measuring Living Standards and Regional Inequality in the Soviet Union — 155

Verena Kröss
Profitability Through Quantification: The World Bank and Rural Development in the 1970s — 183

Rohan D'Souza
Was the Large Dam a "Modern Temple"? Taking Stock of India's Development Tryst with the *Bhakra-Nangal* — 205

III Forum: Alternative Development Indices (ed. Iris Borowy and Corinna R. Unger)

Herman Daly
A Note on the Historical Origins of ISEW-GPI — 229

Hans Diefenbacher
The Origins of the National Welfare Index (NWI) — 235

Karma Ura
GNH-Led Development in Bhutan — 243

Saamah Abdallah
The Happy Planet Index — 251

Nick Cullather
Commentary: The New Epicureans — 259

List of contributors — 269

Iris Borowy, Nicholas Ferns, Jack Loveridge, Corinna R. Unger

Introduction

What Is Development, Why Should We Be Concerned About its History, and Why Is a New Serial Publication Needed?

This is the first volume of the newly established *Yearbook for the History of Global Development* – a serial publication we hope will became a key outlet in this field of research. In an academic world crammed with journals, conference proceedings, websites, and blogs, establishing a new serial publication requires some explanation. As editors, we believe that development is an important subject; that there is a tangible need for more knowledge about the history of development; and that a yearbook is the most appropriate format to publish research on this topic. In the following, we would like to explain why we believe that this is so and how we intend the *Yearbook* to contribute to the future of the field.

What Is Development?

To explain the significance of development may be the most difficult challenge. For a concept that has been as instrumental in shaping worldviews, socioeconomic policies, and the livelihoods of millions of people, the term "development" is remarkably ill-defined. A far from exhaustive overview reveals that existing efforts to arrive at a definition range from the particular to the all-encompassing, from full embrace to passionate rejection of the notion of development. Arguably the most fundamental disagreement among those thinking about the meaning of development is about whether development is an empowering and beneficial phenomenon, or, rather, a destructive and repressive tool. Let us look at this dichotomy in some more detail.

Those who highlight the positive aspects of development, like Hugo Slim, insist that development is "essentially about change: not just any change, but a definite improvement – a change for the better."[1] Mohamed Rabie argues that development "involves the application of certain economic and technical measures to utilize available resources to instigate economic growth and improve people's

1 Hugo Slim, "What is development?," *Development in Practice* 5, no. 2 (1995): 143–148, 143.

https://doi.org/10.1515/9783110730234-001

quality of life."[2] Similarly, the Society for International Development declares its goal to be "a rise in the level and quality of life of the population, and the creation or expansion of local regional income and employment opportunities, without damaging the resources of the environment."[3] Amartya Sen has famously defined development as "freedom," conceived as the capability of individuals to make decisions concerning their own lives, and according to their own values and desires.[4] By contrast, scholars like Arturo Escobar have depicted development as a proto-colonial strategy by industrialized countries to control the Global South.[5] Similarly, Gilbert Rist, while seeking to discredit the very notion of development as an absurd "buzzword," has defined the "essence of development" as "the general transformation and destruction of the natural environment and of social relations in order to increase the production of commodities (goods and services) geared, by means of market exchange, to effective demand."[6]

Interestingly, these contrasting evaluations cut across otherwise very different understandings of what development means. One of the most important disagreements is about whether development should be understood as synonymous with economic growth. Such a view became paradigmatic in many parts of the world in the mid-twentieth century. Although alternative understandings of development gained in strengths and numbers in the last third of the twentieth century and in the early twenty-first century, the idea of development as economic growth is prevalent in many circles still today.[7] Those who do not agree with this view argue that the equation is conceptually flawed. For example, Herman Daly in 1987 argued that "growth is quantitative increase in physical dimensions; development is qualitative improvement in non-physical characteristics. An economy can therefore develop without growing, just as the planet Earth has developed (evolved) without growing."[8] Taking a middle ground, Amartya Sen ar-

---

2 Mohamed Rabie, *A Theory of Sustainable Sociocultural and Economic Development* (New York: Palgrave Macmillan, 2016), 7.

3 Society for International Development, "What is Development," *Issues in Development* (February 17, 2021), accessed February 7, 2022, https://sid-israel.org/en/what-is-development/.

4 Amartya Sen, *Development as Freedom* (New York: Alfred A. Knopf, 1999).

5 Arturo Escobar, *Encountering Development: The Making and Unmaking of the Third World* (Princeton: Princeton University Press, 1995).

6 Gilbert Rist, "Development as a Buzzword," *Development in Practice* 17, no. 4–5 (2007): 485–491, 488. See also Gilbert Rist, *The History of Development: From Western Origins to Global Faith* (New York: Zed Books, 2010[3]).

7 Society for International Development, "What is Development."

8 Herman Daly, "The Economic Growth Debate: What Some Economists Have Learned But Many Have Not," *Journal of Environmental Economics and Management* 14 (1987): 323–336.

gued a decade later that development and economic growth were neither independent of each other nor identical: according to Sen, a certain level of economic productivity was necessary to satisfy human needs. However, it was only in combination with the elements of distribution and freedom that economic output could be translated into developmental wellbeing.[9]

Another disagreement among those debating development focuses on who is, or should be, the target of development. One group regards development as being directed at low-income countries in the Global South with the intention of levelling or fully overcoming existing inequalities, be they economic, cultural, or political in nature. In this view, development appears as "a comprehensive societal process to move the underdeveloped nations from their state of economic backwardness and slow sociocultural change to a dynamic state characterized by sustained economic growth and sociocultural and political transformation that improved the quality of life of all members of society."[10] Contrastingly, a second group considers the focus of development on the real or perceived poor as ruinous. One of its representatives, Gustavo Esteva, argues that "by 1980, it was already clear that there was no correlation between aid and economic growth, and that aid was an obstacle for social transformation."[11] Such a position implies the belief that development in the form of development assistance does more harm than good, and that it presents an uncalled-for intervention that can have unforeseen, often highly problematic, consequences. Thirty years before Esteva made his argument, Gro Harlem Brundtland, then Chair of the World Commission on Environment and Development, had already contested this view, seeing it as unjustifiably narrow and limited "along the lines of 'what poor nations should do to become richer'," and therefore all too easily dismissed as being of concern only to "those involved in questions of 'development assistance'." Instead, she suggested development was "what we all do in attempting to improve our lot."[12]

---

9 Amartya Sen, "The Concept of Development," in *Handbook of Development Economics*, ed. H. Chenery and T. N. Srinivasan, volume L (Amsterdam: Elsevier Science Publishers, 1988), 9–26.
10 Rabie, *A Theory of Sustainable Sociocultural and Economic Development*, 8.
11 Gustavo Esteva, "What is Development?," *Oxford Research Encyclopedia of International Studies* (2018; 2010), accessed May 23, 2022, https://doi.org/10.1093/acrefore/9780190846626.013.360.
12 Gro Harlem Brundtland, "Foreword to World Commission on Environment and Development," in *A Mandate for Change: Key Issues, Strategy and Workplan*, ed. World Commission for Environment and Development (Geneva: World Commission for Environment and Development, 1985), xi.

This brings us back to the question what development is. In his discussion, Hugo Slim pays equal attention to what development is as to what it is not. He insists that development is a lot more than "a matter of economics and economic growth," and that it is not only a "Third world problem but presents a goal for all societies."[13] This discrepancy of whether development is about North-South relations, characterized by asymmetric power relations, or about a challenge and desire shared by all people around the world, is also reflected in disagreements about when development became established as a policy field. Critics like Esteva argue that development started in 1949, "born in the context of the Cold War."[14] This view has come under attack in recent years, as scholars have highlighted the much longer, multicentered history of developmental interventions.

The variety of views derives not only from different opinions but also from the fact that some authors focus on what development should be while others describe the – inevitably much less impressive – existing forms of development, with all the flaws associated with real life. Some authors reflect on this difference in levels of analysis.[15] Others do not. And still others do not even attempt to provide a definition. Nico Schrijver, author of a book on the supposedly positive effect of UN developmental activities, *Development without Destruction*, finds it "appropriate to briefly present a number of basic concepts and principles that will be regularly referred to and further elaborated in the following chapters" but sees no need to include "development" in this list of basic concepts.[16] Meanwhile, Alexandra Brandl argues that there is no point in presenting a definition since, in her view, there is no such thing. Hence, she states, "those overlapping and diverging perceptions of what we mean with development ultimately lead to the understanding that the notion of development can only be interpreted from a certain standpoint rather than pinned down to one precise and at the same time comprehensive definition."[17] Ian Goldin and Kenneth Reinert seem to agree. In a volume called *Globalization for Development*, they point out that understandings have changed over time in "what is meant by 'development'."[18] They also ob-

13 Slim, "What is Development?," 143.
14 Esteva, "What is Development?".
15 Slim, "What is Development?," 143.
16 Nico Schrijver, *Development without Destruction: The UN and Global Resource Management* (Bloomington: Indiana University Press, 2010), 2.
17 Alexandra Brandl, "A Critical Examination of the Notion of 'Development' From a Political Ecology Standpoint," DEVP0020 CGWW7, December 2018, accessed November 15, 2021, https://www.researchgate.net/publication/331248924_A_critical_examination_of_the_notion_of_%27development%27_from_a_Political_Ecology_standpoint.
18 Ian Goldin and Kenneth Reinert, *Globalization for Development* (Washington, D.C., and Houndsmill: World Bank and Palgrave Macmillan, 2007), 15.

serve a "better appreciation than in the past of the roles of institutions, history, the public sector, and human welfare in development processes." In their view, this understanding presents a "middle ground," a degree of common understanding that nevertheless leaves "intellectual room for multiple, successful routes to development."[19]

As these and similar statements suggest, development can mean a variety of things, depending on perspective and interests. It is this ambiguity that, in our view, makes it important to study the history of development. We believe that a historical account of what different actors have meant when they talked about development (or used one of its many synonyms) and how they translated their ideas into practice can help us understand how individuals and societies have perceived socio-economic challenges and how they have approached them. Thus, studying the history of development can provide insight into how societies perceived themselves, into their fears and worries, goals, and visions. Rather than focusing on a specific world region, we aim to encourage a genuinely global perspective that allows us to compare situations and phenomena, and to discover connections as well as ruptures.

Why History?

1 Visions of development have been the driving force behind much of human history

In an article that otherwise focuses on the social sciences, Immanuel Wallerstein argued that "A case can be made for the assertion that the concept of development is not merely one of the central components of the ideology both of western civilization and of world social science but is in fact the central organizing concept around which all else is hinged."[20] Arguably, the hope to improve one's lot has been the overriding motivation underlying virtually all human history, ever since early humans invented the wheel. And even if the claim of development as the basis for practically everything may go a little far, there can be no doubt that the idea of development, however conceived, has provided a powerful driver for decisions and action at the private, local, national, regional, international, and global levels for at least the last 70 years and probably much longer. Countless

19 Goldin and Reinert, *Globalization*, 41–42.

20 Immanuel Wallerstein, "The Development of the Concept of Development," *Sociological Theory* 2 (1984): 102–116, 102.

projects conducted in the interest of some idea of development have left their marks on the world as it exists today.

In many cases this is true in a literal sense, as development efforts have physically shaped the face of the Earth. For thousands of years, humans have transformed land, mainly through agriculture, and the scale and speed at which they have done so has increased substantially in the last centuries.[21] The expansive canal systems of China and England (and elsewhere) were built to accommodate transportation needs at times of economic and demographic expansion; they had a decisive impact on the history of these countries – or, at least, of some of their regions – and still structure present-day landscapes.[22] River rectification projects carried out in the nineteenth and twentieth centuries drastically changed trade possibilities, flood risks, housing, and landscape patterns.[23]

The use of wood for construction and heating has led to the deforestation of some areas and to the planting of timber plantations in others.[24] Other forests were eliminated in order to make room for different forms of land use. Between 1700 and 2018, the world lost roughly one third of its forest, mainly to agriculture, which now covers approximately half of all habitable land.[25] Dams have created artificial lakes, drowned settlements, and displaced millions of people – while providing a large part of the world population with electricity for their socio-economic activities.[26] Mining of mineral and other resources has been practiced for thousands of years but intensified after industrialization increased the need for metals and fossil fuels. In many places across the world, it has led to the removal of vegetation, changes in earth reliefs, pollution, increased erosion, and increased soil and rock instability. According to one observer, "[m]

21 Erle C. Ellis et al., "Used Planet: A Global History," *Proceedings of the National Academy of Sciences* 110, no. 20 (2013): 7978–7985, 7984.

22 Robert Ayres, *The History and Future of Technology* (Cham: Springer, 2021), 125–144; Robert Marks, *China: Its Environment and History* (Lanham: Rowman & Littlefield, 2012), 86–89, 119–121, 209.

23 David Blackbourn, *The Conquest of Nature: Water, Landscape, and the Making of Modern Germany* (New York: W.W. Norton & Company, 2016); Francesco Comiti, "How Natural Are Alpine Mountain Rivers? Evidence from the Italian Alps," *Earth Surface Processes and Landforms* 37, no. 7 (2012): 693–707.

24 Brett Bennett, *Plantations and Protected Areas: A Global History of Forest Management* (Cambridge, Mass.: MIT Press, 2015).

25 Hannah Ritchie and Max Roser, "Forests and Deforestation," *Our World in Data* (2021), accessed March 3, 2022, https://ourworldindata.org/forests-and-deforestation.

26 John R. McNeill, *Something New Under the Sun: An Environmental History of the Twentieth Century* (New York: W.W. Norton, 2000), 157–182.

ining and ore processing are amongst the most important impetus of human development and are regarded as the second worst global polluters today."[27]

These extractive processes, which have drawn on nature as an allegedly infinite "resource," have allowed a growing number of people to enjoy higher living standards and lives made comfortable through various consumer goods. But the way these processes played out has inevitably been shaped by unequal power relations. The destructive effects of extraction activities on the natural environment have disproportionately been borne by those without the possibility to protest or to be listened to. This has been most pronounced in (though not limited to) societies under authoritarian rule. For example, under Soviet auspices, intensive irrigation agriculture in Central Asia resulted in the near disappearance of what once was the fourth largest lake on Earth, the Aral Sea.[28] In China, efforts to jump-start industrialization during the Great Leap Forward (1958–1962) left many mountainous regions deforested, especially in the Northwest of the country, where approximately one third of the forests are believed to have disappeared.[29] Globally, colonial rule served as a driver of interventions into the natural environment. In the French colony of New Caledonia, the discovery of large reservoirs of oxidized nickel (used for constructing airplanes and to generate nuclear power) led to the movement of half a billion tons of rock to mine 100 million tons of ore between 1890 and 1990. The process involved the beheading of mountains, leaving some regions irreversibly changed.[30] Investments in industrialization resulted in the widespread creation of monoculture plantations producing cotton and rubber.[31] Collectively, these and many similar developments efforts have shaped today's world in a profound sense. As people, governments, and corporations around the world have manipulated the natural world in pursuit of energy, raw materials, and labor, the physical landscapes around the world have come to bear witness of development visions. In a less visible but

---

27 Gorazd Žibret et al., "Impacts of mining and smelting activities on environment and landscape degradation-Slovenian case studies," *Land Degradation and Development* 29 (2018): 4457–4470. The ranking was defined as health effects, based on disability-adjusted life years, established by a joint report of Green Cross Switzerland and Pure Earth, published in 2016. See http://worstpolluted.org/, accessed March 3, 2022.

28 S. W. Breckle and G. V. Geldyeva, "Dynamics of the Aral Sea in Geological and Historical Times," in Siegmar W. Breckle et al., eds., *Aralkum – a Man-Made Desert: The Desiccated Floor of the Aral Sea (Central Asia).* Theme issue of *Ecological Studies* 218 (2012): 13–35.

29 Xun Zhou, *Forgotten Voices of Mao's Great Famine, 1958–1962* (New Haven: Yale University Press, 2013), 106.

30 McNeill, *Something New under the Sun*, 31–32.

31 Sven Beckert, *King Cotton: A Global History* (New York: Alfred Knopf, 2014); Stephen Harp, *A World History of Rubber* (Chichester: John Wiley & Sons, 2016).

no less profound way, understandings of development have shaped past and current theories of how the world, past and present, functions.

2 The perceived history of development forms a core component of present world views and the policy decisions that are made in their name

Past developmental decisions have not only affected the state of the world in a direct way through the material manifestations of their results. They have also indirectly (though no less profoundly) influenced international relations by shaping the world views and theories that, in turn, have informed political and economic decisions. Arguably most major ideologies are based, at least in part, on theories formed from perceived developmental patterns. Marxism is firmly based on the belief in a pattern of stages through which all societies will develop as a historical rule. This concept, drawn from a combination of historical observations and predictions into the future, has served both to explain the world and to justify far-reaching political decisions, many of them geared at accelerating the expected pattern of development.[32] It was in explicit response to this theory that Walt Rostow presented his theory of five stages of economic growth in 1960. He argued that societies could be made to jump developmental scales through a combination of financial, technical, and political support from abroad, and that sooner or later all countries would arrive at the supposedly highest stage, liberal capitalism.[33] Collectively, these ideas about how socio-economic transformations would and should take place corresponded to and underwrote political worldviews, which competed with each other in the context of the Cold War. While the Cold War is over, political divisions remain in place, and competing ideas of capitalism, socialism, hybrid and alternative forms, together with their respective interpretations of the past and imaginaries of the future, continue to influence political decisions, alliances, and conflicts until today.

Such diverging interpretations of history and its role for the future have also shaped the various concepts of development that exist today. The usefulness of a historical perspective becomes evident when considering writing on the nature of development. In several publications Amartya Sen outlined his idea that fam-

---

32 B. N. Ghosh, "Karl Marx on Development and Underdevelopment," *Indian Economic Journal* 40, no. 4 (1993): 13–23.

33 Walt W. *Rostow, The Stages of Economic Growth: A Non-Communist Manifesto* (Cambridge: Cambridge University Press, 1960).

ines do not occur in democracies.[34] When critiquing Amartya Sen's seminal 1999 book *Development as Freedom*, Denis O. Hearn pointed out that this argument overlooks famines that were brought about by colonial rule, which Mike Davis depicted so powerfully in his *Late Victorian Holocausts*.[35] Admittedly, this perspective, in turn, overlooks the fact that late nineteenth century Britain can hardly be considered a genuine democracy with an open exchange of information and opinions. Similarly, Gilbert Rist's assertion that development destroyed human relations because "[w]hat used to be freely exchanged within the family circle or among neighbours has been progressively converted into paid employment [...] expensive day nurseries have replaced grandparents in looking after small children" betrays a romantic vision of an unspecified past untouched by slavery, wet nurses, early death, and abandoned children, all of which were common during much of human history.[36]

In short, in as much as any theory is a systematization of perceived historical patterns, all discussion of theory requires a critical historical analysis. Just as the analysis of Rostow's modernization theory informs historical understandings of Western developmentalism in the Cold War era, studying it as a response to Marx's stages of capitalist development reveals the historical evolution of development theory. Similarly, more recent theoretical approaches in development, such as the basic needs, concept have their roots in responses to perceived flaws in modernization theory. This evolution has a history of its own, and understanding this history is vital to the analysis of contemporary development theory.

3 Many of the central challenges of the future are developmental in nature

Challenges deriving from developmental decisions and path dependencies of the past can involve potential threats to human life support systems. Climate change, the result of dramatic increases in fossil fuel use over the last decades, will doubtlessly affect generations of people and other living beings far into the future. Covid-19 has dramatically demonstrated the destructive power of pan-

---

34 Amartya Sen, *Poverty and Famines: An Essay on Entitlement and Depravation* (Oxford: Clarendon Press, 1982).

35 Denis O'Hearn, "Amartya Sen's Development as Freedom: Ten Years Later," *Policy & Practice* 8 (2009): 9–15, 13; Mike Davis, *Late Victorian Holocausts: El Niño Famines and the Making of the Third World* (London: Verso, 2001).

36 Rist, "Development as a Buzzword," 489.

demics, causing not only large numbers of deaths but also enormous economic damage and substantial social disruption. The emergence of pandemics is fuelled by rapid population growth, urbanization, the encroachment of human settlements into formerly remote natural environments, climate change, increasing global mobility, civil conflict, unequal access to education and healthcare, and the fast spread of information, disinformation, and rumors. Together, all of these factors contribute to making pandemic outbreaks more probable and dangerous than in the past.[37]

Ignoring the histories of these processes comes at a cost. Historical analysis offers insight into contemporary developmental challenges that can assist in finding sustainable solutions. This ambition is not new. Already in 2009, Harvard economist Nathan Nunn ended a review of historically informed development literature with the conclusion that "history matters."[38] More recently, the editors of a volume on *International Development* made clear that they hope for their "work to be of practical and not solely of intellectual use."[39] Ultimately, it is difficult to conceive of any study addressing questions of development that does so without reference to past events, ideas, or policies. We believe that a dedicated yearbook on these topics can help to bring the different approaches and findings together in fruitful ways.

Why a New Serial Publication?

The history of development is no longer an exotic topic in the historical profession. The growing establishment of the field is mirrored in the publication of a range of books and overviews in recent years.[40] The increasing interest in devel-

37 Meera Senthilingam, "Seven reasons we're at more risk than ever of a global pandemic," *CNN*, April 10, 2017, accessed March 3, 2022, https://edition.cnn.com/2017/04/03/health/pandemic-risk-virus-bacteria/index.html.

38 Nathan Nunn, "The Importance of History for Economic Development," *Annual Review of Economics* 1 (2009): 65–92, 88.

39 Bruce Currie-Alder et al., eds., *International Development: Ideas, Experience and Prospects* (Oxford: Oxford University Press 2014), xii.

40 For instance: Marc Frey, Sönke Kunkel, and Corinna R. Unger, eds., *International Organizations and Development, 1945–1990* (Basingstoke: Palgrave Macmillan, 2014); Iris Borowy, *Defining Sustainable Development for Our Common Future: A History of the World Commission on Environment and Development (Brundtland Commission)* (Abingdon: Routledge, 2014); Stephen Macekura, *Of Limits and Growth: The Rise of Global Sustainable Development in the Twentieth Century* (New York: Cambridge University Press, 2015); Corinna R. Unger, *International Development: A Postwar History* (London: Bloomsbury Academic, 2018); David C. Engerman, *The Price of*

opment as a historical topic is also evident from the number of related international conferences. Although there is, at present, no association specifically dedicated to the history of development that would host conferences at regular intervals, this has not prevented scholars from organizing meetings in a variety of contexts.

That said, a serial publication dedicated to the history of development does not exist thus far. This is noteworthy since there are at least 40 journals dedicated to "development," mostly addressing concepts and/or policies related to actual or desired changes in socio-economic conditions around the world, usually with a focus on the Global South. Clearly, there was – and still is – ample research space given to questions related to the intertwined challenges of improving living conditions in many parts of the world, of mitigating distributional imbalances, and of safeguarding environmental life support systems. Given that all present global developmental problems are rooted in their historical origins, this lack of historical perspective seems bewildering. The *Yearbook for the History of Global Development* (YHGD) seeks to fill this gap.

The *Yearbook* aims at providing a forum that emphasizes the interconnected nature of past and present development challenges and development approaches. The purpose of the *Yearbook* is to offer a space for the presentation of research on the history of concepts, theories, practices, and experiences concerning development policies in the past that continue to shape present-day attitudes and beliefs. In doing so, it aims at providing an academic home for scholars working on multiple dimensions of a field that is, at present, fragmented but at the same time united by an interest in the core question of how people, institutions, and agencies in the past have envisaged how societies should change and how they have acted on those ideas.

Thus, we hope that the YHGD will help overcome the fragmentation that is clearly detrimental to a deeper understanding of developmental thinking and actions. Colonial policies and development aid programs did not emerge independently of larger ideas regarding how industrialized countries – and, eventually, the world at large – would or should evolve. Similarly, present-day debates about sustainable development and (de-)growth are profoundly shaped by ideas about past and present North-South relations, among others. It is our hope that the *Yearbook* will serve as a forum for debate between different interpretations of development while also revealing connections and interactions that

---

Aid: The Economic Cold War in India (Cambridge, Mass.: Harvard University Press, 2018); Sara Lorenzini, *Global Development: A Cold War History* (Princeton: Princeton University Press, 2019); Corinna R. Unger, Iris Borowy, and Corinne A. Pernet, eds., *Routledge Handbook on the History of Development* (Abingdon: Routledge, 2022).

would otherwise remain hidden. In the long term, the *Yearbook* aims at increasing the impact of the scholarly literature on the history of development around the world.

In addition to serving an academic discipline, one explicit aim of the *Yearbook* is to strengthen the voice of historians in larger societal debates about possible and adequate responses to twenty-first challenges. These challenges include environmental and economic issues but also questions of global inequality and of relations between industrialized (or post-industrial) countries (among them the former colonial powers), today's low-income countries (almost all former colonies), and the growing group of countries of so-called emerging economies. The relations and conflicts between these countries and regions all have a past, and informed debates about future policies require a sound understanding of their historical bases. This, in turn, requires a comprehensive view on development as a multitude of intertwined past concepts and practices.

Within this general framework, the *Yearbook* aims at addressing the following topics in particular, but not exclusively:

- Actors of development, including national governments, international and regional organizations, social movements, individuals, non-governmental organizations, and others;
- Concepts of development, including modernization theory, capitalism, communism, basic needs, development as freedom, sustainable development, degrowth, post-development, etc., and the ways in which these concepts have changed through adaptation to evolving circumstances or new ideas, through hybridization and/or through selective adoption;
- Practices of development, including industrialization, agricultural improvement and intensification, the construction of infrastructure development assistance programs, grassroots efforts, etc.;
- The role of knowledge in development debates, including the role of different types of science and technology, and the transregional, transimperial, and transnational circulation and adaptation of different forms of knowledge;
- The underlying norms and values of developmental thinking, including perceived prosperity, justice, equality, freedom, democracy, happiness, or lack thereof, gender norms, languages, and ethnic and "racial" categories;
- Seeming winners and losers of developmental processes, unequal access to developmental resources and promises, unexpected or unintended side-effects of development projects, and the use of coercive and violent practices in the name of development as well as trade-offs between different, potentially contradictory effects on different groups, or the same groups at different times.

While the *Yearbook's* key discipline is history, contributions from neighboring disciplines are also relevant. These include sociology, anthropology, area studies, political economy, cultural studies, public health, science and technology studies, and economics, among others. Within history, pertinent sub-disciplines include the history of science and technology, colonial, medical, diplomatic, economic, social, global, and cultural history.

As editors, we hope to attract a large number of readers from across the globe and from different backgrounds. By making all volumes available in open-access format, we try to overcome structural inequalities that continue to characterize international academic debate. We invite scholars interested in publishing their work in the *Yearbook* to contact us directly. Furthermore, we encourage colleagues to suggest edited volumes on a given theme in the history of development.

Outline of the First Volume

The first volume of the *Yearbook* consists of three parts: one on "Development and History"; one on "Measuring Development"; and a "Forum on Alternative Development Indices." The rationale is to bring together pieces that reflect the current state of the art in the field, broadly understood, and to highlight some of the themes on which fresh research is currently being carried out.

The section on "Development and History" is dedicated to key questions concerning the history of development: What is development, what has it been in the past, and what can historians learn from studying the history of development? How has the field of the history of development evolved over time, and where should it be going in the future? We have asked a set of renowned experts on the history (or histories) of development to address these questions through the lenses of their respective specializations, from Asian, African, and Latin American history to the history of ideas to the history of religion to the history of colonialism and decolonization.

The section on "Measuring Development" speaks to the interest among historians in the ways in which the concept of development emerged and how it was turned into a quantifiable entity. The last ten years or so have seen a notable growth in the study of quantification and economic thinking. Our section builds on this work and goes beyond it by incorporating different time periods and different organizations and regions than those covered by existing literature. The articles in this section feature Soviet planners, Indian development experts, World Bank staff, and historians of development.

The forum on Alternative Development Indices gives voice to some of those actors who, as scholars and activists, were or are involved in thinking about ways of assessing development in terms other than economic growth. There has been a growing interest in the reactions to the perceived crisis of development that took the floor in the 1970s and 1980s and has stayed with us ever since. Concepts like the Human Development Index have become fully established and institutionalized, while other indices have remained outside the mainstream but have developed a momentum of their own, especially with the growing interest in post-development studies. We consider this forum both a historiographical contribution and as a way of bringing in the experiences of practitioners, and thus as an opportunity to encourage conversations across professional divides.

In closing, we would like to thank our colleagues who have supported our project of establishing this new yearbook in many ways. Rabea Rittgerodt from Oldenbourg De Gruyter took on the project and encouraged us to pursue it. She has been immensely supportive in finding solutions to questions from open access publishing to the more mundane tasks associated with a new serial publication, and we thank her wholeheartedly for all her work and her good humor along the way. Many of our colleagues agreed to serve on the Editorial Board of our yearbook and provided inspiration and suggestions. We thank them kindly for their commitment and their intellectual contributions. Furthermore, we would like to express our gratitude to Shanghai University for generous financial support. Bas Rensen took excellent care of many organizational tasks and helped us to meet the production deadlines; many thanks for that. Last but not least, we are tremendously grateful to all our colleagues who accepted our invitation to write articles for a yearbook they had never heard about, and who were willing to establish it by sharing their expertise and investing their time. And we thank our external reviewers for their valuable comments and suggestions on the articles of the first volume, which, we hope, will inspire interesting conversations and help create new connections across the globe.

I Development and History (ed. Corinna R. Unger and Nicholas Ferns)

Margherita Zanasi

Globalizing Development: A View from Late Imperial China

In recent decades, the history of economic modernization has increasingly moved away from the idea of a Western center serving as a universal model of modernity from which modernization projects were exported to mostly passive and "backward" recipients who had little to offer to the development efforts of their country.[1] Historians have instead shifted their focus toward the space of interaction among the diverse participants and objectives involved in specific development projects and the hybrid forms of economic modernization these encounters generated. While these new historiographical trends have effectively decentralized the history of development and greatly eroded its original Western-centrism, they have not challenged the assumption of the exceptionality of the Europe of the Enlightenment and its unique ability to produce "modern" economic ideas and policies. Even in the post-World War Two period, when the United States took the leadership in international development and after developing countries began to take over their own development projects, the ever-evolving theories of modernization and development continued to derive from a vaguely defined liberalism inspired by an elastic and creative reading of European thinkers such as Adam Smith. As Dipesh Chakrabarti observes, still today, it is impossible to think of modernity "without invoking certain categories and concepts, the genealogies of which go deep into the intellectual and even theological traditions of Europe." Although largely an ideological construct, it is this "genealogy of thought in which social scientists find themselves inserted."[2] Going beyond the realm of the political discourse—Chakrabarti's focus—this European-centered "genealogy of thought" also informed the study of development. The Western narratives, invested with an authoritative aura of scientific modernity, confined to the realm of the "traditional" (i. e., supposedly lacking pragmatism and scientific method) economic notions and practices that did not conform to its language and conceptual framework while using Western categories—often

---

1 This article is primarily based on my book: Margherita Zanasi, *Economic Thought in Modern China: Market and Consumption 1500s to 1937* (Cambridge: Cambridge University Press, 2020); and my article: Margherita Zanasi, "Frugality and Luxury: Morality, Market, and Consumption in Late Imperial China," *Frontiers of History in China* 10, no. 3 (2015): 457–485.

2 Dipesh Chakrabarty, *Provincializing Europe: Postcolonial Thought and Historical Difference* (Princeton: Princeton University Press, 2008), 4–5.

https://doi.org/10.1515/9783110730234-002

inadequately representing local conditions—to reconceptualize the local to fit Western blueprints of modernization.[3]

In this article, I step outside this Western-centered "genealogy of thought" to explore the emergence of ideas of economic development within a different regional, historical, and conceptual context. More specifically, I focus on the writings of Chinese officials and intellectuals in the late eighteenth and early nineteenth centuries—before the Opium War (1839–1842) opened the door to Western imperialism and economic theories—to examine how they independently devised developmental policies which often shared basic themes with Western developmentalism. These Chinese writers focused on solving an economic crisis that was to plague China through the fall of the empire (1911), the Republican period (1912–1949), and the early decades of the People's Republic (PRC). It was at this time that unprecedented growth in population, declining agricultural production, and a massive outflow of silver—a dramatic shift from the previous inflow that had fueled China's commercial growth—brought to an end the dazzling prosperity that had characterized the first century and half of the Qing dynasty (1644–1911).[4] Shocked by this sharp economic reversal, Chinese scholars and officials tried to determine the cause of the crisis and to devise strategies to solve it. Believing the nature of this crisis to be unprecedented, they developed innovative economic plans that departed from previous policies, foreshadowing the Republican developmental state in four main ways.[5] They sought economic growth as a strategy for fighting scarcity and lifting the population of the empire out of poverty. In general, standards of living for the population of the empire were not defined in quantitative terms but were expressed in a descriptive manner. The often used formula of *anju leye* (live peacefully and work happily), in fact, described a situation of social stability in which the state ensured subsistence and a peaceful environment for productive citizens. It was only with the arrival of Western social sciences in the early nineteenth century that Chinese officials and reformers began to embrace "social surveys" and use

---

3 For a discussion of how the language of development led to the obliteration of the local past, see Jonathan Crush, "Introduction: Imagining Development," in *Power of Development*, ed. Jonathan Crush (London: Routledge, 2005, 1995[1]), 1–23; Emery M. Roe, "Development Narratives, or Making the Best of Blueprint Development," *World Development* 19, no. 4 (1991): 287–300.

4 For a discussion of the economic crisis that began at the turn of the nineteenth century, see Richard von Glahn, *The Economic History of China from Antiquity to the Nineteenth Century* (Cambridge: Cambridge University Press, 2016), 348–399.

5 For a discussion of the Republican Developmental State, see William C. Kirby, "Engineering China: Birth of the Developmental State, 1928–1937," in *Becoming Chinese: Passages to Modernity and Beyond*, ed. Wen-hsin Yeh (Berkeley: University of California Press, 2000), 137–160.

new enumerative modalities (such as census), replacing the methodology of evidential and practical studies.[6] This does not mean, however, that the Qing government did not make an effort to collect data. Especially between the early 1740s and early 1850s—when the scarcity crisis began to be felt—it regularly collected data on population and availability of basic staples as well as on the situation of the granary system.[7] Although these data presented several problems, from miscalculation and inaccurate categorization to over or under reporting, they testify to the Qing's commitment to its *minsheng* mandate. In its fight against economic scarcity, the Qing state also introduced the notion of state planning (*ji*) aimed at channeling economic growth in support of state objectives. It also explored new forms of institutional changes in the effort to expand the implementation capacity of the state and, finally, to mobilize the private economy in support of state goals.

By stepping out of Western-centered narratives, I want to contribute to blurring the lines between Western economic modernity and "traditional" local economic thought and policies. As discussed in more details in the first part of this article, the Chinese terminology and conceptual framework—based on the mandate of good government summarized in the trope of *minsheng* (People's Livelihood)—allowed for the formulation of development strategies often very similar to those devised in the West, such as a sophisticated understanding of the market and the need for capital accumulation for economic growth. On the other hand, however, local circumstances and objectives led to reliance on state leadership, departing from the Western liberal capitalist model. This article, therefore, challenges the narrative of the West as the unique source of innovation in an otherwise unchanging global landscape. It, in fact, traces back to the pre-Opium War period the roots of an independent developmental thought which continued to influence state policies through the 1940s and reemerged to some extent in the post-1980 PRC.

The second part of this article focuses on Chinese officials' and intellectuals' reception of Western economic theories in the post-Opium War period. At this time, the Chinese discourse on development came to be gradually re-articulated through Western terminology and the conceptual framework of liberal capitalism. Chinese officials and intellectuals, however, continued to uphold most of the development strategies formulated before the Opium War because, they ar-

6 Tong Lam, *A Passion for Facts: Social Surveys and the Construction of the Chinese Nation-State, 1900–1949* (California: University of California Press, 2011).

7 Pierre-Étienne Will, "Statistical Difficulties and Accounting Methods," in *Nourish the People: The State Civilian Granary System in China, 1650–1850*, ed. Pierre-Etienne Will and Bin R. Wong (Ann Arbor: University of Michigan Center for Chinese Studies, 2020), 233–234.

gued, the Western blueprints for economic modernization did not reflect China's conditions and needs. Finally, the third section argues that the late-Qing developmental ideas consolidated into the Nanjing developmental state (1927–1937) established by the Nationalist Party.

Economic Scarcity and the Mandate of *Minsheng*

Starting in the late eighteenth century, most Qing scholars and officials reached the conclusion that the main cause of the new economic crisis was the unprecedented fast pace of population growth. As renowned scholar and official Hong Liangji (1746–1809) explained, because production grew on a mathematical scale, while population grew geometrically, the gap between the two could not be bridged. For this reason, China faced a future of economic scarcity (*buzu*), chronic poverty, and, consequently, popular discontent and social instability.[8] Hong's bleak view pointed to a systemic crisis rather than one of the many situations of scarcity experienced in the past as the result of failed crops due to droughts, floods, pest invasions, or inclement weather. In those situations, a bounty crop in the following year could bring the empire back to economic stability. The nature of the current crisis, however, was dramatically different. As Emperor Jiaqing (r. 1796–1820) remarked in 1806, according to the Ministry of Revenue, the population of the empire had increased from the previous year by 27,720,119 people, while the total amount of grains harvested and stored had decreased by 294,248 *dan:* "Even if crops were to be good, the people stored plenty of grain, and no natural disaster occurred, food supplies would still be insufficient because of the fast pace of population growth."[9] This scarcity crisis, therefore, was of an unprecedented nature. It could not be resolved with the usual strategies but required unprecedented measures. Foreseeing the coming crisis in the late-1700s, a shocked Qianlong Emperor (r. 1736–1796) declared that the usual policies for solving situations of economic scarcity—land reclamation, tax breaks, and maintenance of flood prevention and agricultural irrigation —would in the future not be enough to support the livelihood of the people.[10]

---

8 Hu Jichuang, *Zhongguo jingji sixiangshi* vol. 2 (Shanghai: Shanghai caijing daxue chubanshe, 1998), 564–566 and 619–620; and Zhao Jing, *Zhongguo gudai jingji sixiangshi jianghua* (Beijing: Renmin chubanshe: Xinhua shudian faxing, 1986), 618.
9 "Renzong Shilu (August 15, 1806)," in *Qingshilu* (Beijing: Zhongguo shuju, 1985), Vol. 30, juan 172, 242–243.
10 "Gaozong Shilu (November 10, 1735)," in *Qingshilu* (Beijing: Zhongguo shuhua, 1985), Vol. 9 juan 3, 194–196.

The crisis struck at the very core of the Qing's mandate of *minsheng* (People's Livelihood), i.e., ensuring subsistence for the population of the empire. Deeply rooted in China's philosophical tradition and supported by most schools of thought, *minsheng* was not just a rhetorical trope aimed at bolstering a dynasty's political legitimacy. It was also a practical strategy for political and fiscal stability aptly expressed by the Qing state with the formula of *guoji minsheng* (State Finances and People's Livelihood). The Qing rulers believed that a hungry population tended to stage uprisings and rebellions, challenging the stability of the empire. An economy of scarcity would also imperil the smooth collection of taxes, jeopardizing the fiscal stability of the state.[11] According to historian Jane Kate Leonard, the Qing rulers' intention in promoting prosperity in the private economy "went to the very heart of Qing strategic views of empire and the intimate connection between economic and strategic power."[12]

Faced with the unprecedented challenge to the stability of the empire posed by the new economic crisis, scholars and officials began to argue in favor of state planning to expand agricultural production in an attempt to meet the needs of the growing population. In an imperial lecture, scholar and official Ren Qiyun (1670–1744) argued that the only solution to the current crisis was for the state to engage in "long-term planning" (*jingjiu zhi ji*). All officials at the prefecture-level should project the size of the population in their jurisdictions for the following year and calculate how much grain was needed to sustain it. Based on these data, they should try to match production with the assessed needs. This could be done, Ren suggested, by expanding the cultivation of basic staples and limiting that of luxury crops, such as tobacco, which were not essential for sustaining the livelihood of the people (*minsheng*).[13] According to Ren, therefore, directives from the provincial authorities should replace market demand and private initiative in deciding what kind of crops to cultivate. The influential scholar, Bao Shichen (1775–1855), also believed that the government should start planning production. Referring to the pro-market policies adopted by ear-

---

11 For a discussion of the history of the idea of *minsheng*, its roots in the Confucian classics, and its various reinterpretations, see Zanasi, *Economic Thought*, 16–50.

12 Jane Kate Leonard, "The State's Resources and the People's Livelihood (Guoji Minsheng): The Daoguang Emperor's Dilemmas about the Grand Canal Restoration, 1825," in *To Achieve Security and Wealth: The Qing Imperial State and the Economy 1644–1911*, ed. Jane Kate Leonard and John R. Watt (Ithaca: Cornell University 1993), 47–73, 50, 53. On this issue, see also Roy Bin Wong, "Chinese Traditions of Grain Storage," in *Nourish the People: The State Civilian Granary System in China, 1650–1850*, ed. Pierre-Étienne Will and Bin R. Wong, 1–16.

13 Ren Qiyun, "Jingyan Jianyi Wupian," in *Wangchao Jingshi Wenbian* 14, ed. He Changling (Zhiti: si, zhengbenxia), http://hanji.sinica.edu.tw/, accessed May 18, 2022.

lier Qing emperors, he lamented that the precedent administrations had left to the people the initiative in agricultural matters, with the dire consequences of mismanagement and wasteful extravagance. Local officials should break this pattern, acquire agricultural expertise, and take charge of agricultural decisions, which "[could] no longer be left simply to the common people."[14] Officials, for example, should intervene in the choice of which crop should be planted in which field, maximizing production by matching crops with the terrains most suited to their cultivation. Bao also suggested that officials introduce more efficient and systematic ways to use manpower as an important technique for increasing land productivity: "The real problem—he explained—is that human work capacity (*li zuo*) has not been utilized efficiently or systematically (*bu ru fa*)."[15] Because increased input of manpower would lead to a proportional increase in yield per acre, Bao argued, local officials should deploy *corvée* labor, not just for land reclamation, but also as additional manpower in the already cultivated land. Bao thus presents as a technology for economic growth the "industrious" mode of production that characterized nineteenth-century China.[16] Bao's view of the importance of a more rational use of labor led Bao to disagree with Hong Liangji. China, he argued, was not facing a population crisis. New agricultural and labor techniques would generate enough economic growth to meet the needs of the population.[17]

Another prominent official and scholar, Yun Jing (1757–1817), also believed that the state could bring about a solution to the population crisis. According to Yun Jing, the scarcity crisis was not a result of population growth but of a growing disparity between the number of producers and consumers. Recent social changes, he argued, had led to the expansion of the consumer group while reducing that of the producers. As a result, production lagged behind while consumption increased. For Yun, therefore, the problem was not rooted in a limited production capacity of the empire's economy but was primarily a social problem. The current crisis, Yun continued, could be solved only by transforming more societal groups into "producers," thus increasing productivity and alleviating the idle consumers' burden on resources. Although Yun did not directly explain

---

14 William T. Rowe, *Speaking of Profit: Bao Shicken and Reform in the Nineteenth-Century China* (Cambridge, Mass.: Harvard University Press, 2018), 82–83.
15 Rowe, *Speaking of Profit*, 82, 90–94; Zhao Jing, *Zhongguo gudai jingji sixiangshi jianghua*, 626.
16 The "industrious" production mode observed in China by several historians generated an intense debate. Kenneth Pomeranz, "Beyond the East-West Binary: Resituating Development Paths in the Eighteenth-Century World," *The Journal of Asian Studies* 61, no. 2 (2002): 539–590.
17 Rowe, *Speaking of Profit*, 82–83, 90–94.

how this change in the composition of society could be brought about, the general context of his writings points to some form of state intervention. Yun blamed the recent economic decline on excessive reliance on the market. Echoing Ren's and Bao's arguments, he believed that production should be planned by the state rather than letting producers decide in response to market demand. The retreat of the government from the economy, he wrote, had caused the deterioration of the agricultural, manufacturing, and commercial sectors. If the people were left alone to decide what to produce, manufacture, and trade, Yun concluded, the economy would inevitably decline.[18]

Bao's and Yun's criticisms of what they described as the recent state's retreat from economic decision-making highlight the extent to which pro-market theories had influenced Qing economic policies before the full extent of the economic crisis became apparent at the turn of the eighteenth century.[19] Their criticisms, however, cannot be read as a call for suppressing market forces. Although discouraging the cultivation of "wasteful" crops that depended on a market-based demand for luxury goods, such as tobacco, they did not aim to de-commercialize the rural economy and revive the model of the self-sufficient rural village. Bao, for example, believed that agricultural production should be integrated with the market to take advantage of its opportunities. He suggested the abolition of domestic custom duties to facilitate the circulation of resources through the market. He also did not advocate for a return to peasants' self-sufficiency but envisioned them as active participants "in the commercial market" and cash cropping. He especially encouraged the cultivation of sericulture and horticulture as a way to improve the agricultural sector.[20]

These plans for solving the scarcity crisis greatly differed in crucial ways from historical precedents of state intervention in situations of famines. They provided systemic and comprehensive strategies rather than targeted *ad hoc* intervention in response to episodic crises. Above all, these writers viewed the economy of the empire as capable of growth, breaking away with the notion of fixed and limited resources that had prevailed in China—as did most premodern agrarian countries—until the commercial revolution of the 1500s.[21] Recognizing the high level of commercialization of the economy and the importance

18 Yun Jing, "Sandai Yinge Lun Wu," in *Dayun Shanfang Ji* (Taipei: Taiwan Zhonghua shuju, 1965), 8b-9b; Zhao, *Zhongguo gudai jingji sixiangshi jianghua*, 624–625.
19 For a discussion of pro-market thought and policies in the Qing period, see Zanasi, *Economic Thought*, 51–108.
20 Rowe, *Speaking of Profit*, 91.
21 For a discussion of the development of the idea of economic growth in China, see Zanasi, *Economic Thought*, 51–108.

of the commercial sector for economic growth, writers like Bao attempted to combine some extent of state leadership with the mature market economy of the empire.

Ren and Bao did not see state intervention as limited in influencing decisions on production. They also envisioned strategies for regulating the distribution of resources, which, they argued, needed to be used frugally and distributed widely and evenly. Both writers discouraged luxury consumption, conceived not just as the acquisition of expensive luxury items but also in terms of the quantity of basic resources consumed by a household. Consumption of more than a proper share of resources by one family would result in scarcity for others. Going beyond the enforcement of traditional sumptuary laws, their plans reached more deeply into society by empowering the imperial system of power brokerage, such as the kinship and *baojia* systems.[22] Ren Qiyun proposed that the *xiangyue* (district regulatory commissions) provide the basic principles and regulations for social behavior to be applied by the *baoijia*. Not-conforming actions were to be detected and reported by the neighbors, who were susceptible to punishment if they failed to denounce any undue activities. This system of mutual surveillance would ensure social stability and eradicate bad customs, among which Ren included luxury consumption and an extravagant lifestyle, i.e., a wasteful use of scarce resources. Bao Shichen suggested that households be categorized according to their economic status. Wealthy households would be required to store an officially regulated surplus of grain—to avoid undue hoarding—and circulate the remaining on the market to keep supplies flowing. Heads of *baojia* would urge rich families to take care of the poorest branches of their lineages. If they failed to do so, they would be labeled "unneighborly," with the consequence of possible expulsion from the group. In years of extreme scarcity, poor families in distress would be authorized to ask the wealthiest families in their area—even if not part of their kinship network—for help in the form of officially regulated loans to be repaid with minimal interest. Bao Shichen's proposal also applied the same system to county-level administrations. In this scheme, "wealthy counties" would aid poorer ones following the same dynamic envisioned for individual households.[23]

22 The *baojia* was a social unit of mutual responsibility generally formed of five families. For a discussion of the system of "power brokerage" in late-imperial China, see Susan Mann, *Local Merchants and the Chinese Bureaucracy, 1750–1950* (Stanford: Stanford University Press, 1987); and the idea of "cultural nexus" in Prasenjit Duara, *Culture, Power, and the State: Rural North China, 1900–1942* (Stanford: Stanford University Press, 1991).

23 Rowe, *Speaking of Profit*, 85–90. For a discussion of Bao's attempt to realize his plans in the town of Nanjing, see Rowe, *Speaking of Profit*, 87.

The development of ideas for state planning and intervention testifies to the flexibility of the conceptual framework offered by the mandate of *minsheng* (People's Livelihood). Rather than being a rigid framework trapping Chinese economic thought in a "traditional" unchanging mode, this mandate allowed significant shifts in understanding the workings of the economy. *Minsheng*, in fact, was not a policy but an objective/mandate as well as a source of political legitimacy. Ideas that broke with the past could assume political legitimacy if they offered a more efficient strategy for achieving the ever-important mandate of ensuring the livelihood of the people and, consequently, social and fiscal stability.

The flexibility of the *minsheng* conceptual framework also dispels the common notion that Confucian thought precluded a pragmatic understanding of the economy and that its supposed inflexible orthodoxy prevented China's economic modernization.[24] In reality, Chinese writers showed remarkable pragmatism in developing new economic ideas as they observed changes in the economy of the empire. Positive views of personal interests (*li*)— traditionally considered a sign of private greed and, consequently, intrinsically opposed to the common good (i.e., the mandate of *minsheng*)—and the idea of the capacity of the market to self-regulate emerged during the Song Dynasty (960 – 1279). This period witnessed the first stage of a commercial revolution that fully developed in the 1500s, after the interruption of the Mongol invasion and anti-commerce policy of the early Ming.[25] The commercial growth of the Song period relied on an improved and expanded canal-based transportation system, which allowed private merchants to move their goods across an increasingly wide portion of the empire at a faster pace and cheaper transportation costs. In cases of famines, merchants —attracted by the possibility of the high profits (*li*) that could be derived from the unusually high prices generated by the local scarcity—were able to move their grains to the affected area. This new influx of grains would soon restabilize prices without the intervention of the state.[26] Starting in the 1500s, Chinese intellectuals and officials had also developed pro-luxury consumption ideas that presented the same logic as that famously articulated in Bernard de Mandeville's *The Fable of The Bees: or, Private Vices, Publick Benefits* (1714). Overcoming

24 This theory was recently perpetuated in Joel Mokyr, *A Culture of Growth: The Origins of the Modern Economy* (Princeton: Princeton University Press, 2016).

25 Von Glahn, *The Economic History of China*, 208 – 254, 295 – 347; Zanasi, *Economic Thought*, 51 – 108.

26 Robert P. Hymes, "Moral Duty and Self-Regulating Process in Southern Sung Views of Famine Relief," in *Ordering the World: Approaches to State and Society in Sung Dynasty China*, ed. Robert P. Hymes and Conrad Schirokauer (Berkeley: University of California Press, 1993), 280 – 309.

the idea that a luxury lifestyle was amoral and, by wasting resources, ran counter to the interest of the common good, philosophers like Lu Ji (1515–1552) and Tang Zhen (1630–1704) argued that luxury consumption actually stimulated economic growth and generated prosperity. In other words, luxury consumption turned from a negative habit, wasteful of resources, into the engine of commercial growth.[27] Historically, therefore, the *minsheng* conceptual framework was able to accommodate dramatic shifts in the perception of the role in the economy of the empire of the market and luxury consumption. It was within the language of *minsheng* that, by the 1500s, Chinese officials and intellectuals were able to develop two economic notions that are considered to be at the very foundations of economic modernity: the self-regulating market and the positive effect on the economy of luxury consumption. It was the same flexibility and pragmatism of the Chinese intellectual discourse that allowed one more change in the understanding of the economy of the empire. The dramatically changed circumstances brought about by the economic crisis led to the formulation of the new idea of state leadership over economic growth and a reinterpretation of frugal consumption.

The theorization of new economic ideas was facilitated by new trends in the philosophical discourse, which, since the late 1500s, came to be dominated by the schools of thought of Evidential Studies (*kaozheng*) and Practical Studies (*shixue*). These two schools criticized Neo-Confucianism—which had gained prominence in the Southern Song (1127–1279) and Ming (1368–1644) periods—for its stress on moral cultivation and the abstract debates it generated. Although they disagreed with each other on many important issues, scholars adhering to these schools shared an interest in practical disciplines directly linked to governmental administration, such as geography, mathematics, water conservancy, and agriculture.[28] Hong Liangji, for example, was a follower of Evidential Studies and specialized in mathematics, as reflected in his sophisticated calculation regarding population growth. Yun Jing and Bao Shichen were also greatly influenced by these new approaches to practical studies and most of their writings reflected their interests in mathematics, governmental policies, and economics.[29]

---

27 Zanasi, *Economic Thought*, 16–50.
28 Both Evidential and Practical studies often overlapped with Statecraft, a term indicating writings on governmental and economic issues. For a discussion of evidential studies and its links to Statecraft and Practical Studies, see Benjamin A. Elman, *From Philosophy to Philology: Intellectual and Social Aspects of Change in Late Imperial China* (Los Angeles: University of California, 2001), 37–86.
29 Rowe, *Speaking of Profit*, 22–41.

By the late nineteenth century, therefore, an indigenous developmental thought had already begun to take shape, influencing the Chinese intellectuals' response to the Western economic ideas that begun to trickle into China as an import, together with merchants and missionaries, of Western imperialism.

The Encounter

Although the Chinese had encountered Western narratives of modernity before the Opium War (1839–1842), it was after the humiliating defeat at the hands of the British and the subsequent pressure from foreign imperialism that Chinese officials and intellectuals actively engaged with Western economic theories. In their quest for understanding the source of power and wealth of the imperialist nations, they began to translate works they believed could offer insights into the reasons for their success. Among them was the prominent intellectual Yan Fu (1854–1921), who had traveled widely and studied in England for three years. In 1901 Yan Fu published a translation of Adam Smith's *The Wealth of Nations*, under the Chinese title *On Wealth* (*Yuan fu*). Yan Fu's translation efforts resulted in a complex and not easily understandable text, since Yan Fu used classical Chinese, rather than the vernacular language, and focused on articulating Smith's ideas with a terminology accessible to Chinese readers.[30] Some of the ideas presented by Smith resonated with Yan Fu. One of them was the relations between savings and capital and cumulation presented in Chapter III of Book II of the *Wealth of Nations*, "On the Accumulation of Capital, or of Productive and Unproductive Labour," which Yan Fu translated as "The work of men that generate profits and that that does not generate profits." In this chapter, Smith discussed the negative influence on the economy of the unproductive groups in society, which wasted important revenue that could have been reinvested into the economy, a theme already common among Qing philosophers.[31] A similar idea of capital accumulation had developed in China since the eighteenth century, framed within the long-standing debate on frugality versus luxury consumption. When prominent official Chen Hongmou (1696–1771) was governor of Shaanxi Province, he advocated frugality among peasant households because, he argued, it would generate savings that could be invested in improving agriculture. Yan Fu agreed with Smith. Unproductive groups in society negatively impacted the econ-

30 For a detailed discussion of Yan Fu's translation of *The Wealth of Nations*, see Benjamin Schwartz, *In Search of Wealth and Power: Yen Fu and the West* (Cambridge, Mass.: Belknap Press, 1983), chapter 5.

31 Smith and Robert, *The Wealth of Nations* (New York: Modern Library, 2000), 360–380.

omy because their consumption—not being balanced by their production—wasted important resources that should instead be reinvested into the economy. Adam Smith's idea of capital accumulation, which, reflecting the early stages of industrialization, was close to China's situation at the time of Yan Fu's translation, was smoothly inserted into the independent Chinese discourse on frugality, although the Chinese term "capital" took a while to stabilize into the Japanese imported *ziben*.

Prominent intellectual Liang Qichao (1873–1929) also paid particular attention to consumption in relation to capital accumulation and economic growth. According to Liang, avoiding poverty and ensuring economic growth could not be achieved by prioritizing consumption, which would result in spending resources rather than accumulating capital. A frugal mode of consumption, instead, would generate savings that could be reinvested into production.[32] The issue of consumption, therefore, was also central to Liang discussion on capital accumulation and economic growth.[33]

The complexity of the Chinese debate on frugality and luxury made the adoption of the Western concept of consumption—translated as *xiaofei*—not easily adaptable. Well into the 1920s and 1930s, many commentators continued to discuss consumption using the ideas of productive frugality—as a tool for capital accumulation—and wasteful luxury. They, in fact, saw the Western idea as representing a modern form of consumption that, even if not necessarily considered luxurious in the economies of abundance of the industrialized West, was still extravagant and wasteful in China's situation of scarcity. While they recognized Western *xiaofei* to be a modern lifestyle to which China might aspire to achieve in the future, most Chinese intellectuals still felt that, at that time, China needed a form of material modernity that more closely reflected its current situation and needs. *Xiaofei* came to be consistently adopted in economic writings by the 1930s when Western-style Economics came to dominate China's academic environment, as an increasingly large number of students pursued studies abroad and Chinese universities established departments and centers devoted to the study of Economics and Economic History based on Western social sciences.[34]

---

32 Liang Qichaho, *Xinmin shuo* (1902), "Section 14: Lun shengli fenli," http://ctext.org/wiki.pl?if=en&res=900281; for a detailed discussion of Liang Qichao's analysis of the various groups of producers and consumers see Lai Jiancheng, *Liang Qichao de Jingji mianxiang* (Hangzhou: Zhejiang daxue chubanshe, 2010), 219–220.

33 Liang Qichao, "Xinminshuo," "Section 14: Lun shengli fenli."

34 Chiang Yung-chen, *Social Engineering and the Social Sciences in China* (Cambridge: Cambridge University Press, 2001).

Western-style consumption (*xiaofei*) was not the only aspect of Western liberal capitalism that Chinese officials and intellectuals believed should not be directly adopted in China. Although humanistic aspirations for freedom and socioeconomic justice led them to support the general idea of economic liberalism, most late-Qing Chinese reformers argued that China's particular situation required an interventionist state.[35] In his discussion of *The Wealth of Nations*, for example, Yan Fu wholeheartedly supported Smith's anti-Mercantilist arguments since he also believed that Mercantilism led to oppressive economic policies and that Smith's model would increase freedom for the citizens. However, Yan Fu argued, while the free-market system Smith advocated was suitable for Western industrialized nations and their economies of abundance, they did not fit China's economy of scarcity, which required the intervention of the state. Smith's aversion to state monopolies, Yan Fu argued, went too far and his free-market system led to inequalities in the distributions of wealth. Because of its population problems and need for an even distribution of resources, he concluded, China should adopt a stronger and more interventionist state than that envisioned by Smith.[36] In his writings, Liang Qichao echoes a similar tension between liberalism/humanism and nation-building goals. While attracted by Smith's anti-despotism arguments, Liang also found himself caught between supporting a free market as an expression of people's freedom and calling for some measure of protectionism and state intervention to meet China's particular needs. At this time, we also find voices supporting more radical forms of state intervention. Liang Qichao's teacher, the official and reformer Kang Youwei (1858–1927)—a main leader of the ill-fated Hundred Days Reforms (June 11 to September 22, 1898) in which Liang also participated—for example, argued that all productions should be planned by the government, which should first collect data on population and average consumption. Based on this data, the government should then distribute resources evenly.[37]

Development strategies formulated during the Self-Strengthening Movement (*Ziqiang*, c. 1861–1895)—a reform movement aimed at strengthening the empire against both Western Imperialism and domestic rebellions through the modern-

---

35 Schwartz, *In Search of Wealth and Power*; Zhang Hao, *Liang Chi-Chao and Intellectual Transition in China, 1890–1907* (Cambridge, Mass.: Harvard University Press, 1971).

36 Hu Jichuang, *Zhongguo jingji sixiangshi*, 77–78.

37 Xia Yande, *Zhongguo jinbainian jingji sixiang* (Shanghai: Shanghai shudian, 1989), 55–66. For a detailed discussion of pro-state intervention arguments, see Zanasi, *Economic Thought*, 109–157.

ization of the military and the adoption of Western technologies[38]—expanded the basic ideas of the pre-Opium War period. For example, Self-Strengthener reformers, like Bao Shicheng, did not see state leadership to be in opposition to a market economy, but believed that the state could help steer market demand in support of state objectives. Prominent officials like Zhang Zhidong (1837–1909), for example, argued that the state could deploy frugality to influence market demand, thus shaping the trajectory of China's economic growth. Frugal consumption, he argued, would lead to a decline in demand for luxury goods, thus indirectly bolstering the production of basic staples.[39]

The nationalist and anti-imperialist goals of the Self-Strengthening Movement, however, brought a reinterpretation of the mandate of *minsheng*. The goal of strengthening China against Western imperialism, in fact, led to refocusing the discourse on the economy from concerns for the stability of the dynasty to the material needs of the nation as it struggled to come out of poverty and find a place in the international scene. Scarcity and poverty became a sign of China's "backwardness." As social Darwinian theories became increasingly popular—especially after Yan Fu translated T.H. Huxley's *Evolution and Ethics* (*Tianyanlun*) in 1898—"backwardness" appeared to threaten the very survival of the Chinese civilization as it lagged behind in the struggle for survival among nations.[40] In this context, the goals of development extended beyond efforts for economic growth aimed at overcoming poverty and social stability.

In addition, in the new global context of the early twentieth century, the debate on development introduced more complex of standards of living. Liberal intellectuals such as the future Minister of Education Cai Yuanpei (1868–1940) envisioned a liberal mode of development that focused on also elevating the intellectual and cultural life of the population going beyond their material needs.[41] These humanistic, *minsheng* visions of development challenged others that prioritized strengthening the military and developing the heavy industry sector at the expense of improving the livelihood of the people. Initially, the Nationalist Party—which was to control the Republican Government from 1927 to 1949—appeared to favor the *minsheng* model, which actually became a central tenet of early Nationalist ideology, since Sun Yat-sen (1866–1925) enshrined it in his fourth lecture on the Principle of the People's Livelihood (*minsheng*

38 The Self-Strengthening Movement was as much a response to the shock of the Taiping Rebellions as to the Opium War.

39 Chen, *Zhongguo jingji sixiangshi*, 245.

40 Rebecca E. Karl, *The Magic of Concepts: History and the Economic in Twentieth-Century China* (Durham: Duke University Press, 2017).

41 Cai Yuanpei (Zimin), "Wenming yu shechi," *Lüou zazhi* (November 15, 1916), 1–3.

zhuyi). Here Sun argued that: "in the evolution of human civilization we can distinguish three stages in the standard of living." The first stage was characterized by the attempt to satisfy basic needs. The second stage was that of achieving comfort and the third saw humanity pursuing luxury. Sun concluded that China was still in the first stage, since the "four hundred million throughout the nation" lacked the bare necessities of life.[42] China's standard of living at the subsistence level, therefore, trapped the country in a premodern stage of evolution. Taking an "evolutionary view of life in the universe," Sun concluded, the state should also ensure food, clothes, housing, and transportation appropriate for a civilized society.[43] Sun's *minsheng* formula—"food, clothes, shelter, and means of transportation" (*shi yi zhu xing*)—remained an important part of the Nationalist rhetoric of development and modernization, although it was dramatically reinterpreted by Chiang Kai-shek (1887–1975). Chiang transformed it into a set of rules for modern living aimed at diverting resources from improving standards of living into the development of a military-industrial complex.[44] It was Chiang's vision that ultimately influenced the Nationalist developmental state, especially after Chiang gained full control of the government in 1935.

The Nationalist Developmental State

Nationalist and anti-imperialist goals had greatly influenced the developmental goals of the self-Strengthening Movement and assumed even greater importance in the Nationalist Government, established in Nanjing in 1927. Regaining tariff autonomy, eliminating foreign concessions, and reversing other clauses unfavorable to China imposed by the "unequal" treaties with Western powers—and later with Japan, after its victory in the First Sino-Japanese War (1894–1895)—became an integral part of the Nationalist plan for economic development.[45] These nationalist goals, however, reinforced, rather than displaced, the trends that emerged at the beginning of the economic crisis and expanded in the Self-

---

42 Sun Yat-sen, "Sanmin zhuyi: minsheng zhuyi, disi jiang," in *Sun Wen xuanji*, vol. 1, ed. Yan Huang (Guangzhou Shi: Guangdong renmin chubanshe, 1924), 654–670.

43 Sun Yat-sen, "Sanmin zhuyi," 635–654.

44 For a detailed discussion of both liberal and military-industrial models of development in the early Republican years and for Sun Yat-sen's and Chiang Kai-shek's reformulation of the trope of *minsheng*, see Zanasi, *Economic Thought*, 158–196.

45 For a detailed discussion of China's efforts to regain control of tariffs, see Felix Boecking, *No Great Wall: Trade, Tariffs and Nationalism in Republican China, 1927–1945* (Cambridge, Mass.: Harvard University Asia Center, 2017).

Strengthening period, especially the ideas that China needed a strong state leadership and could not afford a Western capitalist-style mode of consumption because of its economy of scarcity (poverty).

Nationalist intellectuals and officials also believed that there was no insurmountable contradiction between state planning and market economy. The contradiction between state leadership and market economy could be resolved by cooperation between state and economic elites. A solution for this strategy had already been formulated by Ren Qiyun and Bao Shichen, who had suggested that the local power brokerage system assist the state in achieving its goals. This strategy anticipated those adopted by the Self-Strengthening Movement. Prominent reformer Zheng Guanying (1842–1920), for example, argued that the state and private sector should join forces to fight the "commercial war" against the imperialist aggressor. The state should foster and encourage the private sector, which should focus on the nationalist goal of producing for import substitution, thus strengthening China's export. The government should also establish a ministry of commerce to be linked to local Chambers of Commerce, launch new business schools, publish business journals, and in general help the modernization of trade practices.[46] Kang Youwei also advocated the establishment of provincial merchant associations (*shanghui*). These associations would consult with the state and manage the unified implementation of policies under the control of officials.[47]

It was in this context that Self-Strengtheners provincial governors established new enterprises based on newly imported Western technologies, such as the Kaiping mining complex established in 1877 by Li Hongzhang (1823–1901). Li, like other provincial Self-Strengtheners, also took the lead in improving transportation and infrastructure enlisting private funds and business through the strategies of "state-private cooperation" (*guanshang heban*) or "official supervision and merchant management" (*guangdu shangban*). Arguably the most famous among this kind of enterprise was the China Merchant Steamship Navigation Company (*Lunchaun zhaoshangju*), also launched by Li Hongzhang in 1872. Provincial leadership on economic self-strengthening was not limited to mining, transportation, and infrastructure. It also extended to manufacturing and especially to the revival of traditionally strong Chinese industries aimed at import substitution. Governors Li Hongzhang, Zhang Zhidong, and Zuo Zongtang (1812–1885), for example, set up cotton mills and textile factories in their

46 Hsiao Kung-ch'uan, *A Modern China and a New World* (Seattle: University of Washington Press, 1975), 311–312.
47 Xia Yande, *Zhongguo jinbainian jingji sixiang*, 55–66.

provinces. The cotton industry, in fact, became, together with tea and silk, one of the main focuses for import substitution from the Self-Strengthening period through the Republican years.[48] The strategy of "state-private cooperation" aimed at mobilizing in support of national goals private businessmen's expertise and their capital—at a time when the state lacked appropriate financial resources for footing the bills for economic reforms.

Most of the prewar Nationalist Government's plans for economic "reconstruction" (*jianshe*)—the term used at the time for economic development—rested on the establishment within the government of new economic bodies, such as the National Economic Council (NEC) which institutionalized cooperation with the private sector by establishing industry-wide organizations that included representatives of the government, entrepreneurs, technical specialists, and workers, while extending its control over agricultural production through a network of rural cooperative societies. As was the case with the NEC, however, by the mid-1930s, these corporativist institutions turned from a Self-Strengthening style attempt to mobilize private capital and expertise into a tool for increasing state control over the private economy.[49]

Although foreign experts had flocked to China starting with the Self-Strengthening reforms, as part of the program for knowledge transmission, more structured developmental missions began after the establishment of the Nanjing Government. In those years, the NEC partnered with the League of Nations for three main missions focusing on health, economics and finance, and communications and transit. The NEC also established a more permanent collaboration through the Committee on Intellectual Cooperation which supported educational exchanges.[50] In 1933, the League also sent a fourth mission to help the NEC solve the long-standing problem of agricultural decline and poverty among the peasants. In their final reports, the League's experts offered diverse solutions to the rural crisis, mostly focusing on improving the lives of the peasants through the organization of cooperative societies controlled locally. The NEC, however, did not follow the recommendations of the League's experts, but proceeded in a very different direction. Its network of cooperative societies, rather than empowering the peasants, aimed at extracting resources in support of urban industrialization. Ultimately NEC leaders only sought from the League technical expertise, financial aid, and international support against Japan's escalating

48 Margherita Zanasi, *Saving the Nation: Economic Modernity in Republican China* (Chicago: University of Chicago Press, 2010), 133–174.
49 Kirby, "Engineering China"; Zanasi, *Saving the Nation*, 133–174.
50 Kirby, "Engineering China," 143–148.

imperialist ambitions, rather than a blueprint for solving the rural crisis.[51] The NEC example highlights the limits of China's integration within the Western narratives of development—or better, the diverse views of economic modernity competing in post-World War One West as liberal capitalism came under criticism from different quarters.[52]

By the 1930s, Chinese intellectuals and government officials had completely embraced Western Economics. A new group of Western-trained economists dominated both the academic world and the government bureaucracy, which now prioritized Western-style expertise in its recruiting. Their enthusiasms for modernizing reforms led them to confine to the realm of the "traditional" and unscientific Chinese ideas developed outside the Western conceptual terminology, effectively erasing the early history of Chinese developmental thought.[53] Despite these changes, continuities are striking as Chinese reformers and economists continued to carefully assess Western blueprints for modernization by evaluating whether they fit China's economy of scarcity. During the Republican period, when reformers were most eagerly seeking Western-style economic modernity, China's nation-building and anti-imperialist goals worked against the outright adoption of a Western consumerist capitalist model of development, favoring instead state intervention and frugal consumption as a strategy for capital accumulation. This was not only the case with China. Japan's modernization effort, although considered an unprecedented feat of Westernization in response to Western imperialism, adopted policies very similar to those attempted in China. The newly restructured Meiji state was able to take a decisive leadership over the economy and successfully mobilize private resources both in terms of cooperation with economic elites—as exemplified by the role played by the *zaibatsu* in prewar industrialization—and promotion of frugality as a strategy for diverting resources into economic state goals.[54] More or less formal or institutionalized, state-private cooperation—often aiming at compressing labor costs—remained, together with state leadership, basic traits of the East Asian Development

51 Margherita Zanasi, "Exporting Development: The League of Nations and Republican China," *Comparative Studies in Society and History* 49, no. 1 (2007): 143–169.
52 Zanasi, "Exporting Development."
53 Chiang Yung-chen, *Social Engineering.*
54 The term *zaibatsu* refers to pre-1945 industrial and financial conglomeration which cooperated closely with the government in its industrialization effort. During the economic boom initiated in the 1960s, the South Korean *Chaebol* worked in a very similar fashion.

model throughout postwar Japan, the 1060s rise of the Four Asian Tigers (Singapore, Hong Kong, Taiwan, and South Korea), and post-Mao PRC.[55]

Conclusion

The longue durée approach adopted in this article reveals the complex origins of the East Asian developmental state tracing its origins back to late-eighteenth and early-nineteenth century China. It was at this time that developmental economic strategies emerged, which were soon to be strengthened by anti-imperialists and nation-budling efforts. The adoption in the early-twentieth century of the Western terminology of economics effectively erased the early history of Chinese developmental thought, to the point that in the 1980s the idea prevailed that the PRC's economic reforms, rather than having domestic historical roots, were inspired by the experience of the Four Asian Dragons, and especially by the thought of Singapore leader's Lee Kwang Yew.

Restoring the early history of Chinese developmentalism allows us to go beyond the ideology of the Chinese Communist Party (CCP) and trace the origins of today's (post-1980s) market economy "with Chinese characteristics" in the long-term crisis generated by geopolitical changes—above all population growth and the economy of scarcity (poverty) it created. It was this crisis that inspired new economic views that favored state leadership for stewarding China toward economic growth and out of poverty. The arrival of Western imperialism, and the narrative of economic modernity it brought with it, rather than finding a "blank sheet of paper"—to use one of Mao Zedong's favorite expressions—on which to impress its version of economic modernity, met a well-developed and pragmatic indigenous thought, rooted in a clear analysis of China's circumstances, which mediated the impact of Western ideas.

Recent arguments presenting the "China model" as a more efficient economic system better suited to the contemporary world appear to challenge the Western model that dominates global development today.[56] Recent works have attempted to evaluate "the extent to which China's post 1989 rise, and its more recent emerging narrative of global leadership, might dent Western-style liberal

55 For a discussion of postwar Japan's developmental state see Chalmers Johnson, *MITI and the Japanese Miracle: The Growth of Industrial Policy, 1925–1975* (Stanford: Stanford University Press, 2007).

56 See, most famously, Daniel Bell, *The China Model: Political Meritocracy and the Limits of Democracy* (Princeton: Princeton University Press, 2016).

democracy as teleology of progress."[57] This question, however, remains at the moment unanswered as China's Belt and Road Initiative (BRI)—the main program for the realization of China's aspiration to global dominance—is "more pragmatic than ideological," mostly focusing on creating a network of bilateral Free Trade Agreements.[58] The BRI, therefore, seems to highlight China's economic pragmatism, which, as shown in this article, has deep historical roots.[59] Although the BRI has the potential of "changing the rules of globalization," as the title of a recent book suggests, whether the China model will emerge as an alternative to current neo-liberal developmentalism remains an open question.[60] Some scholars believe that it will probably depend not on China itself, but rather on whether the Western world will grow disappointed with its long-standing highly ideological models and will look for alternative solutions.[61] The China model, as well as the East Asian Development model, might develop some appeal in the West for the tendency it shares with neoliberalism to compress labor costs. The two models, however, greatly differ in the relations between state and economic elites. The hybrid state-market economic systems envisioned by Self-strengtheners and early Republican reformers articulated a liberal version of the developmental state by aiming at cooperation with societal economic elites. In the late-1930s Republican period and post-1980 China, however, the balance between cooperation and coercion and between state leadership and private initiative tended to shift toward more authoritarian solutions.[62]

---

57 Niv Horesh and Kean Fan Lim, *An East Asian Challenge to Western Neoliberalism: Critical Perspectives on the 'China Model'* (London: Routledge, 2019), 12. For a detailed description of the BRI, its goals, structure, and current situation, see Wenxiang Zhang, Ilan Alon, and Christoph Lattemann, *China's Belt and Road Initiative: Changing the Rules of Globalization* (Singapore: Palgrave Macmillan, 2020).

58 Zhang, Alon, and Lattemann, *China's Belt*, 71.

59 With the blatant exception of Mao Zedong's economic campaigns such as the Great Leap Forward (1958–1962).

60 Zhang, Alon, and Lattemann, *China's Belt.*

61 Horesh and Lim, *An East Asian Challenge to Western Neoliberalism*, 2–3.

62 For the complicated relationship between China's private entrepreneurs and the state, see Bruce J. Dickson, *Red Capitalists in China the Party, Private Entrepreneurs, and Prospects for Political Change* (Cambridge: Cambridge University Press, 2001); Kellee S. Tsai, "China: Economic Liberalization, Adaptive Informal Institutions, and Party-State Resilience," in *The Oxford Handbook of Transformations of the State*, ed. Stephan Leibfried et al. (Oxford: Oxford University Press, 2015), 654–670.

Eric Helleiner

Where Did the Idea of International Development Come From? Looking Beyond the Industrialized Core

Where did the idea of international development come from? Scholars addressing this question have devoted much attention to thinkers and policymakers from the United States and Western Europe who were early advocates of the extension of official development assistance to less industrialized regions of the world.[1] Some have focused on US president Harry Truman's 1949 inauguration speech which announced "a bold new program for making the benefits of our scientific advances and industrial progress available for the improvement and growth of underdeveloped areas."[2] Others have challenged that focus by highlighting many earlier American and Western European figures who urged their governments to support economic development in colonial and other contexts between the late nineteenth century and World War Two.[3]

Although these scholarly debates have been important, they have suffered from an important limitation: the relative neglect of thinkers outside the industrialized core of the world economy.[4] This paper analyzes the ideas of five such thinkers who advanced important ideas about international development before World War Two: Dadabhai Naoroji (India), Sun Yat-sen (China), Mihail Manoilescu (Romania), Benoy Kumar Sarkar (India), and José Manuel Puig Casauranc (Mexico). More thinkers of this kind could be examined, but these five are particularly interesting because they each developed quite innovative and ambitious

---

1 In this paper, I focus only the provision of "official" international development assistance rather than wider non-governmental international development assistance. For supporting this research, I thank the Social Sciences and Humanities Research Council of Canada and the Killam Fellowship Program.

2 Harry S. Truman, "Inaugural Address," Harry S. Truman Library and Museum, January 20, 1949, https://www.trumanlibrary.gov/library/public-papers/19/inaugural-address. For examples of this focus, see Wolfgang Sachs, "The Archeology of the Development Idea," *Interculture* 28, no. 4 (1990): 2–32; Arturo Escobar, *Encountering Development* (Princeton: Princeton University Press, 1995).

3 For recent surveys of much of this literature, see Joseph Morgan Hodge, "Writing the History of Development (Part 2: Longer, Deeper, Wider)," *Humanity* 7, no. 1 (2016): 125–174; Corinna R. Unger, *International Development: A Postwar History* (London: Bloomsbury Academic, 2018), 23–48, 49–78.

4 See also Hodge, "Writing," 157–158. Exceptions are noted in the text.

https://doi.org/10.1515/9783110730234-003

ideas about international development. For this reason alone, they deserve a much higher profile in histories of international development thought. But just as important is the fact that their ideas challenge some common views about early international development thought. Specifically, they show that not all early international development thought was rooted in Western thought or linked to efforts to rationalize Western domination of other parts of the world.[5] When the ideas of these thinkers are taken into consideration, the origins of international development thought—both its geography and its content—look quite different than the image portrayed in much literature on the subject.

Naoroji's Pioneering Ideas in Colonial India

The earliest of these neglected pioneers of international development thought was Dadabhai Naoroji (1825–1917). Born into a relatively poor family in colonial India, Naoroji studied at the British-run Elphinstone College in Bombay in the 1840s and subsequently taught mathematics and natural philosophy there. In 1855, he moved to Britain, from which he travelled back and forth to India until 1907. In both India and England, he became a well-known critic of British colonial rule and one of the leading pioneers of the emerging Indian nationalist movement.[6]

In writings between 1867 and 1880, Naoroji developed some very sophisticated evaluations of the economic consequences of British imperialism from the perspective of the colonized. At the center of Naoroji's analysis was the idea that Britain was draining capital from India. Naoroji was not to first to make this point. Indeed, when he first outlined his ideas on the topic in an 1867 lecture, he cited his intellectual debt to "a small band of Hindu students and thoughtful gentlemen" who had discussed this issue "more than twenty years earlier" when they "met secretly to discuss the effects of British rule upon India."[7] J. V. Naik notes that he was likely referring to figures at Elphinstone College such as Bhaskar Pandurang Tarkhadkar who developed prominent econom-

5 For influential statements of this kind, see Wolfgang Sachs, ed., *The Development Dictionary* (London: Zed Books, 1992); Gilbert Rist, *The History of Development*, trans. Patrick Camiller (London: Zed Books, 1997).

6 For a recent biography, see Dinyar Patel, *Naoroji: Pioneer of Indian Nationalism* (Cambridge, Mass.: Harvard University Press, 2020).

7 Dadabhai Naoroji, "England's Duties to India [1867]," in Dadabhai Naoroji, *Essays, Speeches, Addresses and Writings*, ed. Chunilal Lallubhai Parekh (Bombay: Caxton Printing Works, 1887), 33.

ic critiques of British imperialism in the 1840s.[8] But Naoroji's "drain theory" went well beyond these earlier analyses in its depth and detail.

Drawing on his mathematical skills, Naoroji compiled very extensive statistics showing how capital was being exported from India through mechanisms such as the remittances of European employees of the colonial government, payments by the colonial government to Britain for various services, and the export of profits by British investors. He argued that this economic drain not only diminished India's wealth directly but also inhibited the colony's industrialization and economic development over time by creating a shortage of capital. As he put it, "the national capital – or, in other words, its capability of production – is continually diminished year after year."[9]

Naoroji's drain theory directly challenged rosy British narratives about the prosperity of India under their rule at the time.[10] To reinforce this challenge, Naoroji developed the first detailed calculations ever made of Indian standards of living in comparison to those in other parts of the world. His numbers showed that India's per capita income was less than one twentieth that of Britain and much lower than that of other places such as Germany, France, United States, Canada, Australia, Turkey and Russia. He concluded from his calculations that India was, in fact, "the poorest country in the civilized world."[11] His comparative calculations predated by over a half century the publication of Colin Clark's famous worldwide national income statistics in 1939 that helped boost interest in the idea of international development in the 1940s.[12]

Naoroji used his statistics to plead with British authorities that they should promote India's economic development rather than undermine it. He went further to suggest that this was a "duty" of the British in their imperial role.[13] The phrase invoked Queen Victoria's 1858 proclamation in the wake of the Indian mutiny in which she had declared that "it is our earnest duty to stimulate the peaceful industry of India, to promote works of public utility and improvement,

---

8 As Naik notes, other previous thinkers than these also commented on the drain of capital from India, including Rammohan Roy who, earlier in the nineteenth century, criticized India's "tribute" to India; J.V. Naik, "Forerunners of Dadabhai Naoroj's Drain Theory," *Economic and Political Weekly* 36, no. 46–47 (2001): 4428–4432, 4428.

9 Quoted in R.P. Masani, *Dadabhai Naoroji: The Grand Old Man of India* (London: George Allen and Unwin 1939), 129.

10 For these rosy views, see Patel, *Naoroji*, 53.

11 Quoted in Bipan Chandra, *The Rise and Growth of Economic Nationalism in India* (New Delhi: People's Publishing House, 1966), 19; see also Patel, *Naoroji*, 54.

12 See, for example, Heinz Arndt, *Economic Development: The History of an Idea* (Chicago: University of Chicago Press, 1987), 35–36.

13 Naoroji, "England's Duties," 39.

and to administer its government for the benefit of all our subjects resident herein."[14] Underlying this proclamation was a liberal imperialist discourse suggesting that British imperialism was a force for progress and civilizational advancement. In addition to appealing to this ideology, Naoroji cited the ideas of the most famous British political economist of the age (and liberal imperialist), John Stuart Mill, who had highlighted the importance of capital accumulation for industrialization. Naoroji argued that the British were preventing Indian industrialization not just with their drain of capital but also because they failed to create broader conditions for economic progress that Mill highlighted, such as improved education and moderate taxes.[15]

Although Naoroji appealed to Britain's "duties" towards India, he acknowledged that "the British public know very little of their duties towards India, and care less."[16] He summed up some British views of India as follows: "you must remain poor and of few wants [...]. It is we who must have and would have great human wants and human enjoyments, and you must slave and drudge for us like mere animals, as our beasts of burden."[17] Directly confronting the lack of British interest in improving Indian living standards, Naoroji called attention to the human costs of Indian famines and poverty which he blamed on Britain's drain of the colony's wealth. These arguments represented what C.A. Bayly calls a kind of "counter-preaching" that was "designed to subvert the contemporary self-confidence of colonial elites by emphasizing their moral failure as colonial rulers."[18]

In making his case for Britain to promote India's economic development, Naoroji also appealed to British interests. Take, for example, his first 1867 lecture on the subject: "Every penny invested in the development of that vast and naturally rich portion of the British empire will be repaid a hundredfold in a hundred different ways. The greater the prosperity of India, the greater will be the benefits of the commercial and political relations of the two countries." In the commercial realm, he argued that a more prosperous India would provide a rich-

---

14 "Proclamation by the Queen in Council, to the princes, chiefs, and people of India (1858)," Wikisource, last modified June 30, 2017, https://en.wikisource.org/wiki/Proclamation_by_the_Queen_in_Council,_to_the_princes,_chiefs,_and_people_of_India.

15 Dadabhai Naoroji, "The Wants and Means of India [1870]," in Naoroji, *Essays*. For the influence of Mill's work in Naoroji's student community at Elphinston College, see Vikram Visana, "Vernacular Liberalism, Capitalism, and Anti-imperialism in the Political Thought of Dadabhai Naoroji," *The Historical Journal* 59, no. 3 (2016): 775–797.

16 Naoroji, "England's Duties," 40.

17 Quoted in Chandra, *The Rise*, 24.

18 C.A. Bayly, *Rediscovering Liberties: Indian Thought in the Age of Liberalism and Empire* (Cambridge: Cambridge University Press, 2012), 105.

er market for British goods. Politically, he warned that Indians might rebel again "if strenuous and great efforts are not made to develop the resources of the country and thereby ameliorate the material condition of the mass of the population."[19] These passages are notable not just for their appeal to British interests, but also for their early use of the words "development" and "develop" in the modern sense that they came to be employed more widely in the twentieth century. Naoroji did not pioneer this use of these terms, but it is noteworthy they were utilized in this way not just by European thinkers at this early moment.[20]

In what ways did Naoroji want Britain to promote India's economic development? The most obvious was by reducing the "drain" through initiatives such as increased local purchasing by the Government of India, and especially the greater employment of Indians in the colonial civil services (who would be less likely to export their earnings). In addition, he was critical of Britain's imposition of free trade policies on India, given the poverty caused by the drain: "you will easily see that free trade between England and India in a matter like this is something like a race between a starving, exhausting invalid, and a strong man with a horse to ride on."[21]

But Naoroji also urged British authorities to promote economic development actively through government intervention in the Indian economy. Specifically, he suggested that colonial authorities borrow large amounts of capital from Britain to build up new state-owned industries as well as to undertake "vast public works of productive character" As he put it in 1867, "the least that the British people can do is to lend back to India the wealth derived therefrom, in order to develop its resources."[22] Naoroji insisted that British capital needed to be imported to India through public authorities rather than via private investment in order to minimize exploitation, foreign control, and the benefits flowing to foreign investors. As he put it in 1880, "India sorely needs the aid of English capital.

---

19 Quotes from Naoroji, "England's Duties," 39. Naoroji even traveled to Lancashire in 1898 (as Gandhi would later do) to try to convince that region that the promotion of India's development would enable the colony to buy more British exports, see Masani, *Dadabhai*, 407–409.

20 For European uses, see, for example, Mill's reference to the need for "development of the productive resources of India": John Stuart Mill, *Principles of Political Economy* (London: John W. Parker and Son, 1852), 149. In English language literature, references to economic "development" in the modern sense of the word were particularly extensive in the first English translation in 1856 of Friedrich List, *The National System of Political Economy* [1841], trans. G.A. Matil (Philadelphia: J.P. Lippincott and Co, 1856), e. g. 71–73 and elsewhere in the volume.

21 Dadabhai Naoroji, "Poverty of India" [1876] in Naoroji, *Essays*, 217.

22 Quotes from Naoroji, "England's Duties," 41, 39.

But it is English *capital* that she needs, and not the English invasion, to come also and eat up both capital and produce."[23]

Naoroji's innovative appeal to Britain to promote India's economic development in these ways did not trigger the response that he hoped for. But it highlighted how early discourses of international development within colonial contexts did not all stem from the imperial center. Naoroji's ideas were also very different from emerging imperial developmentalism in the late nineteenth and early twentieth centuries. Rather than rationalizing colonial rule, his conception of international development stemmed from a critique of British imperialism.[24] His advocacy of state-led industrialization also went well beyond the dominant Western conceptions of colonial development that were emerging at this time. Indeed, Naoroji himself called attention to the contested meaning of the word "development," criticizing those who used the word to support very different goals than his own. For example, when he was sent a prospectus of a British business venture called "Indian Development Ltd" in the early 1900s, he responded by noting that "the correct title for such companies should be 'Indian Exploitation Ltd'". In a 1903 speech in Britain discussing British private investment, he also asked: "For whose benefit and for what purpose is the development, when all that is produced is carried away to this country?"[25]

Sun's International Development Organization

Historians who focus on the Western origins of international development also sometimes identify the creation of the League of Nations as an important historical event in their story. Gilbert Rist, for example, highlights the importance of Article 22 of the League's Convenant which asserted that the "well-being and development" of peoples in the new mandate territories of the League formed "a sacred trust of civilization" that had to be upheld. This wording was significant because it signaled the first moment when the dominant powers assigned the goal of promoting "development" in less industrialized regions of the world to a multilateral institution. As Rist notes, however, its importance should not be overstated because the task of upholding this goal was assigned to those coun-

23 Naoroji, "Memorandum on a Few Statements in the Report of the Indian Famine Commission, 1880," in Naoroji, *Essays*, 489.
24 In this late nineteenth century period, Naoroji's critique did not extend to a rejection of imperialism altogether. He was an advocate of imperial reform rather than Indian self-rule at this time, see Patel, *Naoroji*.
25 Quotes from Masani, *Dadabhai*, 421–422.

tries that ran the League's mandate territories. In this sense, Rist highlights how the provision really just "legitimatized the internationalization" of European intervention in less industrialized parts of the world.[26] Indeed, imperial ideology infused the passage, which noted that the "tutelage" of peoples in the mandates was to be "entrusted to advanced nations" because those peoples were "not yet able to stand by themselves under the strenuous conditions of the modern world."[27]

Rist is right to highlight this episode in the history of international development, but he makes no mention of another much bolder proposal at this time for creating a multilateral institution with a much more direct and ambitious international development mandate. The proposal came not from Europe or the United States but rather from the prominent Chinese thinker and revolutionary Sun Yat-sen (1866–1925).

At the very moment that the League's convenant was being negotiated by the major industrial powers, Sun developed detailed plans for the creation of a "International Development Organization" (IDO) that would mobilize Western capital and expertise behind the goal of directly promoting China's economic development. This multilateral institution was to be managed by the "various Governments of the Capital-supplying states" which would also be its only members. It would be tasked with signing contracts with the Chinese government to provide funding and skilled personnel to support a large number of specific development projects that Sun outlined in his plans. Although foreigners would help manage and supervise the projects before the loans were repaid, they would be working "under Chinese employment" and would have "to undertake the training of Chinese assistants to take their places in the future." All the IDO-financed projects would be "national undertakings" and the property created by them was to be "state owned" and "managed for the benefit of the whole nation."[28]

Sun's ambition for the projects that he wanted the IDO to support was very high. Some projects were massive infrastructural ones, including irrigation schemes, road-building, the creation of "100,000 miles of Railways," and the construction of three ports equal to New York harbor's capacity. The IDO was also to support China's rapid industrial growth, on which Sun placed very high priority. As he put it, "this miserable condition among the Chinese proletar-

26 Rist, *The History*, 58.

27 Eric Helleiner, *Forgotten Foundations of Bretton Woods: International Development and the Making of the Postwar Order* (Ithaca: Cornell University Press, 2014), 78.

28 Sun Yat-sen, *The International Development of China* (New York: G.P. Putnam's Sons, 1922), 227, 9, 11–12.

iat is due to the non-development of the country, the crude methods of production and the wastefulness of labor. The radical cure for all this is industrial development by foreign capital and experts for the benefit of the whole nation." Sun also outlined many development projects in other sectors such as agriculture, mining, forestry, and energy.[29]

At this time, Sun was a famous figure in China, having served as the first provisional president of the Chinese republic briefly after the country's 1911 revolution. Although he had no formal political position in the country when he was promoting his IDO scheme, he sent his ideas to leading Western officials involved in the Paris Peace conference in early 1919. He also outlined his ideas in English in the *Far Eastern Economic Review* later that year and in a lengthy English-language book published in 1920 (and republished in 1922) titled *The International Development of China*. These publications included detailed maps and plans of his various proposed development projects.[30]

When appealing to Western officials to support his proposal, Sun highlighted its benefits for their countries. Like Naoroji, he argued the economic development of his nation would create new export markets for the West. He also argued that China was "capable of absorbing all the surplus capital" that existed in Western countries after the World War. From a more political standpoint, he argued that the IDO would bring an end to conflicts arising from the rival spheres of influence that foreign powers had carved out in China. As he put it, "international cooperation of this kind cannot but help to strengthen the Brotherhood of Man. Ultimately, I am sure, this will culminate to be the keystone in the arch of the League of Nations."[31]

To his Chinese audience, Sun emphasized how the IDO could provide much-needed foreign capital and expertise but in a manner that avoided past problems associated with private foreign financiers. Whereas the latter had "entirely disregarded the will of the Chinese people," he insisted that no contract would be signed between the IDO and the Chinese government without securing "the confidence of the Chinese people."[32] In other writings, he was extremely critical of Western private financiers for undermining Chinese "independence" and for per-

29 Sun, *The International*, 6–7, 198.
30 Sun, *The International*, 251–259; Harold Schiffrin, "Sun Yat-sen," in *Sun Yat-sen's Doctrine in the Modern World*, ed. Chu-yuan Cheng (Boulder: Westview Press, 1989), 37–38; C. Martin Wilbur, *Sun Yat-sen:* Frustrated Patriot (New York: Columbia University Press, 1976), 322.
31 Sun, *The International*, 8, 9.
32 Sun, *The International*, 9.

petuating foreign "economic domination" of the country.[33] He saw the IDO as a way of securing foreign assistance for China's economic development in a way that avoided this domination. More generally, Sun also emphasized to his Chinese readers at the time the importance of industrialization and economic development for boosting not just China's wealth but also its power to throw off Western "economic oppression" and imperialism that had imposed free trade and threatened "the loss of our country as well as the annihilation of our race."[34]

No Western thinker had outlined a vision of international development as ambitious as this at the time. Indeed, Arndt argues that even Sun's vision of economic development itself outlined in his 1920 book was unprecedented in his scope: "In breadth of imagination, it anticipates by a generation much of the post-1945 literature on economic development."[35] Amanda McVety agrees, noting that Sun was "ahead of his time when he constructed his plan for China's economic development."[36] Where did Sun's innovative ideas come from?

There were certainly important Western influences. For example, the negotiations in Paris to create the League provided a key prompt for Sun to propose a new kind of multilateral institution. He was also likely encouraged to think about how Western nations could cooperate financially by the US government's efforts at the time to create an international consortium of private bankers to lend to China. More generally, Sun's insistence on the importance of state-led industrialization drew direct inspiration from the experience of Western countries (as well as Japan). Sun was very familiar with Western (and Japanese) ideas, policies, and practices arising from his schooling, extensive world travels, and his voracious reading.[37]

It is important, however, not to overstate the Western influences on Sun's thought because he also drew extensively on Chinese intellectual traditions. His advocacy of Chinese industrialization and economic development was deeply rooted in Chinese developmentalist thought that had emerged (with little engagement with Western political economy) in the wake of the Opium Wars. As-

---

33 Sun Yat-sen, *Ten Letters of Sun Yat-sen, 1914–1916* (Stanford: Stanford University Press, 1942), 304; Sun Yat-sen, *San Min Chi I: The Three Principles of the People*, trans. Frank Prince, ed. L.T. Chen (Shanghai: Commercial, 1928), 53.

34 Quotes from Sun, *San Min*, 37, 53.

35 Heinz Arndt, "Economic development: A Semantic History," *Economic Development and Cultural Change* 29, no. 3 (1981): 457–466.

36 Amanda Kay McVety, "Wealth and Nations: The Origins of International Development Assistance," in *The Development Century:* A Global History, ed. Stephen J. Macekura and Erez Manela (New York: Cambridge University Press, 2018), 21–39, 23.

37 See, for example, Marie-Claire Bergère, *Sun Yat-sen*, trans. Janet Lloyd (Stanford: Stanford University Press, 1994); Wilbur, *Sun*.

sociated with the self-strengthening movement of the time, thinkers such as Zheng Guanying had argued that state-led industrialization and economic modernization were needed to boost China's wealth and power in ways that fended off the Western challenge.[38] Sun's first writings about Chinese economic development in the 1890s were developed in the context of his close relationship with Zheng. His ideas, and those of Zheng and others linked to the self-strengthening movement, were, in turn, inspired by earlier Chinese developmentalist thinkers dating as far back as ancient Legalist texts such as *The Book of Lord Shang* and *Guanzi*. The ambition of Sun's ideas about economic development reflected what William Rowe called his "flair for the dramatic," but his core commitment was firmly grounded in Chinese intellectual tradition.[39] Indeed, he went out of his way to challenge Eurocentric understandings of the roots of economics: "Economics initially originated in China, Guanzi was an economist in ancient China."[40]

Even Sun's interest in international institutions had Chinese roots. In the late nineteenth and early twentieth centuries, the prominent Confucian reformist thinker Kang Youwei had predicted a future Great Harmony Age when humans joined together to create a world government and realize the ancient Confucian ideals of universal moral empire. This prediction attracted enormous attention in Chinese intellectual circles and Sun explicitly noted that it helped to inspire his IDO proposal. As he noted in the 1922 edition of *The International Development of China*, the end of World War One had created a situation in which "the hope of the peace-loving nations in the world was raised so high that we Chinese thought that the 'Tatung' or the Great Harmony Age was at hand."[41] Indeed, Sun went out of his way to remind his readers that the cosmopolitanism of Confucian thought was much older than the European cosmopolitan aspirations that some associated with the League of Nations: "Cosmopolitanism has just flowered out in Europe during this generation, but it was talked of two thousand years ago in China."[42]

---

38 See, for example, Eric Helleiner and Hongying Wang, "Beyond the Tributary Tradition in Chinese IPE: The Indigenous Roots of Early Chinese Economic Nationalism," *Chinese Journal of International Politics* 11, no. 4 (2018): 451–483.

39 William Rowe, *China's Last Empire: The Great Qing* (Cambridge, Mass.: Harvard University Press, 2009), 270. See also Eric Helleiner, *The Neomercantilists: A Global Intellectual History* (Ithaca: Cornell University Press, 2021), 232–260.

40 Zhao Jing, "*Fu Guo Xue* and the 'Economics' of Ancient China," in *A History of Ancient Chinese Economic Thought*, ed. Cheng Lin, Terry Peach, and Wang Fang (London: Routledge, 2014), 66–81, 80.

41 Sun, *The International*, 231; see also Bergère, *Sun*, 285.

42 Sun, *San Min*, 98–99.

Manoilescu's International Development Agenda for the League

Although Sun's ideas gained no traction at the 1919 Paris peace conference, Rist and others have shown how Western European officials who dominated the League of Nations became increasingly interested in how the institution could support economic development beyond the context of the mandate territories. Initially, the League's focus was on quite limited initiatives involving technical assistance missions to various less industrialized regions of the world, including China from 1931 onwards. By the late 1930s, however, policymakers within the League discussed more ambitious visions of international development cooperation that went beyond the focus on individual nations that had characterized these missions (and the earlier ideas of Sun and Naoroji). They began to see the promotion of economic development in all less industrialized regions of the world as the basis for the prosperous world economy.[43]

Although scholars are right to note the importance of these discussions in the late 1930s, thinkers from less industrialized regions of the world had already proposed this kind of ambitious international development role for the League years earlier. One pioneer of this vision of broad-based international development cooperation was the Romanian thinker and politician Mihail Manoilescu (1891–1950). Born to a modest family, Manoilescu studied engineering before joining the Romanian government and rising to the position of a government minister in 1930 and governor of the country's National Bank in 1931. Through his government work, he became very interested in international economics and published a book in 1929 titled *Théorie du Protectionisme et de l'Échange International* (The Theory of Protectionism and International Trade) that attracted extensive international attention. During the 1930s, it was translated into five languages and its ideas were invoked by politicians and industrialists across many less industrialized regions of the world, from Eastern Europe to Latin America.[44]

---

43 For League's growing interest in international development, see, for example, Rist, *The History*, 58–66; McVety, "Wealth," 25–28; Margherita Zanasi, "Exporting Development: The League of Nations and Republican China," *Comparative Studies in Society and History* 49, no. 1 (2007): 143–169; Patricia Clavin, *Securing the World Economy: The Reinvention of the League of Nations, 1920–1946* (Oxford: Oxford University Press, 2013).

44 Mihail Manoilescu, *The Theory of Protectionism and International Trade* (London: P.S. King and Son, 1931). For Manoilescu's life and influence, see Joseph Love, *Crafting the Third World* (Stanford: Stanford University Press, 1996).

Manoilescu's book is best known for updating and expanding Friedrich List's famous 1841 advocacy of trade protectionism as a tool for promoting industrialization.[45] But Manoilescu also placed his protectionist ideas in a wider multilateral vision that urged the League of Nations to support the development aspirations of less industrialized countries. Those aspirations, he argued, were undermined by the free trade orientation of the League of Nations which not only prevented industrialization in poorer countries but also endorsed a form of "invisible exploitation" of the latter. In his view, this exploitation arose in any free trade relationship between agricultural and industrial countries because exports of the former embodied more labor than the latter. In this context, industrialized countries were able to "make more men work for them abroad than are put to work at home to create these products." The result, he suggested, was a new kind of slavery: "At the time of slavery this result came through compulsion; at the present time it is obtained by the free exchange of products."[46] Manoilescu's ideas about the exploitation of agricultural countries by industrial ones built on some earlier ones developed and popularized in the late nineteenth century by a Romanian thinker, Alexandru Xenopol, who had also been influenced by List's work but who went beyond it in innovative ways that drew on his Romanian experience.[47]

Because free trade policies contributed to international inequality, Manoilescu argued that the League's endorsement of them could only be justified if "the disadvantages of free-trade to certain nations could be corrected by certain conscious measures of distribution." But he insisted that conscious redistributive initiatives of this kind could be guaranteed only with a unified political entity, whereas "it is impossible to regulate distribution among different nations." In the absence of world political union, he insisted that an international system of free trade would merely be a "system of slavery" in which industrialized countries exploited non-industrialized ones and inter-country inequality grew in politically unsustainable ways. As he put it, "nothing that is unjust can last."[48]

For these reasons, he urged the League of Nations to recognize that the use of protectionist policies was a "reasonable and legitimate" right of all countries. If the League supported less industrialized countries' protectionist policies, greater inter-country equality would result as industrialization spread across

45 Friedrich List, *The National System of Political Economy* [1841], trans. Sampson Lloyd (London: Longmans Green, 1909). List's work is cited throughout Manoilescu's *The Theory.* For the ways his analysis went beyond List's, see Helleiner, *The Neomercantilists*, 109–136.
46 Manoilescu, *The Theory*, viii.
47 Love, *Crafting*, 71–74.
48 Manoilescu, *The Theory*, 221–222, xv.

the world. Like Naoroji and Sun, Manoilescu also argued that state-led industrialization in poorer countries would create larger export markets for wealthier ones as the "buying capacity" of the former grew. For these reasons, Manoilescu argued that the League's endorsement of protectionism would provide the basis for a new kind of international solidarity between nations: "Real solidarity does not mean to let rich countries live on the poverty of poor countries, but the enrichment of poor countries and incidentally also of rich ones."[49]

Manoilescu went further to suggest that industrialized countries should also support poorer countries' industrialization by exporting capital to them. He cited John Hobson's 1902 analysis of England's problem of underconsumption caused by domestic inequality and excessive savings among the rich, and suggested that the same was true of the world as a whole. There were, he argued, "countries that are too rich, which allocate too large a part of their revenue for national savings" alongside "poor countries unable to raise their purchasing power." The solution was clear: "Newly created capital in rich and industrial countries must not remain there in order to augment a production apparatus already far too developed, but must migrate into poorer countries and assist their industrialization. Thanks to this method, poor countries will increase their production and their buying capacity for goods produced by large industrial countries, and a better equilibrium between production and consumption will be realised throughout the world."[50]

Hobson himself had argued that capital exports from rich to poor countries had encouraged imperialist forces. But Manoilescu applauded how capital exports could create a more equal world that benefited all and created "a better equilibrium between production and consumption" at the global level.[51] Unlike Sun, Manoilescu did not discuss how international financial flows would be channeled from rich to poor countries, but his insistence that this "must" happen suggested that he saw a role for the public sector in this process.

Like Naoroji and Sun, Manoilescu's ideas found little immediate support in the industrialized world. After leaving the Romanian government in 1931, Manoilescu continued to press unsuccessfully for international economic reforms.[52] By the end of the decade, however, he embraced the fascist cause and turned his back on his earlier views, supporting Romania's role as agricultural exporter

49 Manoilescu, *The Theory*, 222, 200, 218.

50 Manoilescu, *The Theory*, 209–210. For Hobson's analysis, see John Hobson, *Imperialism* (New York: James Pott and Company, 1902).

51 Manoilescu, *The Theory*, 210.

52 Edward Fertik, "Steel and Sovereignty: The United States, Nationalism, and the Transformation of World Order, 1898–1941" (PhD diss., Yale University, 2018), 247–249.

within the German-led economic bloc being forged through military and economic coercion on the European continent.[53]

Sarkar's "Economic Statesmanship" for Global Transformation

Manoilescu was not the only figure from a less industrialized part of the world who pressed the League to embrace broad-based ideas of international development during the Great Depression. Another was Benoy Kumar Sarkar (1887–1949) who Manu Goswami has described as "the most prominent social scientist in interwar colonial India."[54] Born in Bengal, Sarkar initially became involved in politics through the post-1905 swadeshi movement that urged societal support for Indian industrialization via boycotts of foreign goods and other activities. After traveling extensively in Europe, the Americas, and Asia between 1914 and 1925, Sarkar became a professor of economics at the University of Calcutta and a leading advocate of state-led Indian industrialization.[55]

Like Manoilescu, Sarkar was keen on List's work and even produced the first translation into Bengali of the German thinker's 1841 book.[56] But Sarkar also drew inspiration from non-Western thinkers, including Sun Yat-sen who he praised as "one of the greatest Asians of modern history."[57] He also dedicated his 1926 book *Economic Development* to Mahadev Govind Ranade who had first popularized List's ideas in India and who had helped (with Naoroji) to pioneer modern Indian developmentalist thought in the late nineteenth century (and also provided early support for swadeshi ideas starting in the 1870s).[58] Sarkar dedicated an-

53 Love, *Crafting*, 78, 94–95.
54 Manu Goswami, "Imaginary Futures and Colonial Internationalisms," *American Historical Review* 117, no. 5 (2012): 1461–1485, 1464.
55 Goswami, "Imaginary"; Clemens Six, "Challenging the Grammar of Difference: Benoy Kumar Sarkar, Global Mobility and Anti-Imperialism Around the First World War," *European Review of History* 25, no. 3–4 (2018): 431–449.
56 The translation initially appeared partially as articles in Bengali journals from 1914–1923 and then as a book in 1932: Helleiner, *The Neomercantilists*, 121.
57 Benoy Sarkar, *The Political Philosophies Since 1905* (Madras: B.G. Paul, 1928), 348.
58 Benoy Sarkar, *Economic Development* (Madras: B. G. Paul and Co, 1926). The book was also dedicated to another supporter of the swadeshi movement, Romesh Dutt. For Ranade's early support of swadeshi ideas, see Manu Goswami, *Producing India* (Chicago: University of Chicago Press, 2004), 244; B. N. Ganguli, *Indian Economic Thought: Nineteenth Century Perspectives* (New Delhi: Tata McGraw-Hill Publishing Company, 1977), 203.

other book he wrote on international relations in 1926 to a much earlier South Asian thinker, Kautilya (375 – 283 BCE) who is usually identified as the initial author of the *Arthashastra* (Science of wealth) which advocated the cultivation of state wealth and power through mercantilist policies. Sarkar praised this ancient work of political economy and argued that "the logical apparatus of international diplomacy and the machinery of thinking in regard to the philosophy of foreign politics remain the same as in the days of our old Kautilya."[59]

Sarkar's ideas about broad-based international development emerged from his travels through depression-struck Europe between 1929 and 1931 after which he published *Studies in Applied Economics*. In that book, he urged industrialized countries such as Britain, Germany, and the United States to engage in the "economic statesmanship" of "promoting the economic development of regions which to-day find themselves in different degree of backwardness, for instance, the Balkan states, Russia, China, India, Latin-America, and the African Continent." His reasoning was that these industrialized regions would not be able to address unemployment and poverty at home without expanding foreign markets for their products. The best way for them to do that, he argued, was by exporting capital to these regions in ways that boosted the latter's industrialization and thus their purchasing power. As he put it, "the unemployment-stricken countries of the world are, therefore, called upon to export capital to those regions which are seeking to industrialise themselves."[60]

Sarkar acknowledged that the industrialization of these regions would create new competition for some manufacturers in Europe and America who were making "commonplace goods." But he argued that it would greatly expand demand for the goods of more "specialized industries" making higher quality goods as well as machinery. Indeed, Sarkar argued creatively that the growth of these specialized industries would help to generate a "Second Industrial Revolution" in wealthy countries alongside the "First Industrial Revolution" that was taking place in poorer regions of the world. In this way, complementary economic transformations would take place in both parts of the world that brought rising incomes to all: "the heightening of the standard of living among the working classes in Germany, Great Britain and the U.S.A., is going to become a reality, – but only to the extent and in so far as a simultaneous improvement takes place in the purchasing power, consumption scale etc., of the peasants in the

---

59 Benoy Sarkar, *The Politics of Boundaries and Tendencies in International Relations*, vol. 1 (Calcutta: N. M. Ray Chowdhury, 1926[1], 1938[2]), x.

60 Benoy Sarkar, *Studies in Applied Economics*, vol. 1 (Calcutta: Chuckervertty Chatterjee, 1932), 290 – 291.

Balkan Complex, Eastern Europe, Russia, China, India, Brazil, Chile, Africa etc."[61]

For this reason, Sarkar argued that the Great Depression was not just a "cyclical" crisis but also an "epochal" one which provided an opportunity for "socio-economic transformation" on a global scale. His advocacy of international development was designed to accelerate this transformation:

> This is to be a "long run" phenomenon which is perhaps to be counted in terms of half a generation, a generation or so. It should appear that we are to-day witnessing the transformation of the world's economic and social structure on a monumental scale and its transition to the next stage or epoch of its possibilities. The processes involved are really so many items constituting the final consummation of what may be called the "Second Industrial Revolution" in certain regions and of the "First Industrial Revolution" in others.[62]

During his travels in Europe, Sarkar visited Geneva and spoke with officials from the League of Nations and International Labour Office about his ideas. But he had been disappointed in their reaction: "It is curious that the League of Nations and the International Labour Office have bestowed hardly any attention on these aspects of the world-economy while discussing the present crisis." He implied that these organizations could be doing more to facilitate the epochal global transformation that was underway, if nothing else by identifying it and providing a mental road-map for policymakers to follow. In the absence of that kind of intellectual leadership, Sarkar had taken it upon himself to try to furnish "Indian economic statesmen as well as experts of other countries" with ideas that could "help them to visualize in a concrete manner the basic foundation of genuine world-economy, namely, the export of capital and 'instruments of production' (*Produktionsmittel*) from the regions of the Second Industrial Revolution to those of the First in order that the purchasing power of the men and women of the latter might rise helping thereby to heighten the standard of living of the former."[63]

Puig's Proposals in the Inter-American System

As noted above, League officials did finally begin to endorse the idea of broad-based international development cooperation by the late 1930s. But it was not

61 Sarkar, *Studies*, 292.
62 Sarkar, *Studies*, 268, 262, 269.
63 Sarkar, *Studies*, 297, ft. 33, viii.

until the 1944 Bretton Woods conference that this idea was institutionalized at the international level for the first time with the creation of the International Bank for Reconstruction and Development (IBRD). The bank represented the first international financial institution ever to be created with an explicit international development mandate. In the words of Article 1(i) of its Articles of Agreement, its purpose included assisting "the development of territories of members by facilitating the investment of capital for productive purposes, including [...] the development of productive facilities and resources in less developed countries."

The IBRD is often depicted as the brainchild of the American official Harry Dexter White, who developed a first draft of the institution in early 1942 and who was the lead US negotiator in the subsequent international discussions that produced the Bretton Woods agreements. But it is important to recognize that White and other supporters of the IBRD proposal drew on earlier ideas advanced by thinkers from less industrialized regions of the world. For example, Sun's IDO proposal was invoked by Chinese officials involved in the Bretton Woods negotiations as well as by some prominent American supporters of the creation of an international development institution in the early 1940s.[64] The much more important inspiration, however, came from Latin America in the form of proposals for an inter-American bank dating back to the early 1930s.[65]

Proposals for an inter-American bank had been advanced much earlier in the late nineteenth century but without any kind of development mandate. One with the latter feature first appeared prominently in a proposal put forward by Mexico's José Manuel Puig Casauranc (1888–1939) at an inter-American conference at Montevideo in 1933. Initially trained as a medical doctor (like Sun), Puig assumed various positions in the Mexican government after the country's revolution, including the position of foreign minister by the time of the Montevideo meeting. At that meeting, Puig took a leading role in criticizing American proposals to expand free trade as a solution to the economic chaos of the Great Depression. At a time when many Latin American countries were suffering from severe external debt and payments crises, he argued that protectionism was necessary given that the economy of Latin American countries was "of the colonial type [...] exporting raw materials and necessarily importing manufactured products."[66]

---

64 Helleiner, *Forgotten*, 190, 192, 198.

65 Helleiner, *Forgotten*, 52–79.

66 Christy Thornton, *Revolution in Development: Mexico and the Governance of the Global Economy* (Berkeley: University of California Press, 2021), 55.

Puig also devoted considerable attention to the need for international financial reform. He insisted on the need for "a new legal and philosophic conception of credit" at the international level that recognized it as "a 'social function' the same as property."[67] In Christy Thornton's words, he wanted recognition not just that "lenders needed to make productive use of their surplus capital" but also that "borrowers needed capital for their industrialization and development efforts." Thornton explains how his proposal was rooted in the ideas of his country's revolution: "Much as Mexico's revolutionary constitution of 1917 redefined property rights as vested not in the individual, but in the nation, Puig's proposal sought to reveal the *social* character of international finance, and to create institutions that would serve its social function."[68] Puig also emphasized other values from the Mexican revolution such as "inviolability of the principle of national autonomy" and the fact that his reforms were "something logically, decidedly, systematically and firmly on behalf of 'the many' as against the unjust privileges and interests of the few."[69]

A number of the specific reforms that Puig advanced were designed to address Latin America's external debt problem, such as a moratorium on debt payments, acceptance of the Drago Doctrine (which prohibited the use of force to collect debt repayment), and the creation of "public international organizations to take care of debts negotiations and agreements, in order to exclude thereby the intervention of Bankers' Committees."[70] But Puig also recommended the establishment of an inter-American bank that the Mexican delegation suggested would be "authorized to intervene effectively in the exchange, liquidation, and discount operations among the American countries and contribute, thus, to the development of agriculture, industry, and commerce."[71] Other Latin American governments were also interested in this idea, with one Peruvian delegate suggesting that it could help "the definite economic liberation of Latin America." After some discussion, two subcommittees of the conference recommended the creation of an inter-American bank that could grant credit facilities, "mobilize" capital, and "improve the onerous conditions in which many of the Latin American countries negotiate their foreign loans."[72] The conference as a whole then

67 Christy Thornton, "'Mexico Has the Theories': Latin America and the Interwar Origins of Development," in *The Development Century*, ed. Macekura and Manela, 263–282, 269.
68 Thornton, "Mexico," 269.
69 Thornton, *Revolution*, 48, 54.
70 Helleiner, *Forgotten*, 53.
71 Thornton, *Revolution*, 62–63.
72 Helleiner, *Forgotten*, 54.

recommended further consideration of the creation of an inter-American bank at the next Pan-American financial conference.

It is important to note that the enthusiasm for this idea came from Mexico and other Latin American governments, not the United States. While supporting further study of the idea, the US delegation made clear that their country was not willing to commit to participate in a future bank of this kind. The new Roosevelt administration was focused on the domestic economic troubles of the United States and wary of multilateral financial commitments, including those that might involve it directly in the negotiation of Latin American debts to Wall Street investors. US officials continued to oppose the proposal after this and only relented in 1939 when Mexico and other Latin American governments pressed once more for the idea at an inter-American meeting at the start of World War Two. In a new geostrategic context where US officials were trying to cultivate Latin American support, finally backed the establishment of an Inter-American Bank (IAB). US and Latin American officials then quickly negotiated the convention and by-laws of such a bank by 1940 whose mandate included the promotion of "the development of industry, public utilities, mining, agriculture, commerce, and finance in the Western Hemisphere."[73] Once again, Latin American officials saw the bank as pioneering a new pattern of international financial relations, one that would bolster their sovereignty and support their development aspirations in ways that American private investors had not. As the lead Mexican advocate at this time, Eduardo Villasenor, put it in 1939, the bank had to "avoid in all cases the aspect of hegemony or privilege that [foreign] investment could represent in the internal economy."[74]

At the center of these negotiations was Harry Dexter White who declared that the new institution's "principal importance will lie in investigating and facilitating rather long-term development projects in other American republics."[75] The IAB was never approved by US Congress, but it served as a key template for White's later Bretton Woods plans. His IBRD draft of early 1942 built directly on this earlier proposal but transformed its international development mandate from a regional context to a global one. Interestingly, Puig in 1933 had hoped for this eventual outcome, noting that his new conception of international finance "may perhaps come to have some effect of a universal order."[76]

When White's IBRD plan was discussed in the Bretton Woods negotiations, Latin American governments showed particular interest in its development lend-

73 Helleiner, *Forgotten*, 64.
74 Thornton, *Revolution*, 68.
75 Helleiner, *Forgotten*, 64.
76 Thornton, *Revolution*, 54.

ing mandate and compared it to the earlier IAB plan. Led once again by Mexico, they also worked hard to ensure that the IBRD's commitment to lending for European reconstruction would not dilute its development focus.

Because they made up almost half of the 44 governments represented at the conference, their views had to be taken seriously by the Americans and other delegates. The final text of the IBRD's charter that refers explicitly to assisting "less developed countries" was a product of Mexican lobbying, as was a clause that committed the bank to give "equitable consideration to projects for development and projects for reconstruction alike."[77] The IBRD's development mandate, thus, had strong Latin American roots.

Conclusion

The idea of international development was invented not just by figures from the United States and Western Europe who wanted their governments to support the economic development of less industrialized regions of the world. It was also pioneered by thinkers from the latter who wanted their societies to receive assistance from those same governments (and/or from international institutions they controlled). It is curious that the thinkers analyzed in this paper have received relatively little attention from historians of international development. Not only did these thinkers each develop ambitious and innovative ideas on the topic, but some of their ideas also influenced thinking in the United States about international development such as the Sun's IDO plan and inter-American bank proposals of Puig and other Latin American thinkers.[78] The diffusion of ideas about international development, in other words, flowed not just from the industrialized core to the rest of world but also in the reverse direction.

What explains the relative neglect of these thinkers in histories of international development? No doubt, it is partly a product of the fact that the broader history of economic thought devotes so much more attention to American and Western European thinkers than to those from countries such as India, China, Romania, and Mexico. But it may also be because so many scholars of international development have embraced the thesis that international development was invented in the leading Western powers to legitimate their domination of

77 Helleiner, *Forgotten*, 165. See also 163–164.

78 Harry Dexter White had also read Manoilescu's book but apparently was critical of it; David Rees, *Harry Dexter White* (New York: Coward, McCann and Geoghegan, 1973), 39. It is also noteworthy that Naoroji's ideas were widely known in European and American anti-imperialist circles in the late nineteenth century and turn of the twentieth, see Patel, *Naoroji*, 223–236, 251.

other parts of the world. The idea that key pioneers of this concept came from regions of the world suffering from that domination challenges that thesis. Even more unsettling may be the fact that these pioneers were leading critics of that domination, and saw international development as a tool for overcoming it.

The content of the ideas of these thinkers also undermines the common notion that international development was rooted in only Western traditions of thought. Although all five of these thinkers were familiar with Western thought, their ideas were not merely derivative of it. Not only did they innovative intellectually in important ways in response to local contexts, but they also drew inspiration from earlier thinkers from their own parts of the world. Some of the earlier thinkers they cited were part of autonomously-generated, non-Western developmentalist intellectual traditions, including those that dated back to ancient times in China (in the case of thinkers cited by Sun) and South Asia (in the case of Kautilya cited by Sarkar).

The case for devoting more attention to these thinkers, then, is not just to build a more comprehensive history of the intellectual origins of international development. The study of their ideas also encourages scholars to see those origins in a new light. In addition to showing the wider geographical sources of early ideas of international development, it reveals greater diversity in the content of those ideas and intellectual traditions that informed them.[79] In short, the birth of international development thought looks more complicated than much conventional wisdom suggests when its history includes thinkers from outside the industrialized core of the pre-World War Two world economy.

---

79 For others who have called for more attention to this diversity, see Hodge, "Writing"; Stephen Macekura and Erez Manela, "Introduction," in *The Development Century*, ed. Macekura and Manela, 1–18.

Dena Freeman

Entangled Histories of "Development," "development," and "Christian development"

Introduction

While the origins of international development are many and diverse, as the articles in this volume attest, this paper seeks to explore certain aspects of development thinking and practice that can be traced back to nineteenth century European Protestant missionaries, in their entangled relations with both European governments and non-Western colonial subjects, in the context of European colonialism and Empire. It seeks to show that the idea of development did not burst into the world with President Truman's 1949 speech, as is often assumed, but rather has roots which extend much further back, and which cannot be separated from Protestant ideas about providence, civilization, and the practice of overseas mission. It also seeks to show how the various different meanings that are given to the term "development" in the contemporary context in part arise from the historical collaborations and contradictions between these secular and Christian actors in the nineteenth and early twentieth centuries.

Academic discussions about "international development" often exhibit a disciplinary dichotomy, with scholars from different disciplines using the term to mean quite different things. Those in international relations, political science, and economics, broadly speaking, tend to conceive of development as political-economic relations within and between states aimed at promoting industrialization and modernization in poorer countries and increased trade between poorer countries and richer countries. In this article I will refer to that as "Development," with a capital D. Scholars in development studies, and to some extent sociology and anthropology, and indeed much of the general public, more often consider development as a genuine concern to improve the lives of poor people, as a way of making society better, or as a set of techniques to improve human capacities, wellbeing, and quality of life. I shall refer to that as "development," with a small d. When these meanings are conflated, which they often are, I will talk about "D/development." And recently, there has been a surge of scholarly interest in the area of religion and development, focusing on the activities of (mainly Christian) faith-based development organizations and the ways that

https://doi.org/10.1515/9783110730234-004

faith, culture, and meaning impact on development. I will refer to this third strand as "Christian development."

This article aims to consider all of these different meanings of development, and to shed light on their entangled and mutually constituted histories, in order to unravel the way that various actors, secular and Christian, governmental and non-governmental, have contributed to the contemporary manifestation of the field of "international development," in its wide diversity, as an inspiring idea, as a set of practices, and as a discourse that legitimates relations of extraction and exploitation.

The Emergence of Protestant Social Action and Evangelism in the Context of Industrialization and Empire

The roots of contemporary ideas about international development can be traced back to the late eighteenth and early nineteenth centuries and the tumultuous societal changes brought about in Britain and other parts of Europe by industrialization, expanding imperialism and the institutionalization of international industrial capitalism. The re-organization of society and economy that these processes ushered in, both nationally and internationally, led to increasing wealth and affluence for some (mainly the capitalist entrepreneurs), and dramatically worsening living and working conditions for others (mainly the urban proletariat laboring in the factories and mines in Europe, and the slaves laboring in mines and plantations in the colonies). In this context, new ideas about social reform and societal improvement started to emerge in certain sectors of European society, most notably amongst Protestant Christians.[1]

Since the Enlightenment, Christianity had been somewhat in a state of flux. New ideas about science and evolution were gaining ground, and many Europe-

1 Catholics also have a long history of involvement in social improvement, mission, and development. See Elisabeth Foster, *African Catholic: Decolonization and the Transformation of the Church* (Cambridge, Mass.: Harvard University Press, 2019); Peter Stamatov, "Activist Religion, Empire, and the Emergence of Modern Long-Distance Advocacy Networks," *American Sociological Review* 75, no. 4 (2010): 607–628; Charlotte Walker-Said, "Science and Charity: Rival Catholic Visions for Humanitarian Practice at The End of Empire," *French Politics, Culture & Society* 33, no. 2 (2015): 33–54. For an analysis of the role of more conservative evangelical missionaries in development, see Dena Freeman, *Tearfund and the Quest for Faith-Based Development* (London: Routledge, 2019), 18–37.

an Christians were experiencing a profound crisis of faith.[2] European society was slowly starting to secularize and the Protestant church needed to re-imagine itself and its role in social life. And thus, even as large numbers of people left the church, a huge number of revival movements swept across Europe in what has since become known as the nineteenth century "Great Awakening." These revival movements demanded that Christians engage more deeply and passionately with their faith in their own lives and also work towards the manifestation of Christian values in society.[3] Thus the Protestant churches began to re-fashion themselves as institutions that demanded and facilitated intense spiritual experience on the one hand, while also dedicating themselves to social reform and the improvement of society on the other.

Throughout the nineteenth century the idea that society can and should be improved began to grow, and several social reform movements came into being, most of them initiated by Protestant Christians and inspired by Christian values. Most of these movements focussed either on improving working conditions in the mines and factories at home, or abolishing the transatlantic slave trade and ending slavery in the colonies. For example, in Britain Lord Shaftesbury, a prominent nineteenth-century evangelical Protestant politician, passed acts in the British parliament to prohibit the employment of women and children in coal mines and to establish a ten-hour day for factory workers.[4] Other prominent British evangelicals, such as John Wesley and William Wilberforce, worked tirelessly to abolish the transatlantic slave trade and bring about the end of slavery. For nineteenth-century evangelical Protestants, in Britain, as in Germany, Scandinavia, and elsewhere, the improvement of society came to be understood as part and parcel of the practice of Christian faith. Charles Finney, a leading mid-nineteenth-century American evangelical revivalist, summed up the sentiment when he wrote:

2 Richard Helmstadter and Bernard Lightman, eds., *Victorian Faith in Crisis: Essays on Continuity and Change in Nineteenth Century Religious Belief* (Basingstoke: Macmillan, 1990); Michael Watts, *The Dissenters: The Crisis and Conscience of Nonconformity* (Oxford: Oxford University Press, 2015).

3 David Bebbington, *Evangelicalism in Modern Britain: A History from the 1730s to the 1980s* (London: Routledge, 1989); Earle Cairns, *An Endless Line of Splendors: Revivals and Their Leaders from The Great Awakening to the Present* (Eugene: Wipf and Stock, 1986); Fred Van Lieburg, "Interpreting the Dutch Great Awakening (1749–1755)," *Church History* 77, no. 2 (2008): 318–336.

4 Geoffrey Finlayson, *The Seventh Earl of Shaftesbury, 1801–1885* (London: Methuen, 1981); Kathleen Heasman, *Evangelicals in Action: An Appraisal of their Social Work in the Victorian Era* (London: G. Bles, 1962).

> The great business of the church is to reform the world. The Church of Christ was originally organised to be a body of reformers. The very profession of Christianity implies the profession and virtually an oath to do all that can be done for the universal reformation of the world.[5]

These "awakened" Christians also placed a renewed emphasis on personal spiritual experience and many began to develop a strong desire to share their experience with others, in the belief that it could bring them salvation. This renewed evangelical zeal, in the context of expanding colonial empire and increasing awareness of the existence and nature of "distant others" overseas, started a theological debate within the Protestant world about the importance of spreading the gospel. Up until then mainstream Protestant Christian thinking was that the "Great Mandate" to spread the gospel had ended with the apostles and that salvation depended on election by God and was not something that could be influenced by worldly activity or personal faith. But in 1792 William Carey, widely known as the father of Protestant missions, wrote a small booklet called *An Enquiry into the Obligations of Christians, to Use Means for the Conversion of the Heathens*, which argued that the "Great Mandate" had not ended with the apostles and that new methods had to be discovered in order to fulfil it in the present.[6]

Carey's booklet led to the founding of the Baptist Missionary Society (BMS) later that year, and to the founding of many other missionary societies in the subsequent years.[7] The London Missionary Society (LMS) was formed in 1795, the Church Missionary Society (CMS) in 1797, the Wesleyan Methodist Missionary Society in 1813, the Basel Evangelical Missionary Society in 1815, the Berlin Mission in 1824, the Swedish Missionary Society in 1835, the Norwegian Missionary Society in 1842, and many others.[8] The birth of these missionary societies represented a major sea change in the Protestant world. As the nineteenth century American missionary Rufus Anderson noted, "It was not until the present centu-

5 Cited in Melvin Tinker, "Reversal or Betrayal? Evangelicals and Socio-Political Involvement in the Twentieth Century," *Churchman* 33, no. 3 (1999): 254–276.

6 Roberto Catalano, "Missionary Societies in the Evangelical Churches: Origins and Characteristics," *Annales Missiologici Posnanienses* 19 (2014): 107–135, 112.

7 The one missionary society that was founded earlier was the Society for the Propagation of the Gospel in Foreign Parts (SPG), that had been formed at the start of the eighteenth century in order to provide Christian services to colonial settlers in North America and it only started to evangelise the "heathens" later in the nineteenth century.

8 William Richey Hogg, *Ecumenical Foundations: A History of the International Missionary Council and its Nineteenth Century Background* (Eugene: Wipf and Stock, 1952), 5–14.

ry that the evangelical churches of Christendom were ever really organised with a view to the conversion of the world."[9]

In many cases missionaries from one country had first trained in another country, and there were strong links of cooperation between many of the missionary societies. Throughout the nineteenth century a series of interdenominational missionary conferences in Europe, America, and in the colonies further helped to develop a shared vision about the goals and techniques of missionary work across most of these Protestant missions, with the result that they operated in many fundamental respects in broadly similar ways.[10] It has thus often been noted that nineteenth-century Protestant missionaries formed a network of religious actors extending over the colonial space, and often acted in opposition to, or at least in tension with, the other existing networks, of colonial administrators and of European settlers.[11]

Nineteenth century evangelical Protestants were inspired to both improve society and to spread the gospel, and to a large extent they understood both elements to be part of a broader process of social and spiritual change leading towards salvation.[12] Thus bringing Christianity to the heathen did not just involve matters of gospel and belief, but also included the work of "civilization," a broader project which included changing people's dress, lifestyle, social practices, and working habits. As Stanley puts it, "To bring to the 'heathen' the gospel of the cross of Christ was to open before them not only the prospect of eternal life but also the road to unlimited social and economic development."[13] Although the term "development" was not used until much later, some of the basic ideas underlying it were already beginning to take shape in the nineteenth century.

9 Catalano, "Missionary Societies," 108.

10 Hogg, *Ecumenical Foundations*, 15–50.

11 Stamatov, "Activist Religion," 614; Zoe Laidlaw, *Colonial Connections, 1815–45: Patronage, the Information Revolution and Colonial Government* (Manchester: Manchester University Press, 2005); Alan Lester, *Imperial Networks: Creating Identities in Nineteenth-Century South Africa and Britain* (London: Routledge, 2001).

12 Missionary societies sought to raise funds and to educate people by publishing information bulletins, with letters and diaries from the different missions. In this way they mobilized a mass movement in Britain, Switzerland, the German states, and elsewhere, in which people felt called to be involved in the mission enterprise by financially and spiritually supporting their missionaries overseas. See Catalano, "Missionary Societies," 118. This mode of operation was later adopted by humanitarian and development NGOs in the twentieth century.

13 Brian Stanley, "'Commerce and Christianity': Providence Theory, the Missionary Movement, and the Imperialism of Free Trade, 1842–1860," *The Historical Journal* 26, no. 1 (1983): 71–94, 71.

But at this point in time there was little idea about exactly how the "civilizing" or "developmental" process would actually take place. The initial focus of the missionaries was on spreading the gospel. But it quickly became clear that for people to be able to take in the gospel message they first needed reasonably healthy bodies, and second needed to be able to read the bible. And therefore almost all of the missionaries got to work providing basic medical care and teaching literacy. These can be seen as the first "development" activities, with missionaries of all persuasions opening schools, running clinics, and seeking to "improve" and "civilize" the bodies and souls of the people in the colonies.

According to the providentialist worldview that was common among most Protestants at this time, this process of "civilizing the heathens" was part of God's plan for the world and would ultimately lead to the salvation of humanity.[14] Viewed through this lens, nineteenth-century Protestants understood the expansion of European empires as part of God's plan to redeem mankind. Empire, along with growing international commerce, facilitated their spreading of the Christian message, which would ultimately lead to the spiritual and material development of everyone and the salvation of humanity.

It is worth pointing out that at this point in time most colonial administrators and secular traders in what have been referred to as the "secular imperial networks" did not share the missionaries' view of the purpose of empire. In their view the primary purpose of empire was to enrich themselves and the metropole. They had little interest in the spread of Christianity or of "civilization" or of any other scheme for "social improvement" in the colonies. Stamatov summarizes the distinction between the dominant views in the secular and the religious networks very aptly when he says,

> secular networks, agents of governance and settlers, were largely driven by the logic of economic profit. This reckless drive for profits engendered, in turn, double moral standards that legitimized the exploitation and dehumanization of non-Europeans [...] In many cases, however, religious imperial networks were guided by a very different logic in which imperial 'others' were potential or actual Christians, and thus fellow human beings entitled to dignity and rights.[15]

Thus in these early years the relationship between missionaries and the colonial administration was often rather fraught, with missionaries frequently being imprisoned or expelled.[16] While the colonialists sought to exploit the colonies for

14 Stanley, "Commerce," 73.

15 Stamatov, "Activist Religion," 614.

16 Andrew Porter, *Religion Versus Empire? British Protestant Missionaries and Overseas Expansion, 1700–1914* (Manchester: Manchester University Press, 2004).

their own benefit, the missionaries sought to improve them in a way that they believed would lead to mutual benefit.[17] And while the colonialists saw local people as a source of cheap labor and as little more than commodities, missionaries saw them as potential or actual Christians and thus as fellow human beings entitled to dignity and rights.[18] Andrew Porter, in his masterful study of the tensions and entanglements between missionaries and government officials in the British Empire, gives the example of the missionary, John Philip, who struggled with British imperial officials and white settlers in what is now South Africa, about the treatment of black workers. While the officials and settlers argued that the local people were fit only to work, Philip contended that they were humans and Christians and as such deserved rights. Philip took his pleas all the way back to Britain and to the British parliament, supported by the London Missionary Society and the influential Clapham Sect. At the center of this struggle, and indeed of many other similar struggles detailed by Porter, was the "debate about the meaning of "civilization" and especially the possibility of civilizing, or improving the conditions of, non-European peoples."[19]

So here we see the beginning of the divide between secular and religious, and governmental and non-governmental, ways of viewing the colonies and the purpose of European activities in them. Secular governments were interested in pursuing their own national interests, mainly expanding production for export, which we can see as an early precursor to the idea of "Development," while religious non-governmental actors were seeking to bring about a genuine improvement in the lives of local peoples, which we can understand as the first glimmers of the idea of "development."

"Commerce and Christianity" as the Route to World Salvation

In the 1830s Protestant ideas about how to "civilize" the heathen took on a new shape. Rather than just focus on medical care and literacy, alongside preaching

17 The "natives" in the colonies generally also had their own ideas about what was good for them, and there were of course long processes of negotiation between missionaries and local leaders and communities. For one of the best explorations of the clash between missionary and "native" worldviews, see Jean Comaroff and John Comaroff, *Of Revelation and Revolution: Christianity, Colonialism and Consciousness in South Africa* (Chicago: University of Chicago Press, 1991).

18 Stamatov, "Activist Religion," 615.

19 Porter, *Religion Versus Empire?*, 92.

the gospel, a new idea emerged about the civilizing power of commerce. As David Livingstone put it: "we ought to encourage the Africans to cultivate for our markets as the most effectual means next to the Gospel for their elevation."[20]

The idea of "commerce and Christianity" initially emerged as a solution to two problems that troubled nineteenth century Protestants – how to abolish the transatlantic slave trade and how to "civilize" the heathens. The vision was most ably put forward by Quaker MP Thomas Fowell Buxton in his book, *The African Slave Trade and Its Remedy* (1840), which set out a plan to put an end to the slave trade by improving the situation in Africa, through developing its "vast, though as yet undeveloped, resources" and "enlightening its population":[21]

> Let missionaries and schoolmasters, the plough and the spade, go together, and agriculture will flourish; the avenues to legitimate commerce will be opened; confidence between man and man will be inspired; whilst civilization will advance as the natural effect, and Christianity operate as the proximate cause of this happy change.[22]

In this way it would prove more profitable, and more ethical, to keep Africans in Africa, where they would work the land and sell the resources to the British, rather than to sell them as slaves to work for the colonists in the Americas. And thus the slave trade could be replaced with a supposedly "legitimate trade," not of slaves but of resources. At the same time new markets could be opened up for British goods through African consumption. Africa could be developed by a program "to encourage her commerce; to improve the cultivation of her soil; and to raise the morals, and the minds of her inhabitants."[23] At first, this seemed like a "win-win" situation, in which the interests of the imperialists could coincide with those of the missionaries, and in which benefits could be generated both for the metropole and for the local people living in the colonies. And infused with the Calvinist work ethic, many European Protestants at this time were delighted that their capitalist economic interests could indeed be fully in line with their Christian faith.

This type of program required a combination of entrepreneurial and missionary effort. And thus between the 1830s and the 1860s relations between col-

20 Brad Faught, "Missionaries, Indirect Rule and the Changing Mandate of Mission in Colonial Northern Nigeria: The Case of Rowland Victor Bingham and the Sudan Interior Mission," *Canadian Society of Church History Historical Papers* (1994): 121–141, 122.

21 Thomas Buxton, *The African Slave Trade and Its Remedy* (London: John Murray, 1840), 301–302.

22 Buxton, *The African Slave Trade*, 511.

23 Buxton, *The African Slave Trade*, 310.

onialists and missionaries improved considerably. Colonialists began to see the missionaries' "civilizing" or "developmental" work as rather useful, particularly their endeavors to promote literacy, to encourage a Calvinist ethic of hard work and to improve agricultural production. And so from the 1830s onwards missionaries, and their worldview, became co-opted into the colonial project.[24] During this period the Protestant idea that the fundamental purpose of European empires was to improve the world – by bringing the people of Africa and Asia both social and economic progress and spiritual salvation, while at the same time encouraging a mutually beneficial trade between Europeans and the colonies – was effectively co-opted by the secular colonialists to legitimate their imperial activities. From the mid-nineteenth century onwards Protestant understandings of empire in terms of providence, progress, and civilizing mission became the established framework of European imperial discourse.[25] Here we can see the beginnings of a pattern of rhetoric whereby discourses about social improvement or humanitarianism (be that "civilization" or "development") are used to legitimate relations of extraction and exploitation.

The Late Nineteenth-Century Divergence between Missionaries and Colonialists

However, during the 1860s the alliance between commerce and Christianity gradually fell apart and the aims and interests of religious and secular actors began to diverge. For a variety of reasons many European countries shifted their colonial strategies away from "commerce and Christianity" towards improved secular governance of the colonies and the extraction of resources.

Nonetheless, the discourse of "civilizing mission" remained central to the European colonial project in this period. Even though colonial involvement in "civilizing" was markedly lower, the power of the discourse and the uses to which it could be put were becoming much clearer. For example, public support for British and German colonial interventions in East Africa could be aroused by contrasting the European approach of "civilizing Africa" with the Omani/Swahili

---

24 Stanley, "Commerce and Christianity," 76; Jörg Haustein, "Development as a Form of Religious Engineering? Religion and Secularity in Development Discourse," *Religion* 51, no. 1 (2021): 19–39, 22–23; Jörg Haustein and Emma Tomalin, "Religion and Development in Africa and Asia," in *Routledge Handbook of Africa-Asia Relations*, ed. Pedro Amakasu Raposo, David Arase, and Scarlett Cornelissen (London: Routledge, 2017), 76–93, 78.
25 Stanley, "Commerce and Christianity," 94.

slave-traders who were characterized as "barbarian." Using this rhetoric, German colonialists, for example, were able to secure parliamentary support for military action to quash the uprising against the German East Africa Company in 1888. And Hermann von Wissmann, who would later lead the German military conquest of the East African coast, enthusiastically supported the call for a Christian "crusade" against Arabs in inner Africa and publicly proclaimed his wish to "see freed the enslaved race [...] and to truly open Africa to the influence of our civilization."[26] The rhetoric of "civilizing mission" provided the moral cover for European colonial exploitation and was fundamental in securing widespread European public support for this project.

At the same time, on the missionary side, Christian confidence in the redemptive function of commerce had begun to wane. They observed that engaging "the natives" in commerce often failed to support their spiritual development as Christians. Instead it seemed that many people were converting simply to gain improved access to trading possibilities and as a result the quality of their faith was poor and superficial. Therefore a growing body of Christian opinion in the later part of the nineteenth century began to repudiate the association with such material matters as commerce, and to reconceive of the missionary task as purely spiritual and focussed solely on evangelism.[27] Thus after the 1860s most of the classical missions disentangled themselves from commercial activities and returned to their earlier focus on spiritual conversion alongside basic humanitarian and developmental activities such as healthcare and education. For many of the classical missions at this time education and health came to be seen as lofty goals in their own right, and not just as a means to evangelism, as the missions began to see humanitarianism (another precursor term to "development") as a central part of their work.

During this period, and despite the ongoing rhetoric of "civilizing mission," most European governments did very little to develop or improve the colonies or the lives of those living there. Britain, for example, followed a policy of "colonial self-sufficiency," whereby the colonies were required to finance their own economic development from the proceeds of sales of their export crops and whatever private international capital they could attract, and funding would not be sent from the metropole. The result was that very little government money was spent on economic development, and what was spent was used to finance endeavors which would be profitable for the colonialists, with little regard to their impact

26 *Deutsche Kolonialzeitung* 1888, 355, quoted in Jörg Haustein, "Development as a Form of Religious Engineering?," 24.
27 Brad Faught, "Missionaries," 122; Brian Stanley, "'Commerce and Christianity'," 92.

on the local people or the local society. The Dutch approach was even more exploitative, particularly in colonial Indonesia, with a focus on state-directed, large-scale agricultural enterprise, which had little benefit for the local people.[28]

Instead, at this time, it was the classical missionaries who were the main agents of both material and spiritual development across the colonial world. In sub-Saharan Africa, for example, over 90% of Western education during the colonial period was provided by missionaries.[29] In this way missionaries were critical to the early spread of literacy and Western scientific thought and their efforts helped to create a modernizing African elite.[30]

By the early twentieth century the classical mission societies had grown hugely in scale and resources and had established a professional bureaucracy and structure which would later be copied by most non-governmental development NGOs. Each missionary society employed large numbers of European and local staff and ran several institutions in the colonies. The CMS, for example, in 1906 had an annual income of £300,000, and was responsible for 975 missionaries and 8,850 "native agents," 37 theological and training colleges, 92 boarding schools, 12 industrial institutions, 2,400 elementary schools, 40 hospitals, 73 dispensaries, 21 leprosaria, 6 homes for the blind, 18 orphanages, 6 other homes and refuges, and 17 presses or publishing houses.[31]

Each missionary society also maintained its own publishing arm and distributed a primary journal to keep its European supporters informed. Much of what the average European person knew about Africa or Asia in the late nineteenth and early twentieth centuries came from reading the bulletins and periodicals of the missionary societies. The mission societies also hosted meetings and exhibitions that were designed to stimulate interest and to generate financial sup-

---

28 Suzanne Moon, *Technology and Ethical Idealism: A History of Development in the Netherlands East Indies* (Leiden: CNWS Publications, 2007).

29 Francisco Gallego and Robert Woodberry, "Christian Missionaries and Education in Former African Colonies: How Competition Mattered," *Journal of African Economies 19*, no. 3 (2010): 294–329.

30 Several graduates of this missionary education later went on to become the first generation of African nationalist leaders. The mission background of many of the first generation of African leaders added a significant Christian content to the development programs they sought to implement after independence – Kenneth Kaunda's Presbyterian heritage shaped his brand of humanism for Zambia, and Canaan Banana, formerly a Methodist minister and then first president of Zimbabwe, developed an explicit theology of development. See David Maxwell, "Post-Colonial Christianity in Africa," in *World Christianities c. 1914-c. 2000*, ed. Hugh McLeod (Cambridge: Cambridge University Press, 2006), 401–422, 401, 414.

31 Brian Stanley, "Where Have Our Mission Structures Come From?" *Transformation* 20, no. 1 (2003): 39–46, 42.

port. In this way, rather like contemporary non-governmental development NGOs, mission societies played an important role in providing information to the European public about the rest of the world as part and parcel of their fund-raising activities.[32] And, whilst promoting support for their mission work they, often unintentionally, also promoted public support for the imperial project, as by now the quite distinct notions of "Christian mission" and imperial "civilizing mission" had become almost totally conflated in European public discourse.

Early Twentieth-Century Rapprochement between Missionaries and Colonialists in the Pursuit of "Development"

Throughout the nineteenth century colonial "Development" had primarily been a matter of resource extraction from the colonies for the benefit of the metropole. The term "development" was mainly used in the context of the "development of resources." Towards the end of the nineteenth century this began to change. The Dutch government developed an "Ethical Policy" which promoted social welfare projects to support what was coming to be known as "the development of the native peoples."[33] British colonial government officials began to talk about the "development of estates" or territories, meaning the development of the colony itself. Thus in a speech given on August 22, 1895, Britain's new Secretary of State for the Colonies, Joseph Chamberlain, said:

> I regard many of our Colonies as being in the condition of undeveloped estates, and estates which can never be developed without Imperial assistance [...]. I shall be prepared to consider very carefully [...] any case which may occur in which, by the judicious investment of British money, those estates which belong to the British Crown may be developed for the benefit of their population and for the benefit of the greater population which is outside.[34]

This speech marked the beginning of a new approach to colonial development, or what I call "Development," in two other ways. Firstly, it brought the idea that

---

32 Patrick Harries and David Maxwell, eds., *The Spiritual in the Secular: Missionaries and Knowledge about Africa* (Grand Rapids: Eerdmans, 2012), 1.

33 *Moon, Technology and Ethical Idealism, 1.*

34 Quoted in George Abbott, "A Re-Examination of the 1929 Colonial Development Act," *The Economic History Review* 24, no. 1 (1971): 68 – 81, 68. See also Joseph Morgan Hodge, *Triumph of the Expert: Agrarian Doctrines of Development and the Legacies of British Colonialism* (Athens: Ohio University Press, 2007).

colonial development should be for the benefit of the local native population in the colony as well as for the benefit of the metropole. And secondly, it marked a break with previous policies of "colonial self-sufficiency," and a move towards a new approach where the metropole would play an important part in financing the economic development of the colonies.

While this speech marked the beginning of the public recognition of a new principle of imperial responsibility for colonial development, it was only with the passing of the Colonial Development Act in 1929 that these ideas began to be formalized into a more consistent set of policy and practices.[35] The Act established a fund for colonial development of between £750,000 and £1 million per annum, and most of this was spent on transport, communications, and infrastructure projects where labor requirements could be met through exporting British workers, thus easing British unemployment problems.[36] There was however little real engagement with social change or improvement for the natives in the colonies. This, as we shall see, has remained a key aspect of "Development," in contrast to "development."

As conditions in the colonies failed to improve and as social unrest and calls for independence began to spread, colonial officials in many European countries realized that they needed to change their approach if they did not want to risk losing the colonies. Thus they decided to invest more seriously in developing the colonies for the benefits of the native population in order to calm unrest.[37] This led to the British Colonial Development and Welfare Act of 1940, and the French *Fonds d'Investissements pour le Développement Economique et Sociale* (Investment Fund for Economic and Social Development) in 1946, which both allocated more serious financial resources and focussed on improving the living and working conditions of workers so that both their productivity and their standard of living would increase. These acts marked a shift from pre-war extractive colonial policy married to a legitimising discourse of "civilizing mission" to a more balanced approach combining economic development and welfare, with

---

35 Abbott, "A Re-Examination," 70.

36 Abbott, "A Re-Examination," 74; Charlotte Riley, "Monstrous Predatory Vampires and Beneficent Fairy-Godmothers: British Post-war Colonial Development in Africa" (PhD diss., University College London, 2013), 73.

37 Frederick Cooper, "Modernising Bureaucrats, Backward Africans and the Development Concept," in *International Development and the Social Sciences: Essays on the History and Politics of Knowledge*, ed. Frederick Cooper and Randall Packard (Berkeley: University of California Press, 1997), 64–92, 67.

the aim that there would be benefit to both the colony and the metropole.[38] Science and technology, bureaucracy and large, state-led projects, often in the agriculture sector, were at the core of this new approach of colonial "Development."

As imperial governments became more interested in the development of the colonies, missionaries from the classical mission societies were again foregrounding humanitarian, or "developmental," activities as the core of mission. And so in the early decades of the twentieth century they again started to work closely with colonial administrations to carry out what was now coming to be called "D/development." Adjusting to the new opportunities offered by changing colonial policies, they began to shift their activities from a narrow focus on education and health to work more broadly on developmental activities, such as agriculture and welfare, in order to receive the government grants that were now made available.[39]

As the classical missionaries became more and more involved in D/development work, now mainly funded by European governments, they formulated their own concepts of "development," based on the liberal incarnational theology and the social gospel. Ideas were discussed and exchanged at missionary conferences, including the large and formative Edinburgh Missionary Conference in 1910, and proliferated through all of the churches and organizations in the newly forming Ecumenical Movement, forming a reasonably coherent theory of "Christian development."

In this alternative view, development was the holistic change of the "whole person," body and soul, towards living a comfortable and meaningful "abundant life." The role of the missionary was to mimic Christ's example as a "servant" to the other in his ministry of care to the "whole person." Most fundamentally, they believed in the combination of secular science and technology with Christian compassion and spirituality, or in their terms, "science in the hands of love," which could lead to "wholeness."[40] And fundamentally, they believed that conversion to Christianity was both the most important method and the central goal of development, because it brought about a change in worldview in the develop-

38 Riley, "Monstrous Predatory Vampires," 75; Kathryn Tidrick, *Empire and English Character* (London: Tauris Parke, 1990).

39 Similarly, Catholic missionaries began to receive funding from the French government's Fund for Economic and Social Development to carry out development activities in their African colonies. Foster, *African Catholic*, 3.

40 Rebecca Hughes, "'Science in the Hands of Love': British Evangelical Missionaries and Colonial Development in Africa, c. 1940–60," *Journal of Imperial and Commonwealth History* 41, no. 5 (2013): 823–842.

ing person, thus leading to a sustained shift in actions and behaviors, which they claimed was far more important than small material improvements.[41]

With this alternative conceptualization of "development," the classical missionaries criticized the colonial state and its large-scale, secular, technological "Development" projects. They argued that development needed to consider persons as well as forms of production. For people to develop, they argued, they needed to change their worldviews, their beliefs, and the structures of their communities. For example, in contrast to imperial "Development" policies, that sought to displace small scale hoe agriculture and replace it with large scale mechanized agriculture, British CMS missionaries instead developed a "theology of the soil" to guide their approach to agricultural development, in which religious conversion combined with small-scale technical inputs would lead to improvements in agricultural productivity and harmonious rural communities. The type of progress they promoted was to deliver greater crop yields in order to satisfy human need rather than to make profit and riches for the metropole.[42]

So we can see that during this period the basic outlines of two very different approaches to "D/development" began to crystallise. On the one hand was large-scale, state-led, technology-driven "Development" projects whose aims were primarily to increase productivity and export to the metropole, with at best, perhaps some benefit to the local people; and on the other hand was small-scale, Christian, people-or community-centered "development" approaches which focussed almost entirely on improving the lives and livelihoods of local people. While both types of activities went under the name of "D/development," they were fundamentally different in rationale, organization, and purpose. The conflation of the terms used to refer to these two very different activities led to much confusion, and the beginnings of much discussion and debate about the nature and purpose of "D/development," both in policy circles and in broader European civil society.[43]

---

41 I have made similar arguments with regard to Pentecostal development approaches in the late twentieth century. See Dena Freeman, "The Pentecostal Ethic and the Spirit of Development," in *Pentecostalism and Development: Churches, NGOs and Social Change in Africa*, ed. Dena Freeman (London: Palgrave Macmillan, 2012), 1–38; Dena Freeman, "Affordances of Rupture and their Enactment: A Framework for Understanding Christian Change," *Journal of the Finnish Anthropological Society* 42, no. 4 (2017): 3–24.

42 Hughes, "'Science in the Hands of Love'," 832–833.

43 Hodge, *Triumph of the Expert.*

The Post-War Fall of Empire and the Rise of "D/development"

After the Second World War, and particularly after 1956, European empires began to wane. While it would take another 20 years for most colonies to achieve independence, the direction of travel was becoming clear. And as the idea of empire as the best way to organize relations between Europe and the rest of the world began to decline, in its place arose the new idea of "international development." President Truman's speech in 1949 widely publicized the notion of "international development" as the idea that the richer or "developed" countries would help the poorer or "under-developed" countries in the post-war and post-colonial era. As has been shown above, the roots of D/development thinking and practice extend much further back into history, but what Truman's speech did was to launch the idea that "international development" would become the main reason for the ongoing involvement of Europe and North America in the economic matters of the former colonies. In effect, Truman co-opted the already-existing idea of D/development and used it to legitimate future post-colonial relations of extraction and exploitation, in a similar way to how the Christian idea of "civilizing mission" had been co-opted to legitimate earlier colonial relations of extraction and exploitation. And the fact that "D/development" itself was already a contested term, used by different actors to mean quite different things, made it a particularly suitable term, rich in rhetorical possibilities and social and moral valence.

And as in the nineteenth century, many people in the public and in civil society were taken in by this legitimating discourse. The new field of international development began to flourish. Even as large, state-led "Development" projects, such as the Sukumaland Development Scheme and the Tanganyika Groundnut Scheme, were funded by Western governments and implemented by the new governments of independent countries in Africa and Asia, a plethora of non-governmental organizations emerged to take forward the vision and practice of small-scale, people-centered "development."

Throughout the 1950s, many voluntary humanitarian associations that had been established after the First World War to help war refugees, such as Save the Children and Plan International, began to re-orient themselves to focus on providing aid to the poor in the colonies and former colonies. Newer voluntary associations that had been established after the Second World War to provide relief to the war-wounded and to refugees in destroyed communities in Europe, such as Oxfam, Christian Aid, and War on Want, also began to shift their activities to providing aid to the poor in the newly decolonizing countries of Africa and Asia.[44] At the same time many explicitly Christian development NGOs formed alongside their secular peers, including Christian Aid, formed in the UK in 1942; Brot für die Welt, founded in Germany in 1959; Bread for All, established in Switzerland in 1961; and Inter-Church Organisation for Development Cooperation (ICCO), formed in the Netherlands in 1964, amongst many others.[45]

Whereas "development" had been a fundamentally Christian idea and practice during the colonial era, in the post-colonial years it was self-consciously secularized. European society had become increasingly secular, and there was a marked decrease in support for efforts to convert people to faith. In secular public discourse the notion of "mission" was now reduced to "evangelism," and was discredited and de-legitimized both due to its conversionary focus and due to its association with imperialism and colonialism. Instead, the notion of "development" took its place, as the moral concern for the wellbeing of far-away others, but now secularized and cleansed of any colonial or religious connotations. Thus what had been "Christian development" was subtly transformed into secular "development."

However, the secularization of "development" was far less clear in practice than it was in discourse. Most development NGOs, whether secular or Christian, in effect worked in similar ways, building on the approaches of the classical missionaries before them. In fact, most of the organizations that were working on the ground overseas continued to be the classical missionaries. And virtually all of the NGOs, whether supposedly secular or Christian, initially operated by raising funds in Europe and then making grants to missionaries overseas to do small-scale development work.[46] In response, many of the classical missionaries re-positioned themselves as providers of secular development services and began to downplay their religious nature in order to conform to newly emerging

44 Gilbert Rist, *The History of Development: From Western Origins to Global Faith* (London: Zed Books, 1997), 70–79.

45 Major Catholic development NGOs also formed at this time, including Caritas Internationalis, established in 1951 and now a network of over 160 Catholic relief and development organizations focussing mainly on humanitarian aid, and CIDSE (Coopération Internationale pour le Développement et la Solidarité), founded in 1967 to coordinate the development priorities identified by the Second Vatican Council, which today has 16 member organizations in Europe (and a further two in America), including Trocaire in Ireland, Misereor in Germany, Fastenopfer in Switzerland, CAFOD in the UK, Cordaid in the Netherlands, and Manos Unidas in Spain.

46 Maggie Black, *A Cause for Our Time: Oxfam, The First 50 Years* (Oxford: Oxfam Publishing, 1992); Mark Luetchford and Peter Burns, *Waging the War on Want: 50 Years of Campaigning Against World Poverty* (London: War on Want, 2003); Firoze Manji, "The Missionary Position: NGOs and Development in Africa," *International Affairs* 78, no. 3 (2002): 567–584.

mainstream development paradigms.[47] They began to place less emphasis on spiritual matters and more on material matters. Most classical mission societies either set up new departments for relief and development or transformed entirely into secular development NGOs (or shut down entirely).[48] Thus by the 1960s many of the classical mission societies had been subsumed into the development sector, and the spiritual or evangelistic aspect of "Christian development" had been firmly excised from the new secular "development."[49]

By the 1960s colonial empire had almost completely given way and a host of new countries had gained independence. The concept of "international development" had indeed taken hold as the central discourse through which relations between richer and poorer countries, now framed as "developed" and the "developing" countries, was articulated. And of course, in the context of the burgeoning Cold War, the new discourse of D/development, and to some extent its practice, sought to encourage the newly independent post-colonial states to retain relations with their former colonial rulers rather than to develop new relations with the communist Soviet Union. The Western governments continued to push forward the idea of Development, and now the governments of the post-colonial states in Africa and Asia also began to call for assistance with D/development. The multiple meanings of the term meant that many people used it to refer to very different things, varying from activities that sought political and economic benefits for Western states (e.g., through access to natural resources and the inclusion of the former colonies in the Western geo-political bloc), activities that aimed for economic benefits to African and Asian states (e.g., funding and technology transfer for large-scale energy and infrastructure projects), and activities that attempted to lead to the improvements of the lives and livelihoods of poor people in communities in Africa and Asia (e.g., small-scale projects using appropriate technology in local communities). This multiplicity of meanings, often in tension if not outright opposition with each other, led to "D/development" becoming both a very widely used term and also an extremely imprecise and cloudy one.

47 Oscar Salemink, "The Purification, Sacralisation and Instrumentalisation of Development as a Religious Enterprise," in *Religion and the Politics of Development*, ed. Philip Fountain et al. (London: Palgrave Macmillan, 2015), 35–60, 51.

48 Andrea Paras, "Between Missions and Development: Christian NGOs in the Canadian Development Sector," *Canadian Journal of Development Studies* 35, no. 3 (2014): 439–457, 443.

49 Alastair Ager and Joey Ager, "Faith and the Discourse of Secular Humanitarianism," *Journal of Refugee Studies* 24, no. 3 (2011): 456–472, 457; John Stuart, "Overseas Mission, Voluntary Service and Aid to Africa: Max Warren, the Church Missionary Society and Kenya, 1945–63," *The Journal of Imperial and Commonwealth History* 36, no. 3 (2008): 527–543, 537.

In 1960 the United Nations launched the Decade of Development and many European governments, and the newly emerging European Economic Community, set about putting new "development infrastructures" in place, often at the behest of the United States. In the coming decades they set up Development programs for a variety of reasons, according to their domestic concerns and geopolitical interests.[50]

Meanwhile, by the late 1970s and early 1980s local development NGOs had started to form in big numbers in countries in Africa, Asia, and Latin America, staffed primarily by local people rather than expatriate Europeans, and without links to earlier missionary organizations. At this point most of the major European development NGOs stopped making grants to missionaries and started instead to work in partnership with these local development NGOs. The Christian origins of "development" were largely forgotten, or swept under the carpet, as development NGOs were hailed in the 1980s as a "magic bullet" to solve the problems of the under-developed countries in a modern, efficient, and highly technical manner.

But only twenty years later, in the early 2000s, in the context of the "global resurgence of religion" and talk of the "post-secular society,"[51] interest in religion began again to appear in the mainstream development field. Many in the NGO "development" field were becoming frustrated that even small-scale development projects often did not work and were beginning to come to the realization that culture, values, and beliefs played an important role in shaping people's actions and thus their social and economic behaviors.[52] At the same time Western governments were pushed into thinking about the ongoing relevance of religion in the world after the 9/11 terrorist attack on the World Trade Center in New York and the subsequent "war on terror." Thus practitioners of both "development" and "Development" began to consider the role of religion and religious organizations in D/development.

---

50 Carol Lancaster, *Foreign Aid: Diplomacy, Development, Domestic Policies* (Chicago: University of Chicago Press, 2006), 213; Andrew Jones, "British Humanitarian NGOs and the Disaster Relief Industry, 1942–1985" (PhD diss., University of Birmingham, 2014), 22.

51 Jose Casanova, *Public Religions in the Modern World* (Chicago: Chicago University Press, 1994); Richard Falk, "A Worldwide Religious Resurgence in an Era of Globalization and Apocalyptic Terrorism," in *Religion in International Relations: Culture and Religion in International Relations*, ed. Pavlos Hatzopoulos and Fabio Petito (New York: Palgrave Macmillan, 2003), 181–208; Thomas Scott, *The Global Resurgence of Religion and the Transformation of International Relations: The Struggle for the Soul of the Twenty-First Century* (Basingstoke: Palgrave Macmillan, 2005).

52 Freeman, "The Pentecostal Ethic."

In 2001 the Faith Based and Community Initiatives Act was passed in the US, which enabled faith-based organizations to apply for funding for overseas relief and development work, leading to a huge increase in the number of evangelical Christian development NGOs receiving US government money to carry out international development. Governments in the UK, Switzerland, the Netherlands, Denmark, and Sweden, as well as the World Bank, also started to increase their funding to mainly Christian faith-based organizations.[53] By the mid-2000s the term "faith-based organization," along with the acronym "FBO," had emerged and become widely used in development circles and FBOs had become recognized as significant players in the development sector.[54]

But as is by now a recurring theme in the history of D/development, practitioners of "Development" and "development" had contrasting ideas about the role of religion in D/development. For most government actors and funders, the main interest was in using local, national, and transnational religious networks as a means to get a fundamentally secular and Western developmental message down to local communities, so that the messages would reach even remote villages and would be presented by trusted local religious leaders.[55]

For many Christian NGOs, on the other hand, considering the role of religion in development meant bringing (back) questions of faith and meaning into the project of social and personal change and improvement. Several leading Christian FBOs, particularly those coming from the evangelical wing of the Protestant church, such as Tearfund and World Vision, began to re-consider the Christian basis of "development" and to (re)-formulate ideas of "Christian development." Going by various names, such as "integral mission" or "transformational development," these new approaches sought to put Christianity back into development, to (re)-combine material change with spiritual change, or "development"

---

53 Gerard Clarke, "Agents of Transformation? Donors, Faith-Based Organisations and International Development," *Third World Quarterly* 28, no. 1 (2007): 77–96, 82; Gerald Deacon and Emma Tomalin, "A History of Faith-Based Aid and Development," in *The Routledge Handbook of Religions and Global Development*, ed. Emma Tomalin (London: Routledge, 2015), 82–93, 74; Katherine Marshall, "Development and Religion: A Different Lens on Development Debates," *Peabody Journal of Education* 76, no. 3–4 (2001): 339–375; Ben Jones and Marie Juul Petersen, "Instrumental, Narrow, Normative? Reviewing Recent Work on Religion and Development," *Third World Quarterly* 32, no. 7 (2011): 1291–1306; Gerard Clarke, "The Perils of Entanglement: Bilateral Donors, Faith-Based Organisations and International Development," in *International Development Policy: Religion and Development*, ed. Giles Carbonnier (Basingstoke: Palgrave Macmillan, 2013), 65–78.

54 Elisabeth Ferris, "Faith and Humanitarianism: It's Complicated," *Journal of Refugee Studies* 24, no. 3 (2011): 606–625.

55 Ben Jones and Marie Juul Petersen, "Instrumental, Narrow, Normative?".

with "evangelism," in order to (re)-create a model of holistic change that would transform the whole person, body and soul.[56] As such they effectively re-created something very similar to the original model of "Christian development" formulated by the classical missionaries in the 1940s and 1950s, and out of which secular "development" later emerged.

Conclusion

This overview of the histories of "Development," "development," and "Christian development" has shown the entanglements, interactions, and confusions between these overlapping but contrasting projects. It has made three core arguments.

Firstly, it has shown that the very idea of a coordinated project of global improvement – what we now call "development" – first emerged as a nineteenth-century Christian response to the ills of industrial capitalism and empire. Its first agents, or practitioners, were Protestant missionaries, who sought to develop people, rather than resources, through the twin activities of education and evangelism, in order to bring about what they called "civilization." In the early to mid-twentieth-century the Protestant missionaries expanded their approach into a more coherent and multi-faceted approach to transform the whole person, body, and soul, which they called "development," and we can term "Christian development." And then later, after the end of European empires, secular development NGOs secularized "Christian development" into "development," by removing the elements of faith and evangelism, and took over the structural position of the missionaries in the world system. And most recently, there has been a turn (back) to religion, with Christian FBOs (re)-formulating an explicitly faith-based form of "Christian development."

Secondly, it has argued that the nineteenth-century Christian idea of coordinated global improvement, as a moral project, has been repeatedly appropriated by Western governments as a smokescreen to legitimate their trade and business activities in other parts of the world. This happened first in the appropriation of the idea of "civilizing mission" by colonial governments to legitimate the imperial project, and later in the appropriation of the idea of "development" to legitimize ongoing relations of domination and exploitation in the post-colonial pe-

56 Freeman, *Tearfund*; Dena Freeman, "From 'Christians doing Development' to 'Doing Christian Development': The Changing Role of Religion in the International Work of Tearfund," *Development in Practice* 28, no. 2 (2018): 280–291.

riod, in the project of "Development." Rather than offering a brave new approach to dealing with the injustices of the world, post-World War Two ideas about "Development" can instead be seen as a re-working and re-positioning of earlier ideas about empire, resource extraction, and Christian social improvement.

And thirdly, it has argued that the multiplicity of meanings given to the term "D/development" make it a remarkably effective, and confusing, rhetorical construct that can, and has been, used and mis-used to a variety of different ends, throughout its relatively short history. Bringing this rhetorical confusion into focus, and highlighting the history of its different meanings, is important for those who still believe in the moral validity of the development project but feel frustrated with the realities of contemporary Development.

Frederick Cooper

Development, Modernization, and the Remaking of an Imperial World Order

The word "development" has many meanings and its use serves different purposes. Examining its varying deployments can give historians insight into important transformations in recent history.[1] Economic development, in some views, is a long-term, self-propelled process, as in "capitalist development," or else it is self-conscious actions of a state or international financial institutions to correct failures in capitalist development.[2] Development can be a short-term intervention to enable poor states or regions to participate fully in a market economy or a long-term alternative to market mechanisms – socialist as opposed to capitalist development. Some view development positively as a global project of uplift, while others are negative. One negative view comes from the left: development continues the colonialist projects of imposing an unwanted modernity on subordinated people. Another negative view comes from the right: development is a deviation from market principles. Development has been called depoliticizing, turning conflict over control of resources into a technical question, and it has been deemed a political notion, a demand by impoverished people for the state to provide them with resources to improve their lot or a demand by impoverished states for the global redistribution of resources.[3] Development initiatives

---

1 Previous assessments of the field include Frederick Cooper and Randall Packard, eds., *International Development and the Social Sciences: Essays in History and Knowledge* (Berkeley: University of California Press, 1997); Frederick Cooper, "Writing the History of Development," *Journal of Modern European History* 8, no. 1 (2010): 5–23; Joseph Hodge, "On the Historiography of Development (Part 1: The First Wave)," *Humanity* 6, no. 3 (2015): 429–463; and Joseph Hodge, "Writing the History of Development (Part 2: Wider, Longer, Deeper)," *Humanity* 7, no. 1 (2016): 125–174.
2 Michael Cowen and Robert Shenton, *Doctrines of Development* (London: Routledge, 1996).
3 See the contrasting views, both based on studies of Lesotho, of James Ferguson, *The Anti-Politics Machine: Development, Depoliticization, and Bureaucratic Power in Lesotho* (Cambridge: Cambridge University Press, 1990), and John Aerni-Flessner, *Dreams for Lesotho: Independence, Foreign Assistance, and Development* (Notre Dame: University of Notre Dame Press, 2018). Ferguson could be right about the depoliticizing tendencies in development organizations and bureaucracies, while Aerni-Flessner could be right about the importance of development in the politics of Lesotho. One could postulate that the argument *against* development programs – trying to shield world markets from intervention to benefit the poor – is the true anti-politics machine. See Quinn Slobodian, *The Globalists: The End of Empire and the Birth of Neoliberalism* (Cambridge, Mass.: Harvard University Press, 2018).

https://doi.org/10.1515/9783110730234-005

have given rise to questions of who benefits – raising issues of race, class, and gender, as well as of patron-client relations. Some observers think of development more as a discourse – a reinscription of hierarchy – than a genuine effort to bring about material improvement for the poor.[4] Others insist that as long as many people lack water, electricity, decent medical care, and good schools, development will be a claim by those who lack it and a moral obligation on those who have the means to help.

Development is both an actor's category and an analytic category. It has been an explicit demand and an explicit promise by political actors in different times and places. It is a category used by scholars to delineate a field of inquiry, a phenomenon to be explained, and a project that the possessors of knowledge can help to direct in fruitful ways – producing an overlap between the concept as actor's category and as analytic category.

This chapter brings out three themes, with emphasis on African examples: 1. the relationship of development history to another theme in historical studies, on empire, especially the end of colonial empires; 2. the continuity question – how much postcolonial development differed from the colonial variety; and 3. the alternative developments question, specifically whether "African" or "decolonized" versions can be usefully distinguished from a "western" or "orthodox" model of development. Behind these themes is a larger issue: the asymmetrical nature of global economic relations. Development presumes inequality. The question is whether thinking with this category suggests ways of reducing inequality – or at least ameliorating the lives of the worst off – or else reifies the distinction between developed and underdeveloped.[5] I will be reflecting on the kinds of questions historians are asking about the changing nature of asymmetrical economic relationships.

Empire, Decolonization, and Development

The concept of development is essential to understanding one of the most important transformations of the twentieth century, the end of colonial empires and the formation of a world in which the territorial, national state is the general

4 Arturo Escobar, *Encountering Development: The Making and Unmaking of the Third World* (Princeton: Princeton University Press, 1995); Wolfgang Sachs, *The Development Dictionary: A Guide to Knowledge as Power* (London: Zed Books, 1992).
5 The tension between the goal of reducing global inequality and that of meeting minimal needs is emphasized in Samuel Moyn, *Not Enough: Human Rights in an Unequal World* (Cambridge, Mass.: Harvard University Press, 2018).

norm. We need to understand not only the geopolitical conflicts and reconfigurations that this transition entailed, but how people at the time could think about it. Empires have been around for thousands of years, and ending them was more than the seizure of power by the colonized from the colonizer, but a transformation – a radical one – in the normative framework in which sovereignty, governance, and participation in international relations could be conceived of and talked about throughout the world.[6] In the twentieth century, imperial elites had worked hard to cultivate the idea that the people of Africa or Asia were not capable of governing themselves. The development concept was critical to the contested process of turning static hierarchy into dynamic politics, a reformulation of inequality that seemed to promise its elimination or at least reduction. Development talk helped to formulate a language in which Africans and Asians could make claims and Europeans could convince themselves of their essential role in meeting them.

Historical studies of development and of the crisis in empire were mutually constitutive. Although useful studies of the administrative and political history of development programs of London and Paris go back to the late 1960s,[7] by the 1990s and early 2000s historians were both broadening the inquiry to include the global crisis of empire and narrowing it to examine the politics of development projects as played out in specific parts of Africa.[8] Imperial rulers had long sought to channel wealth into their own hands, and sometimes took action to enhance the wealth-producing capacity of the territories over which they gained control – think of the roads and aqueducts built by the Roman Empire. When British prime minister Joseph Chamberlain wrote in 1895 of the need to develop the Empire's "estates" he was thinking like a landlord investing in fences or fruit trees.[9] European empires were not the only political entities that acted to increase material resources. Cyrus Schayegh points out that in Chamberlain's

---

6 On empire history, see Peter Fibiger Bang, C. A. Bayly, and Walter Scheidel, eds., *The Oxford World History of Empire*, 2 vols. (Oxford: Oxford University Press, 2021); and Jane Burbank and Frederick Cooper, *Empires in World History: Power and the Politics of Difference* (Princeton: Princeton University Press, 2010).

7 J. M. Lee, *Colonial Development and Good Government* (Oxford: Oxford University Press, 1967); Michael Havinden and David Meredith, *Colonialism and Development: Britain and Its Tropical Colonies, 1850–1960* (London: Routledge, 1993).

8 On the empire perspective, see Frederick Cooper, "Reconstructing Empire in Post-War French and British Africa," *Past and Present* 210, no. 6 (2011): 196–210. A pioneering study focused on a mega-project in Africa is Monica van Buesekom, *Negotiating Development: African Farmers and Colonial Experts at the Office du Niger, 1920–1960* (Portsmouth: Heinemann, 2002).

9 Corinna R. Unger, *International Development: A Postwar History* (London: Bloomsbury Academic, 2018), 34.

time the Ottoman empire sought to enhance the productive capacity of its frontier regions, investing in railroads and telegraph lines as part of its competition with rival empires.[10] African empires – most strikingly Ethiopia in the late nineteenth century – could mount projects to improve technology and expand production.[11]

Whether the actions that European empires took in the early twentieth century to improve transportation or healthcare amount to a development policy is not clear. When some of the most influential British and French colonial officials of the 1920s proposed to pull together various initiatives intended to increase the productivity of the colonies into a coherent policy funded with revenue from the French or British taxpayer, both governments rejected the plans, and further attempts along these lines were either refused or put forth in limited form. Resources were supposed to go from colony to metropole, not the reverse.[12]

Historians of development have made clear that ideas of "improving" colonized people had roots outside of government policies. European missionaries and other humanitarian activists promoted conversion and education and sometimes fought back against the claims of settlers, business interests, and colonial officials that Africans were inferior beings who could be exploited – even worked to death – at will.[13] However authoritarian and exploitative, empires were also incorporative. Having made certain peoples into British or French subjects and insisting that they remain that way, rulers needed to convince people at home of the legitimacy of the project done in their name, and in certain circumstances they wanted to give fractions of conquered people a stake in the imperial order. They sometimes claimed to pursue a "civilizing mission." Recent scholarship has

---

10 Cyrus Schayegh, "Imperial and Transnational Developmentalism: Middle Eastern Interplays, 1880s-1960s," in *The Development Century: A Global History*, ed. Stephen J. Macekura and Erez Manela (Cambridge: Cambridge University Press, 2018), 61–82, esp. 61–67.

11 Ruth Rempel, "Colonialism and Development in Africa," in *The Palgrave Handbook of African Colonial and Postcolonial History*, ed. Martin Shanguhyia and Toyin Falola (New York: Palgrave Macmillan, 2018), 569–619, esp. 570–572. While it makes sense to look beyond a narrow and Eurocentric definition of development, there is a danger in putting any kind of innovation or enhancement of productive resources into that framework, since it could cease to be clear what the added value of the development concept is.

12 For concise reviews of development in colonial Africa (on which the following paragraphs are based), see Unger, *International Development*; Rempel, "Colonialism and Development in Africa"; and Corrie Decker and Elizabeth MacMahon, *The Idea of Development in Africa: A History* (Cambridge: Cambridge University Press, 2021).

13 On the other side—the death and misery caused by European attempts to construct an infrastructure for extracting African commodities—see James P. Daughton, *In the Forest of No Joy: The Congo-Océan Railroad and the Tragedy of French Colonialism* (New York: Norton, 2021).

emphasized how contested the ideas were that Africans were permanently locked in a state of racial subservience. Colonizing elites sometimes claimed that Africans could be advanced in the scale of civilization – perhaps part way, perhaps eventually to a position of equality – if only the proper policies were applied.[14] All this can be fit into the longue-durée of development history, and the relationship of projects of improvement and progress at home and overseas can be fruitfully debated.[15] Meanwhile, Africans were economic actors in their own right, particularly in expansion and innovation in cash crop production – histories that might be seen as within a development framework or as an alternative to it.[16]

The strands of stories about economic initiatives of different actors and political conflict and change come together in the late 1930s and 1940s. It was then that the colonial regimes of France and Great Britain put their money where their mouth was: The Colonial Development and Welfare Act of 1940 in the British case and the creation of the *Fonds d'Investissement pour le Développement Economique et Sociale* of 1946 in the French case. Both of these enactments – controversial in their respective countries – marked a crucial break with the doctrine of colonial self-sufficiency.

The new legislation, bureaucracies, and funding came together when the future of empire was in question in a way it had not been before. Strikes and riots in the British West Indies and African cities after 1935 were the direct impetus for the Development Act of 1940; the French act was part of an attempt to reconfigure imperial rule, including the granting of citizenship rights to the inhabitants of the colonies. Erupting in a long-colonized region and in urban centers in Africa, the anger at living conditions could hardly be attributed to the "primitive" nature of the people involved. Poverty – especially the poverty of wage laborers

---

14 On the relevance to development history of doctrines of racial thinking, see Decker and MacMahon, *Idea of Development in Africa*, 58–78. Helen Tilley and Alice Conklin have complicated the picture by showing that "scientific racism" never achieved consensus among scientists in both Britain and France. Helen Tilley, *Africa as a Living Laboratory: Empire, Development, and the Problem of Scientific Knowledge, 1870–1950* (Chicago: University of Chicago Press, 2011); Alice Conklin, *In the Museum of Man: Race, Anthropology, and Empire in France, 1850–1950* (Ithaca: Cornell University Press, 2013).

15 On the influence – both ideas and personnel – of colonial development initiatives on development projects in the metropole, see Matthew Wendeln, "Contested Territory: Regional Development in France, 1934–1968" (PhD diss., New York University, 2011).

16 On cash crop production, see Gareth Austin, *Labour, Land, and Capital in Ghana: From Slavery to Free Labour in Asante* (Rochester: Rochester University Press, 2005).

– was a crisis of empire.[17] In short, the initiative for an active – and funded – project of development on the scale of empire did not come from on high, but from contestation. Development was very much a political question.

In 1945, thoughtful people around the world understood that empire had come into question, but they didn't know if the empires would reconfigure themselves, weather the storm as they had after World War One, break up along the boundaries set by the colonizing states, or give way to some kind of federal or confederal grouping larger than the former colonies. Who should control economic development – where to find capital and where to invest it, in what kinds of projects, with what kinds of provisions for social welfare – was at the heart of debates at the time. Colonial regimes tried to take the initiative, but whether their efforts would ward off challenges or produce more conflict was an open question. To the extent that development gave opportunities to European and indigenous elites to exploit more land with greater efficiency it deprived people with weak land rights of access and produced alienation and anger – a major factor in the Mau Mau revolt in Kenya in the early 1950s. Development politics fostered the idea that control of the state was crucial to economic progress, raising the stake in the argument that only Africans could ensure that the state would organize development in the interests of the majority.

During the 1950s, anthropologists and other social scientists became fascinated with social change, looking beyond the old conception of "tribal" Africa, investigating the effects of labor migration on family lives, the harshness of living conditions in mushrooming cities, and also the adaptation of people and social structures to the situation. Publications from that era are now primary sources for both social and intellectual history: on-the-ground inquiries into development in action and analysis of the categories through which western – and eventually African – social scientists tried to intellectually tame a world whose trajectories were not clear. A critical literature has exposed the limitations of the "modernization" concept, but the point remains that it emerged in the context of radical uncertainty, in which western intellectuals both welcomed and

---

17 Frederick Cooper, *Decolonization and African Society: The Labor Question in French and British Africa* (Cambridge: Cambridge University Press, 1996). Rempel points out that nutrition also came under consideration as a problem of empire in the mid-1930s: Rempel, "Colonialism and Development," 580–581. On development and nationalist politics in India, see Sugata Bose, "Instruments and Idioms of Colonial and National Development: India's Historical Experience in Comparative Perspective," in *International Development*, ed. Cooper and Packard, 45–63.

feared the emergence of colonized people from the political, social, and cultural constraints of the colonial situation.[18]

The politics of independence was not just about national liberation, but of making something of political liberation, and that required transforming international order – what Adom Getachew calls "worldmaking."[19] The leaders of the already "developed" states greeted the collapse of colonial empires with anxiety as well as a sense of new possibilities. Some hoped that a world of nation-states would be more stable than a world of rival imperial powers and that a new order could be constructed without rigid racial hierarchy.[20] For economic liberals, a post-imperial world promised open markets rather than imperial preference – a potential advantage to American businesses and perhaps an easing of burdens on former colonial powers that had recently assumed the cost of development.

For rulers of the new states, as well as some of the elites of the Latin American states that had experienced their own "decolonization" around 140 years earlier, the end of empire opened the possibility of reconfiguring international institutions, through the UN and the ILO for instance, to promote the raising of the standard of living of ex-colonial states, not their exploitation. Whether ex-colonial states could act collectively against global inequality was an intensely debated political issue between the Afro-Asian Conference in Bandung in 1955 and the defeat of the drive by Asian, African, and Latin American states for reform of global economic relations known as the New International Economic Order (NIEO) around 1980. Among the demands coming from the ex-colonial states were for each country to have control of its economic resources and more favorable rules for participation in world markets, for restrictions on multinational corporations to claim property rights to minerals and unchecked opportunities for acquiring property and repatriating profits, and for additional funds to promote development directed from the richer countries to the poorer.[21]

---

18 Frederick Cooper, "Development, Modernization, and the Social Sciences in the Era of Decolonization: The Examples of British and French Africa," *Revue d'Histoire des Sciences Humaines* 10 (2004): 9–38; Michael Latham, *Modernization as Ideology: American Social Science and "Nation-Building" in the Kennedy Era* (Chapel Hill: University of North Carolina Press, 2000); George Steinmetz, *Sociology and Empire: The Imperial Entanglements of a Discipline* (Durham: Duke University Press, 2013).

19 Adom Getachew, *Worldmaking after Empire: The Rise and Fall of Self-Determination* (Princeton: Princeton University Press, 2019).

20 Giuliano Garavini, *After Empires: European Integration, Decolonization, and the Challenge from the Global South 1957–1986* (New York: Oxford University Press, 2012).

21 Getachew, *Worldmaking after Empire.*

Development and modernization were all part of a necessary process of rethinking the world's political order, deployed by bureaucrats and politicians as well as social scientists. Modernization and development allowed European elites to embrace the possibility that enough Africans, in a not too distant future, could make the transition from uncivilized to sufficiently educated for Europeans to enter a post-colonial relationship with them conducive to continued economic ties and to common participation in international organizations. It also implied that Africans who failed to make this transition had themselves to blame.[22]

Britain and France, in particular, had thought that seizing the initiative on development would enable them to relegitimize colonialism, at least until an indefinite future date. Instead, it both made control of development into a more compelling issue and its escalating costs forced colonial officials to undertake for the first time a serious account of the benefits and costs of colonial rule.[23] The accounting exercises favored maintaining British or French interests by means other than direct rule. Equally important, the assertion that Africans could be turned into modern men and women with a western education and a desire to participate in industrial employment, market economies, and parliamentary governance helped Europeans to imagine – in however problematic a relation to reality – that they could cede power to the people they could claim to have molded.

There were other threads in the development story. Eric Helleiner points to one coming out of Latin America in the aftermath of the depression and world war, where intellectuals and a few statesmen, the proud inheritors of sovereignty over a century previously, were aware of economic dependence on the United States and Europe and the prevalence of poverty. They sought to influence new international institutions – including the World Bank and the International Monetary Fund – to address global economic order. For a time, the United States saw possibilities in such initiatives for better trade and diplomatic relations, but by the early 1950s that viewpoint was eclipsed by political reaction at home and Cold War priorities abroad.[24] Leaders in India also looked to development to strengthen a new nation coming into being, and sought both to influence international organizations and to make its exit from empire into an opportunity to

---

22 On the politics of blame for failed development initiatives, see Felicitas Becker, *The Politics of Poverty: Policy-Making and Development in Rural Tanzania* (Cambridge: Cambridge University Press, 2019), 6, 195.

23 Cooper, *Decolonization and African Society.*

24 Eric Helleiner, *Forgotten Foundations of Bretton Woods: International Development and the Making of the Postwar Order* (Ithaca: Cornell University Press, 2014).

benefit from different development models and access to multiple sources of investment and aid instead of just one.[25]

That development shifted from an imperial construct to a national one marked both a set of new possibilities and a constraint. The national form in which political movements in the colonies gained power – after attempts at federal structures or other forms of wider groupings – put into place vulnerable states, some small, most poor, facing a world of wealthy states, corporations, and international financial institutions that could exercise choice in where they would invest, whom they would aid, and whom they might attempt to undermine. The leaders of each new state had to worry about the fragility of their power base at home and their need for favorable relations with "developed" states that were pursuing their own interests and rivalries. The quest for the NIEO reflected many leaders' awareness of the problem, but the failure of the initiative reflected the fragility of their connection to each other and the dependence on wealthy nations that development was supposed to overcome.

The Continuity Question

Whether political decolonization implied economic decolonization was a question posed shortly after most of Africa became independent. Kwame Nkrumah's book of 1965, *Neo-colonialism: The Last Stage of Imperialism*, encapsulated in a single word the argument that the exploitation of Africa's material resources and people was continuing.[26] This has been a controversial argument, but it has led to more nuanced questions about different elements of post-colonial relationships. The question is complicated by the argument, cited above, that the "colonial economy" was itself not fixed, but was changing in particularly important ways after 1945. Some people, as I did in 2002, posited a "development era" that extended from the 1940s to the mid-1970s, when the advocates of free market orthodoxy gained the upper hand in international policy debates and international financial institutions preached austerity, free movement of capital, removal of tariff barriers, and other such measures, while pressuring indebted governments

---

25 David Engerman, *The Price of Aid: The Economic Cold War in India* (Cambridge, Mass.: Harvard University Press, 2018). Engerman points out that both the US and the USSR started out with condescending views of India and only slowly came to see it as an important element in the postwar world. On the framing of development questions in post-war British Asia, see Unger, *International Development*, 64–66.

26 Kwame Nkrumah, *Neo-colonialism: The Last Stage of Imperialism* (London: Nelson and Sons, 1965).

– including most of Africa – to pull back from government efforts to improve the standard of living of Africans. But the apparent closing of a development era was followed by its apparent reopening in the early 2000s, as some of the same institutions and economists who had backed away from development two decades before proposed ambitious global initiatives. The effect of this shift was overshadowed by the impact of China's surge in demand for African raw materials and its investment in projects in Africa, something considered by some to be a new element and others a repeat of an old pattern, with more than a tinge of colonialist attitudes and the same orientation toward extraction as western development strategies.[27] In some eyes, China was itself a model of successful development as well as a source of investment; since the 1970s, it has reduced poverty by historically extraordinary levels. While China in the days of Mao had been a model for some radical Africans, today it is not altogether clear what it is a model of. Rapid growth and poverty reduction in China did not come about through either the liberal capitalism that ideologues in the West promoted or the social democratic variant that promised to correct capitalism's ills, but via a decidedly authoritarian version of state-controlled capitalism that provides an alternative that is, to some political elites, attractive and to others frightening.[28]

A point so obvious that it is rarely made is that the effects of decolonization were shaped by the particular form it took: to nation-states based on colonial boundaries. The pattern enhanced the fragmentation of the African continent and made politics into a zero-sum for the maintenance of control of each territorial unit. African leaders in the 1950s, including Nkrumah and Léopold Sédar Senghor, had warned of these dangers, but their attempts at forging larger units – Nkrumah's United States of Africa or Senghor's Franco-African confederation – did not win out. Colonial development policies enhanced the role of the state; sovereignty took the process further. The extremes of inequality between the internal economy of each African state and the outside world encouraged elites to use the biggest asset they controlled – sovereignty – to pursue strategies of gatekeeping to cement their role at the interface of the two, a strategy that often led to conflict over control of the gate. Senghor had urged Africans to combine "hor-

27 Compare the two editions of my book *Africa since 1940: The Past of the Present* (Cambridge: Cambridge University Press, 2002, 2019). The rise, decline, and resurrection of development initiatives are catalogued in Ruth Rempel, "Development History and Postcolonial African Experience," in *The Palgrave Handbook of African Colonial and Postcolonial History*, ed. Shanguhyia and Falola, 881–926.

28 Literature on Chinese-African relations is growing. See for example Ching Kwan Lee, *The Specter of Global China: Politics, Labor, and Foreign Investment in Africa* (Chicago: University of Chicago Press, 2018).

izontal solidarity" – Africans with each other – with "vertical solidarity" – relations with the most affluent and powerful parts of the world – to avoid the choice between unity in poverty and continued dependence. Decolonizing into nation-states made horizontal solidarity a more difficult objective, underscoring the power of the vertical. African leaders have at times tried to put together alternatives, through the Organization of African Unity and later the African Union and regional organizations like ECOWAS (Economic Community of West African States), but the jealousy with which elites guard their sovereignty combined with the extremes of structural inequality in the world makes this a difficult task.[29] Such questions have come to the fore in an international arena in demands such as that in the 1970s for the NIEO, a demand by poorer nations working together that could not overcome the horizontal solidarity of the rich and the dependence of the poor on vertical relations for immediate survival.[30]

Independence did not end asymmetrical economic relations, but it did give African states choices among would-be patrons. Abou Bamba has shown how the Côte d'Ivoire, sometimes considered a client-state of France, skillfully played the United States against France and diversified its possibilities for investment and trade.[31] Cold War rivalries created competition among patrons, at the risk of making states subject to political tests for aid or investment as well as getting caught in shifting rivalries.

Also revealing is what became known in the late 1970s as the "Kenya debate." Both sides drew on a process that began at the end of the 1940s: as the colonial government of Kenya loosened racial restrictions that prevented Africans from growing the most lucrative export crops, small to mid-sized African producers began to grow higher proportions of these crops. After independence, the government supported land acquisitions by Kenyans, particularly those close to President Jomo Kenyatta, and as part of the independence agreement Great Britain provided financing to enable some of these Kenyans to buy out white

---

29 Frederick Cooper, *Citizenship between Empire and Nation: Remaking France and French Africa, 1945–1960* (Princeton: Princeton University Press, 2014), and Cooper, *Africa since 1940: the Past of the Present* (Cambridge: Cambridge University Press, 2019). Decker and McMahon pick up Senghor's use of these metaphors in a speech from 1961, but don't mention that he first used this language in 1948 and that it lay behind his efforts throughout the 1950s to find an alternative to both colonial empire and the nation-state: Decker and McMahon, *Idea of Development in Africa*, 143.

30 On the NIEO, see Getachew, *Worldmaking after Empire.*

31 Abou Bamba, *African Miracle, African Mirage: Transnational Politics and the Paradox of Modernization in Ivory Coast* (Athens: Ohio University Press, 2016). Engerman makes the point that independence gave India the possibility of looking to multiple sources of investment and aid: Engerman, *Price of Aid*, 6.

farmers. Some Kenyans moved into other sectors of the economy. The Kenya debate focused on whether this pattern constituted a form of development that was truly capitalist: African capitalists gaining control of the means of production. Advocates of a classic Marxism said yes. Scholars influenced by dependency theory – a Latin American school that was acquiring followers in Africa – argued that Kenya's capitalists remained dependent on multinational corporations, who controlled the export markets and whose investments in import substitution industrialization put Kenyans in secondary roles.[32] This argument tacked close to others being made at the time: that most Africans entered into a "state bourgeoisie" whose position depended solely on their position relative to a sovereign state. In those terms, sovereignty had its consequences, but not as a step toward capitalist development. The Kenya debate was resolved not by academic combat, but by political events in Kenya: after Kenyatta's death and the coming to power of Daniel arap Moi – from a different region with a different set of connections – the entrepreneurs connected to the old regime were systematically pushed out in favor of a new batch of entrepreneurs, demonstrating – or else creating – a class more akin to a state bourgeoisie than a semi-autonomous capitalist class.[33]

The overtaking of an academic debate by an historical process makes clear the need not to treat the "post-colony" as a singular entity and the post-colonial period as a single period, but to trace dynamics in all their complexity. Other studies have shown how people in different contexts work with whatever possibilities they have. Kara Moskovitz for example finds that neither a state-centered model nor a prefabricated notion of capitalist development fits ways in which rural people in western Kenya developed their own networks, sought out relations with organizations that might provide resources, struggled against land grabbing by other Kenyans, and tried to work within a regional context toward a modest measure of economic resilience. Felicitas Becker points out that people in the middle in Tanzania – mid-level bureaucrats and party cadres – are not embodiments of "the state" but actors in their own right, working in a region not

---

32 A pioneering text bringing Latin American dependency theory to Africa comes from the Guyanese historian Walter Rodney, who taught for a time in Tanzania: Walter Rodney, *How Europe Underdeveloped Africa* (London: Bogle-L'Ouverture Publications, 1972). Dependency arguments were applied to Kenya in Colin Leys, *Underdevelopment in Kenya: The Political Economy of Neo-Colonialism, 1964–1971* (Berkeley: University of California Press, 1974).

33 For a recent retrospective noting the durable influence of this scholarship, see John Harbeson and Frank Holmquist, "The Lessons and Legacies of the 'Kenya Debate'," in *The Oxford Handbook of Kenyan Politics*, ed. Nic Cheeseman, Karuti Kanyinga, and Gabrielle Lynch (Oxford: Oxford Handbooks Online, 2020), 451–464.

well endowed with resources or transportation infrastructure, improvising more than following a development script.[34]

Studies such as these point to neither an African miracle (as claimed in the "Africa rising" thesis) nor an African debacle (as Africa has been viewed by many for decades). There are certainly examples of the latter, particularly in zones beset by armed conflict, and there are examples of successful African entrepreneurs and businesses (for example cell phones) that not only make their owners rich but provide a useful service to vast numbers of people. Such examples point to the value of focusing on the specifics of place and time, at how people confront possibilities and constraints, how situations change, how people do something with what they have and struggle against others trying to take that away. To do so is to examine both the particularity of social relations in local context and connections – regional, national, global. Relations of inequality are relations nonetheless, and they produce different trajectories.

Historical research has also pointed to continuities in personnel. Véronique Dimier and Joseph Hodge describe the movement with decolonization of significant numbers of colonial civil servants into European or international institutions engaged in fields like economic development, health, and education.[35] These civil servants were coming out of the final phase of colonial bureaucracy, when administrations had shifted away from the "man who knew his natives" to the technical expert – someone who had something to offer other than his race and his skill at keeping Africans in their place. Given the miserable record of colonial regimes until their very last years in providing advanced education to Africans, newly independent countries as well as international institutions had reason to seek their services. Whether these veterans of colonial service were bringing a colonial outlook to development work or whether development work was bringing them into a new conception of international order is more complicated than an either-or question. Dimier makes clear that European Economic Community bureaucrats built on personal connections to African elites who were also taking an initiative in shaping the interaction, underscoring the importance of relationships to the study of development.

On the African side is a generational question. In the last years of colonial rule, panicked colonial administrators grasped the need to "Africanize" their

---

34 Kara Moskowitz, *Seeing like a Citizen: Decolonization, Development, and the Making of Kenya, 1946–1980* (Athens: Ohio University Press, 2019); Becker, *Politics of Poverty.*

35 Véronique Dimier, *The Invention of a European Development Aid Bureaucracy: Recycling Empire* (London: Palgrave Macmillan, 2014); Joseph Hodge, *Triumph of the Expert: Agrarian Doctrines of Development and the Legacies of British Colonialism* (Athens: Ohio University Press, 2007).

civil services if their claims to presiding over a more inclusive and progressive colonialism were to have any plausibility.[36] The regimes that replaced them had good political reason to put their constituents as rapidly as possible into positions of responsibility. The United States, the Soviet Union, and allies of both sides in the Cold War put in programs of training and university education in the hope of getting people who thought the proper way into important positions in Africa.[37] Most people who seized these opportunities were young and would be in their positions – or better ones – for years. Taken together, the generation coming of age in the late 1950s and 1960s had an opportunity for upward mobility available to neither an older nor a younger generation.

Decolonization put an end to the rivalry, often deadly, of European empires, but that rivalry had been cross-cut by a shared notion of European competence and superiority and the possibility of collaboration. From the 1890s, the International Colonial Institute brought together people from administrations, businesses, and academia to discuss what might be termed best practices of colonial rule.[38] After World War One, the League of Nations Permanent Mandates Commission, the International Labour Office, and other international organizations became sites where laws and actions of colonial regimes could be discussed, with some input – usually sidelined – from humanitarian organizations and activists and petitioners from the colonies themselves. After World War Two, international organizations followed the technical direction of colonial policies, resulting in new forms of inter-empire cooperation, not without tension. Jessica Pearson has shown how French officials hesitated between welcoming the help of the World Health Organization and the United Nations in addressing the enormous burden of bringing decent healthcare to the colonies and insisting that France must do things its own way. After decolonization, the question became whether the relationship of new states to international organizations would ratify their sovereignty or undermine its substance.[39]

---

36 Michelle Pinto, "Employment, Education, and the Reconfiguration of Empire: Africanization in Postwar French Africa" (PhD diss., New York University, 2013).

37 Constantin Katsakioris, "Creating a Socialist Intelligentsia: Soviet Educational Aid and Its Impact on Africa (1960–1991)," *Cahiers d'Études Africaines* 226 (2017): 259–288; Robyn D'Avignon, Elizabeth Banks, and Asif Saddiqi, eds., "An African-Soviet Modern," Special Issue of *Comparative Studies of South Asia, Africa and the Middle East* 41, no. 1 (2021).

38 Florian Wagner, *Colonial Internationalism and the Governmentality of Empire, 1893–1982* (Cambridge: Cambridge University Press, 2022).

39 Jessica Lynne Pearson, *The Colonial Politics of Global Health: France and the United Nations in Postwar Africa* (Cambridge, Mass.: Harvard University Press, 2018). See also Eva-Maria Muschik, "Managing the World: The United Nations, Decolonization, and the Strange Triumph of State Sovereignty in the 1950s and 1960s," *Journal of Global History* 13, no. 1 (2018): 121–144.

Independence did not bring a rapid end to the masculine bias of development thinking in colonial regimes. Even if there had long been a complex gender division of labor in many agricultural systems and women's role in food production was well known, colonial agronomists tended to see export production as an affair for men, supposedly more oriented toward markets and technological innovation. The view of the male as the "modern" producer tended to die hard, but it has long been questioned. Ester Boserup published a book on women and development in 1970[40] the journal *Gender and Development* is now in its twenty-ninth year. Studies of microcredit, sustainable agriculture, and "informal" economies point to the importance of the gender dimension in a wide range of development questions.[41] The "experts" who plan development and the scholars who examine the process come from their own regimes of gender relations, with their burdens of inequality and prejudices and struggles to overcome them, and they intersect with the gender regimes of the diverse societies that are the object of intervention. Efforts to bring together advocates of approaches to development that take gender equality seriously confront layers of assumptions about the gendered nature of "traditional" and "modern" values.

Was development becoming an international industry that would bring the theories, administrative practices, personnel, and capital – as well as biases – of Europe and North America to fulfill claims of improving the lives of Africans, or would internationalization follow what the word implied and include – in its operations as well as goals – people from the former colonial world? The organizations themselves attracted personnel from the former colonies. Eventually, a Ghanaian became head of the United Nations and an Ethiopian head of the World Health Organization, but the question of how much of a new perspective personnel at all levels brought to such institutions and how much the institu-

---

40 Ester Boserup, *Woman's Role in Economic Development* (New York: St. Martin's Press, 1970). For more recent interventions, see Martha Nussbaum, *Women and Human Development: The Capabilities Approach* (Cambridge: Cambridge University Press, 2000); Barbara Bush, "Motherhood, Morality, and Social Order, Gender and Development Discourse in Late Colonial Africa," in *Developing Africa: Concepts and Practices in Twentieth-Century Colonialism*, ed. Martina Kopf, Gerald Hödl, and Joseph Hodge (Manchester: Manchester University Press, 2014): 270 – 291; Janet Momsen, *Gender and Development* (Abingdon: Routledge, 2020[3]).

41 A notable insight into the relevance of gender to economic change is Aili Mari Tripp's finding that women's economic role in the "informal sector" of an African country became more prominent in a situation where global recession and structural adjustment policies cut into wage employment, where men had predominated: Aili Mari Tripp, *Changing the Rules: The Politics of Liberalization and the Urban Informal Economy in Tanzania* (Berkeley: University of California Press, 1997). A Kenyan woman's powerful role in the politics of the environment was recognized in the awarding of the Nobel Peace Prize to Wangari Maathai in 2004.

tions created a framework of thinking and practice into which people from the former colonies had to fit does not have a simple answer.

Africa and Development Knowledge

Is there a "development discourse" or a "development episteme," a shared vision emerging out of the asymmetrical international order? Or is there more of a "development arena," in which different conceptions of what goals should be and how they should be attained are in play, albeit without equal chances of being implemented?

The free-market critique of development in the 1980s had powerful backing in the world of finance, although even in that world the eclipse of development was temporary.[42] During the same period, critique of development also came from the left, but it had more impact on the academy than on institutions that actually had resources. Historians' reception of these arguments has been mixed, for the anti-development arguments of both left and right have one important dimension that goes in a different direction from the predilections of historians: both operate at a level of abstraction that leaves little room for locatedness in time and space.

The most widely cited development-bashing (and state-bashing) text is James Scott's *Seeing Like a State*. Scott contrasted "high-modernism" – systematic development directed by a state – with what he called, using the Greek expression, *mētis:* ideals and practices based on the messiness and personal interchange of local life. He argued that states seek to make complex situations "legible" so that they could intervene in them. He did not see all development efforts as high modernism – that concept demanded an ideological consistency not always found – but his examples revealed the problematic nature of his approach.[43] His African example is the program of forced villagization by Tanzania in 1970s, a policy which had few defenders after the fact. But specialists in Tanzanian history find his portrayal of high modernism to have little basis. Politics

42 Among the academic critics of development from the standpoint of market economics is William Easterly, *The White Man's Burden: Why the West's Efforts to Aid the Rest Have Done So Much Ill and So Little Good* (New York: Penguin, 2006). On the historical context in which such arguments developed, see Slobodian, *The Globalists*. A leading economist who at one time pushed market discipline but returned to the development fold is Jeffrey Sachs, *The End of Poverty: Economic Possibilities for Our Time* (New York: Penguin, 2005).
43 James Scott, *Seeing Like a State: How Certain Schemes to Improve the Human Condition Have Failed* (New Haven: Yale University Press, 1998).

in Tanzania was messy, pulled in different directions by regional political party leaders, by young men in search of a role. Much of what happened on ground level was improvised, as people confronted the impediments to improving production or marketing. The Tanzanian case is hardly a developmental success but not because of the excesses of ideological purity or state quests for legibility.[44] On the other end of Scott's spectrum, one could cite examples of *mētis* that exhibit the complexity and interactivity Scott seems to advocate, but with decidedly awful results. Mobutu's Zaire comes to mind – a domestic politics built on patron-client political relations and predatory economic actions, connections to affluent states and corporations revealing considerable skill in playing off the obscurity of international relations and domestic politics.

The best example of high-modernism in Scott's book is Scott himself, who forces complex politics into "legible" containers.[45] But dichotomies like his have had considerable appeal. The recent book of Corrie Decker and Elisabeth McMahon discusses stages and instances of the history of development in Africa with considerable subtlety and narrative complexity, but at the beginning and end they insist on a neat separation of "African" conceptions and the "development episteme."[46] The dichotomy understates the complexity of both sides. They can accurately point to ethnographic work that suggests African communities could look at progress in terms of the collective good. But they could have cited examples of African kings who enriched themselves in the slave trade and colonial-era chiefs who accumulated land at the expense of "their" people. As in most of the world, the mix of individual (or familial) greed and commitment to a collectivity in Africa is too varied and too embedded in historical circumstances to fit a continent-wide generalization. The "development episteme" is also hard to pin down, for theories and approaches have come and gone over the decades – for and against central planning, for and against industrialization,

---

44 Priya Lal, *African Socialism in Postcolonial Tanzania: Between the Village and the World* (Cambridge: Cambridge University Press, 2015); Leander Schneider, *Government of Development: Peasants and Politicians in Postcolonial Tanzania* (Bloomington: Indiana University Press, 2014); Becker, *Politics of Poverty.*

45 I put a critique of Scott in the context of a more extensive discussion of the concept of "modernity": Frederick Cooper, *Colonialism in Question: Theory, Knowledge, History* (Berkeley: University of California Press, 2005), 140 – 142. See also Fernando Coronil, "Smelling Like a Market," *American Historical Review* 106 (2001): 119 – 130.

46 Decker and McMahon trace the development episteme from the Enlightenment, through the racial ideologies of the nineteenth century, and civilizing missions of the colonial era. At one point they refer to development programs being "inflicted on Africans": Decker and McMahon, *Idea of Development in Africa*, 15.

for participatory development schemes or for meeting basic needs.[47] The critique of trade policy developed since the 1940s by Raúl Prebisch and the Economic Commission for Latin America has as much claim to be part of development discourse as the pro-trade policies they criticized. International NGOs can be rightfully criticized, as Decker and McMahon do, but such organizations have brought different imaginaries, recruited people with different agendas, and to greater or lesser degrees worked with African organizations and individuals.[48] The basic problem with NGO involvement isn't that they think or act within a certain episteme but that they are accountable to their donors rather than the people whom they claim to help. And what does one do with African development economists, whether trained at the University of Chicago or in Moscow, or with organizations like the Economic Commission for Africa or the African Development Bank, whose intellectual underpinnings might come from western universities or financial institutions mixed in with individual and collective experiences and goals rooted in their personal, political, and social connections in different parts of Africa? On the ground level, as Felicitas Becker makes clear, understanding development in the light of regional ecology, the intersecting trajectories of different people, the ups and downs of markets, and the vagaries of state policies calls for an analytic strategy that emphasizes interaction, adaptation, and confrontation, with outcomes that might range from mutual benefit to heightened exploitation, modest reductions in poverty to immiseration.[49]

The development question is not going away. It is hard to see how a country like Niger could educate its people or provide for their health with its own resources. The institutions with resources will have more power to shape not only the interaction but the ideological and cultural framing of it than the people and places in need. That is the development dilemma, and the study of development history is part of the history of global inequality.

As soon as one tries to explain why some places lack what others have or how projects to lessen inequality are conceived, one is looking beyond any

---

47 Different approaches and programs are described in Unger, *International Development*; Rempel, "Development Experience."

48 See also Gregory Mann, *From Empires to NGOs in the West African Sahel: The Road to Nongovernmentality* (Cambridge: Cambridge University Press, 2015); Benedetta Rossi, *From Slavery to Aid: Politics, Labour, and Ecology in the Nigerian Sahel, 1800–2000* (Cambridge: Cambridge University Press, 2015).

49 Becker, *Politics of Poverty*. Becker points out that even in a very poor part of Tanzania, development programs produce some winners as well as losers. She sees the process "bumping along" rather than producing a decisive breakthrough or complete failure. Becker, *Politics of Poverty*, 268, 276.

one place, with all its particularities, and at questions of political economy that entail all scales of connection, from the neighborhood to the globe. Development history is closely linked to the study of how some parts of the world came to be wealthier than others, and how inequality is reproduced or reduced. Divergent trajectories across the world have intrigued scholars, for example Kenneth Pomeranz, Thomas Piketty, and Walter Scheidel.[50] In the post-World War Two era, the remarkable divergence between South Korea and other Southeast Asian countries from most countries in Africa raises questions about the effectiveness of different strategies. The Southeast Asian story is not one of market miracles, but of a relationship of interventionist state policies, international connections, and specific forms of class relations.

Meanwhile, the economic historian Morton Jerven has reposed the question of Africa's trajectory. He argues that what needs to be explained is not "slow growth" but "growth spurts," triggered mostly by positive responses to external demands for a succession of African products (slaves, palm oil, cocoa, minerals) followed by periods of stagnation or retrogression.[51] That leaves the question of whether this or any other analysis of when African economies grow – which must be refined by region and even locality – has implications for how, in the future, states and international institutions might affect strategies to promote equitable growth or mitigate averse affects. To understand the origins, processes, and consequences of development initiatives is to look beyond the study of "development" as a specific object and toward a wider analysis of political economy. At the same time, looking broadly at the history of economic interaction and change requires going beyond self-propelled economic processes and toward the action of collective and individual actors, that is to "development."

That question is much more complicated than growth. "Underdeveloped" countries exhibit extremes of inequality, between a small number of people whose lifestyles and connections are those of a global and cosmopolitan bourgeoisie, versus people living with extreme deprivation. Africanists are now giving due attention to land issues, including the land grabbing in the past by white settlers, the land-grabbing in independent countries like Kenya of elites connect-

50 Kenneth Pomeranz, *The Great Divergence: China, Europe, and the Making of the Modern World Economy* (Princeton: Princeton University Press, 2000); Thomas Piketty, *The Economics of Inequality*, trans. Arthur Goldhammer (Cambridge, Mass.: Harvard University Press, 2015); Walter Scheidel, *The Great Leveler: Violence and the History of Inequality from the Stone Age to the Twenty-First Century* (Princeton: Princeton University Press, 2018).

51 Morton Jerven, "African Economic Growth Recurring: An Economic History Perspective on African Growth Episodes, 1690–2010," *Economic History of Developing Regions* 25 (2010): 127–154.

ed to power, and the recent influx of foreign investment in large land parcels in some African countries. Some have argued that various forms of communal land tenure stand in the way of potentially progressive farmers who could use land more productively, but it is far from clear that individual land titles will result in the economic dynamic that decades after the generalization of private land ownership led to prosperous economies in western Europe or only to the immiseration that accompanied that process. Studies based on extensive fieldwork are showing how small-scale cultivators try not only to defend their land rights, but to grow new crops and use new techniques when those possibilities arise, that they engage with state development projects when they have something to offer, and they can work collectively among themselves or with local or international NGOs when the state abdicates its responsibilities to its citizens.[52] One can make similar observations about urban economies: the "official" economy and the "informal" economy are not clearly demarcated; development projects, individual entrepreneurship, collective self-help, gangs, and protection rackets are overlapping modes of action as many people struggle to get by and others to enrich themselves.

Conclusion

Economic relations are rarely symmetrical. How this unevenness affects people in different circumstances and whether asymmetry is contained or reproduces itself are difficult questions. Development, as the word came to be used in mid-twentieth century to delineate a project of state governments and international agencies, comes into the picture because market mechanisms will not in themselves correct asymmetries. Whether such actions work to reduce or augment inequality is the crucial question. One can on the one hand point to the modest gains, especially in education and health, that came about during the "development era" of 1945 to 1975 and to the way in which the anti-development politics imposed on African states in the era of structural adjustment (late 1970s and 1980s) made the destructive effects of global economic crisis in the 1970s worse. Neither structural adjustment policies nor autarchy – withdrawal from economic relations, however asymmetrical they were – has been of much help to poor countries.[53] Denouncing or defending development at a high level of generality does not get us very far.

52 For example, Moskowitz, *Seeing Like a Citizen.*
53 Thandika Mkandawire, *Africa Beyond Recovery* (Legon-Accra: Subsaharan Publishers, 2015).

Historians of development have brought out the intersections of different conceptions and interests at local, national, regional, and global levels. "Development" became a concept distinguishable from "economy"– over the resistance of many economists[54] – at a moment when the imperial order was under challenge. It remains a definable and controversial concept because its central premise is the need for intervention to do what market mechanisms do not. Because so much of the once-colonized world bears the weight of a colonial histories and often lack basic resources, development necessarily poses the problem of relationships across lines of difference and inequality. Development is a quintessentially political concept, a quintessentially human one. To understand what development has meant historically and what it can mean in the future is to probe human thought and action across the divisions that are themselves produced historically – across continents, differences of language and culture, hierarchies, affinities, and antagonisms.

54 Robert Tignor, *W. Arthur Lewis and the Birth of Development Economics* (Princeton: Princeton University Press, 2006).

Ruth Rempel

Which Speeches Matter? Reflections on the Invention of Development

When was development invented? A frequent answer has been 1949, in the inauguration speech of American President Harry Truman. This answer appears in scholarly publications, particularly by authors with a critical perspective, and in some undergraduate textbooks.[1] Gilbert Rist's *The History of Development: From Western Origins to Global Faith* is an important reason for this answer.[2] The other widely cited reason is *The Development Dictionary* (1992). The authors of many of its entries state that the "age of development" began on January 20, 1949, the date of Truman's speech.[3] Between these two books Arturo Escobar published his influential *Encountering Development*, which also started with Truman's speech.[4]

Rist, Escobar, Wolfgang Sachs, and the other *Development Dictionary* authors belong to the Post-Development school, which emerged in the late 1980s.[5] While a diverse school, its members share a comprehensive rejection of development, citing its economistic and Eurocentric essence, and its destructive impacts. One of the school's most influential contributions has been the argument that development is a discourse, a historically situated way of seeing and speaking about the world. As Aram Ziai explained:

> knowledge about and representations of the social world are not neutral, but have a certain perspective and imply relations of power. Knowledge about "development" therefore al-

1 Juhani Koponen, "Development: History and Power of the Concept," *Forum for Development Studies* 47, no. 1 (2020): 1–21, 2. For a textbook example, see Paul Haslam, Jessica Schafer, and Pierre Beaudet, eds., *Introduction to International Development Studies: Approaches, Actors, Issues, and Practices* (Don Mills: Oxford University Press Canada, 2017).

2 Gilbert Rist, *The History of Development: From Western Origins to Global Faith* (London: Zed Books, 1997[1]). The book is a translation of *Le Développement, Histoire d'une Croyance Occidentale* (Paris: Presses de Sciences Po, 1996). All following quotes from this book are from the 1997 edition unless stated differently.

3 Wolfgang Sachs, "Introduction," in *The Development Dictionary: A Guide to Knowledge as Power*, ed. Wolfgang Sachs (London: Zed Books, 2019[3]), Kobo e-book, 5/21.

4 Arturo Escobar, *Encountering Development: The Making and Unmaking of the Third World* (Princeton: Princeton University Press, 2012, 1995[1]), 3.

5 For example, Arturo Escobar, "Preface to the 2012 Edition," in idem, *Encountering Development*, vii-xliv, vii.

https://doi.org/10.1515/9783110730234-006

> ways implies a claim on how other ("underdeveloped") people should live and how their lives can be improved, and thus a justification of intervention (knowledge as power).[6]

In making this argument Post-Developmentalists needed to identify the historical context in which development discourse emerged and gained power. Their outline of this context has become the accepted history of development for many in development studies, most of whom have social science backgrounds. While some social scientists have a long-standing interest in the history of thought in their disciplines, including ideas about development, many do not read research on development by historians.[7]

Over the last two decades historians have become interested in development. The picture painted by their research is, not surprisingly, more complex than the Post-Developmentalists' outline. It also challenges that outline at several points; most strongly on the origin of development. There is a consensus among historians that development as a concept and a program of action existed well before 1949, while its invention by Truman in 1949 remains a core principle of Post-Development.[8]

At the turn of the millennium historians were optimistic that using history to study phenomena like modernization offered "a way to write about development without accepting its clichés."[9] At that point development studies was still polarized by debates that neoliberalism's ascendency triggered, debates that reframed but did not reverse the fragmentation of development thought that occurred in the 1970s and 80s. Even if historians do not follow these debates within development studies, they cannot easily escape them. The definitions of development historians adopt and the initiatives they choose to research play into those debates.

---

6 Aram Ziai, "'I Am Not a Post-Developmentalist, but...': The Influence of Post-Development on development studies," *Third World Quarterly* 38, no. 12 (2017): 2719–2734, 2721. This special issue marked the twenty-fifth anniversary of *The Development Dictionary*'s publication and discusses Post-Development's legacy.

7 For an overview of development's history of thought, see Joseph Hodge, "Writing the History of Development (Part 1: The First Wave)," *Humanity* 6, no. 3 (2015): 429–463, 431–434. Michele Alacevich and Mauro Boianovsky, "Writing the History of Development Economics," *History of Political Economy* 50, Annual Supplement 1 (2018): 1–14 offers a recent look at the history of thought in a key development discipline.

8 Frederick Cooper, "Writing the History of Development," *Journal of Modern European History* 8, no. 1 (2010): 5–25, 8; Ziai, "'I am not a Post-Developmentalist'," 2721.

9 Nick Cullather, "Research Note: Development? It's History," *Diplomatic History* 24, no. 4 (2000): 641–653, 642. For a more nuanced view see Cooper's "Writing the History of Development."

This article takes a critical look at Post-Development's outline of development history, which has been most fully elaborated by Gilbert Rist. It will summarize Rist's argument, for readers not familiar with it, and evaluate his claims using the criterion of novelty, which Rist considered important. Additional criteria suggested by agency-based definitions of development and by discourse analysis—the intentions of the speaker and their capacity to initiate change, as well as the purpose and context of a speech—will also be applied. Identifying parallels between the Post-Development view of development history and Cold War-focused histories of development will be the final task of this article.

Seeing Development as a Discourse

Despite its title Rist's *History of Development* was primarily a critique of development. This was not surprising given that Rist was a political scientist with an interest in anthropology. Rist's critique followed established Post-Development lines, aiming to ensure the development's rejection. He decried development's obsession with economics and growth, and lamented the destruction it wrought by assuming that Western ways were superior to those of other cultures. He was deeply critical of the dominant theories of development, produced either by individuals from the global North or within the UN system—implicitly dominated by the North. The only Southern contributions to development were dependency theory from Latin America and Tanzania's *ujamaa* policy.[10] The former Rist dismissed as a variant of modernization; of the latter he said that it represented "a *diversification of 'developments'*," but was nonetheless a top-down initiative that failed to achieve its goals.[11] Although Rist organized the objects of his critique chronologically, outlining the history of development took only four of the first edition's 13 chapters. Rist prepared new editions in 2001, 2007, and 2013, with English translations following in 2002, 2008, and 2014. In all the later, longer editions the four chapter history section remained and was unrevised.

Development for Rist was a discourse, an idea that had the "power to seduce in every sense of the term [...], but also to abuse, to turn away from the truth, to deceive."[12] Reality was not created by words, Rist added, but

10 Gilbert Rist, *The History of Development: From Western Origins to Global Faith* (London: Zed Books, 2014[4]), 198.

11 Rist, *History of Development*, 109–111, 137–139, 154.

12 Rist, *History of Development*, 1.

> certain forms of discourse express more accurately than others a reality in the making, because certain texts bring out more clearly than others the episteme of an epoch, and finally —this is the performative aspect of the text—because *power does not necessarily involve changing reality, but, rather, inserting it into a different problematic*, proposing a new interpretation to kindle the illusion of change.[13]

Rist did not provide a more detailed explanation of discourse, though the concepts and methods of critical discourse analysis were developing in the early 1990s.[14] As Jan Nederveen Pieterse noted, for Post-Development scholars discourse analysis was an "ideological platform" rather than a methodology.[15]

Religion was another term Rist used to describe development, though it was a metaphor rather than an analytic category he pursued in depth. He used religion to highlight development's Western origins, arguing that development shared characteristics with European Christianity as he saw it. It was a belief system that set out "indisputable truths" that compelled or determined behavior, creating a "collective certainty" that it would be improper to question, at least in public.[16] Religion was later a metaphor with which to stress compulsion rather than seduction as Rist sought to explain the continuing power of development.[17]

Post-Development's Outline of Development's History

Like any respectable Western phenomenon, development needed a civilizational genealogy. Rist's history started with a standard one: Aristotle, Augustine, and several Enlightenment thinkers. Social evolutionism, the progenitor of development, was their child.[18] Social evolutionism was implemented by the "great powers" of Western Europe between 1870 and 1940 via their empires.[19] The League of Nations provided new legitimation for European imperial interventions, but the League lacked the capacity to fully implement its mandate system and become

13 Rist, *History of Development*, 78, emphasis in the original.
14 For example, Ruth Wodak, "What CDA is About—A Summary of Its History, Important Concepts and Its Developments," in *Methods of Critical Discourse Analysis*, ed. Ruth Wodak and Michael Meyer (London: Sage, 2001), 1–13.
15 Jan Nederveen Petersie, *Development Theory* (Los Angeles: Sage, 2010^2), 15.
16 Rist, *History of Development*, 44, 22.
17 Rist, *History of Development*, 214–215.
18 Rist, *History of Development*, 40–41.
19 Rist, *History of Development*, 47.

the institutional expression of an internationalized imperialism. A glance at texts like Victor Hugo's speech on the abolition of slavery (1879), a presentation on *mise en valeur* by Jules Ferry (1885), and the League of Nations Covenant (1919) allowed Rist to characterize this era.[20] It was the annunciation of these ideas, rather than their embodiment in policy, that interested Rist.[21]

While the colonial era's practices and rationales had similarities to and continuities with the development era that succeeded it, Rist argued there were crucial differences. Some Post-Developmentalists said colonization had been primarily a cultural project, while development was an economic one, but Rist disagreed—and provided a more detailed analysis.[22] He focused on agency rather than on the minimization of economic motives in colonization. "The initiative of turning the colonies 'to account'," Rist said, "could [...] be taken only by the metropolitan countries," within an "openly asymmetrical, hierarchical and non-egalitarian relationship" that was distinctive to "the colonial enterprise."[23] In the era that followed, all peoples and states possessed agency, but it was notional because development held them—or their leaders, at least—in deepening thrall.[24] The other differences were the absence of the United States, which Rist said did not participate in colonization, and the absence of development.[25]

Truman's inauguration speech, nicknamed Point Four for its final point, which announced a development initiative, initiated profound change. It also "gave the impetus" to the adoption of development by the United Nations, which, unlike the League, was able to institutionalize development.[26] While other Post-Developmentalists assumed the UN was the US writ large, Rist described the transfer of American-invented development to the UN, using John F. Kennedy's speech proposing a "Decade of Development" to represent this.[27] Rist ended his historical outline with a selection of material, mostly from the

---

20 Rist, *History of Development*, 50–51, 60–61.

21 While Rist was writing there were already studies of *mise en valeur*'s translation into policy. Alice Conklin, *A Mission to Civilize: The Republican Idea of Empire in France and West Africa, 1895–1930* (Stanford: Stanford University Press, 1997) was published one year after Rist's first edition.

22 For example, Wolfgang Sachs, "On the Archaeology of the Development Idea," *The Ecologist* 20, no. 2 (1990): 42–43, 42. Escobar, like Rist, saw continuities between colonial and developmental discourse; Escobar, *Encountering Development*, 9.

23 Rist, *History of Development*, 58.

24 Rist, *History of Development*, 79.

25 Rist, *History of Development*, 66, 68.

26 Rist, *History of Development*, 88.

27 Rist, *History of Development*, 90; on the UN as an embodiment of American hegemony see Sachs, "On the Archaeology," 42.

1991 and 1992 UN Development Programme's (UNDP's) *Human Development Reports*, which he said became "the basis of all discourse on 'development'."[28]

Evaluating Speeches and Truman's Invention of Development

By what criteria might we judge the impact of Truman's Point Four speech and Post-Development's claim that it constituted the invention of development? Evidence of novelty would be one: was the word development being used for the first time, or used in a new way? For Rist this was an important issue, and thus a criterion worth including. Further criteria for evaluation are suggested by reflection on human agency, in particular the intention and capacity to act.[29] Since the intent to change has become important to definitions of development, this adds weight to the intentions of a speech's authors as a criterion for judging its impact.[30] In addition, critical discourse analysis suggests that the purpose of a speech is important. So are the context in which it was delivered and the event's participants. This kind of analysis works outward from the content of a text (written or spoken) to the social relations, processes, and circumstances in which it is embedded.[31]

The capacity to act is linked to the issue of power, a core concern for the Post-Development school and of great interest to others who research development.[32] While financial resources are an imperfect proxy for an actor's capacity, a look at changes in the allocation of money by or to actors named in a speech would help understand the capacity of the speaker (and their backers or allies) to institute the changes of which they spoke. I have argued elsewhere that

---

28 Rist, *History of Development*, 90–91.

29 For example, Mark Schlosser, "Agency," in *Stanford Encyclopedia of Philosophy*, ed. Edward Zalta et al. (Stanford: Stanford University, 2021), accessed May 19, 2022, https://plato.stanford.edu/entries/agency/.

30 Petersie, for example, defined development as "organized intervention in collective affairs according to a standard of improvement": Petersie, *Development Theory*, 3. The focus on intention in defining development originated with Michael Cowen and Robert Shenton, whose work is discussed in the next section.

31 Thao Lê and Quynh Lê, "Critical Discourse Analysis: An Overview," in *Critical Discourse Analysis: An Interdisciplinary Perspective*, ed. Thao Lê, Quynh Lê and Megan Short (New York: Nova Science Publishers, 2009), 3–16, 5–6; Ruth Wodak, "The Discourse-Historical Approach," in *Methods of Critical Discourse Analysis*, 63–94, 65.

32 Rist does not explain what he means by power, but Escobar indicates his understanding of power is based on Foucault in Escobar, *Encountering Development*, 5.

changes in resources are a tool for periodization in development history.[33] If a speech constituted a turning point in development history, significant changes in access to and allocation of resources would be indicators.

Related to this, the implementation of key elements of the speech via the creation of new practices or organizations, or significant alteration in existing ones, would be a fourth criterion for evaluation. The institutionalization of any such changes would be a further sign of the speaker's capacity to effect change, and to persuade others to adopt it. For Post-Developmentalists, though, implementation was not important. As Sachs put it, development was a "cast of mind" more than "a socio-economic endeavor," and like other "myths and fantasies" it rose and fell "independent of empirical results."[34] To the extent that Rist considered institutionalization, he looked at the UN system rather than the US, so the UN will be the focus in the latter part of this paper. What follows is a brief look at each of these criteria for evaluation, supported by a mix of sources from the 1950s, literature contemporaneous with the Post-Development classics, which were researched in the late 1980s and early 1990s, and more recent studies of Truman's speech and the Point Four Program that followed it.

Development and Underdevelopment—New Terms or Concepts?

Rist argued that Point Four in Truman's speech was an instance of "*terminological innovation.*"[35] Instead of looking at use of the noun development, he focused on use of the adjective underdeveloped "as a synonym for 'economically backward' areas." Rist qualified his claim for novelty by noting Truman's speech was the first time underdevelopment had been used in this way "in a text intended for such wide circulation."[36] The *Oxford English Dictionary* (OED) supports this, listing Truman's speech as the first usage example of underdeveloped in this sense.[37]

However, Rist's argument for innovation was mostly based on the distinction between development as an "intransitive phenomenon" and a "transitive mean-

33 Ruth Rempel, "Periodizing African Development History," *African Economic History* 36, no. 1 (2008): 125–158, 129.
34 Sachs, "Introduction," Kobo e-book, 5/21.
35 Rist, *History of Development*, 72, emphasis in the original.
36 Both quotes from Rist, *History of Development*, 72.
37 Oxford English Dictionary Online, Entry "under-developed, adj.", accessed May 19, 2022, https://www-oed-com.eui.idm.oclc.org/view/Entry/211564?redirectedFrom=under-developed&.

ing" of development. In the former development "simply 'happens'," and nothing can be done to alter the evolutionary process through which it is achieved. In the latter, action can be taken to bring about development; it becomes "possible to 'develop' a region."[38] This is the distinction that Michael Cowen and Robert Shenton made, also in 1996, between development as an immanent process and development as intentional change.[39] They built a powerful argument for the nineteenth century birth of development as an accepted term for intentional change, an argument supported by numerous nineteenth century OED usage examples of develop as a transitive verb, together with an argument for the nineteenth century birth of underdevelopment.[40] Responding to the *Development Dictionary*'s just-published argument about Truman, Cowen and Shenton said the late 1940s was a time when "when 'development' had become so accentuated that many are led to believe that it was then discovered."[41]

Rist also made a broader claim about conceptual innovation, arguing that Truman's speech "radically altered the way the world was seen."[42] The world was no longer divided between the colonizers and the colonized; after Point Four it was divided between the developed and the underdeveloped. This divide was new in that all nation-states were recognized as theoretical equals. Developed countries had the lead in economic, social, and political matters, but underdeveloped countries could act to alter their status—they could catch up by undertaking development.[43] It was this action, tied to a model of Western modernization, for which President Truman offered American assistance.

---

38 All quotes are from Rist, *History of Development*, 73.

39 See, for instance, Michael Cowen and Robert Shenton, *Doctrines of Development* (London: Routledge, 1996), viii-ix, 25. Sections in Cowen and Shenton's book were published prior to 1996, and thus available when Rist's first edition was being written and translated. For example, Michael Cowen and Robert Shenton, "The origin and course of Fabian colonialism in Africa," *Journal of Historical Sociology* 4, no. 2 (1991): 143–174; Michael Cowen and Robert Shenton, "The Invention of Development," in *Power of Development*, ed. Jonathan Crush (London: Routledge, 1995), 27–43.

40 Oxford English Dictionary Online, Entry "develop, v.", accessed May 19, 2022, https://www-oed-com.eui.idm.oclc.org/view/Entry/51427?redirectedFrom=develop. For a critique of Rist's argument based on these insights see Michael Cowen, Review of *The History of Development: From Western Origins to Global Faith*, by Gilbert Rist, *Canadian Journal of African Studies* 32, no. 1 (1998): 240–244.

41 Cowen and Shenton, *Doctrines of Development*, 7–8.

42 Rist, *History of Development*, 73.

43 Rist, *History of Development*, 74.

The Intent to Develop

Rist's argument for the 1949 invention of development would be strengthened if it were clear that Truman intended to create something new and announced it in his speech. To understand Truman's intentions, it is important to know a bit about the context of his 1949 inauguration. Harry Truman was Roosevelt's last Vice-President and was thrust into the top office with little preparation when Roosevelt died in April 1945. Truman ran for the presidency in his own right in 1948, in an election so hard fought that several newspapers initially declared his Republican opponent the victor. Truman came into office with an ambitious agenda of social reform that built on Roosevelt's New Deal.[44] However the Democratic Party, though it regained control of both Congress and the White House, was divided, while the Republicans were embittered. Truman, who had faced disdain and ridicule from within his own party as well as from opponents, was buoyed by a powerful sense of vindication. He was aware, though, that both voters and legislators would need to be coaxed if the reforms on which he campaigned were to be implemented.[45] The crowd of more than a million who gathered to witness his inauguration was Truman's initial, intended audience. And the inauguration was historic: Truman announced that African Americans were welcome to attend, and the ceremony was broadcast on television.[46] Both "firsts" likely encouraged Truman to focus on his national audience; they were certainly among the social processes in which the speech was embedded.

The idea of technical assistance to underdeveloped areas—the speech's fourth point—was not intended to significantly alter American foreign policy or recast international relations. It was added because Truman and his advisors felt the speech needed a "dramatic highlight."[47] As a State Department official who helped generate ideas for the speech later explained, it was "a public-relations gimmick, thrown in by a professional speech-writer to give the speech more

---

44 For example, Ken Hechler and George Elsey, "The Greatest Upset in American Political History: Harry Truman and the 1948 Election," in *White House Studies Compendium*, vol. 6, ed. Anthony Eksterowicz and Glenn Hastedt (New York: Nova Science Publishers, 2008), 81–92.
45 Robert Donovan, *Tumultuous Years: The Presidency of Harry S. Truman, 1949–53* (New York: Norton, 1982), 17, 22–23.
46 Amanda McVety, *Enlightened Aid: U.S. Development as Foreign Policy in Ethiopia* (Oxford: Oxford University Press, 2012), 92.
47 *New York Times*, June 26, 1949 as quoted in Tarun Bose, "The Point Four Programme: A Critical Study," *International Studies* 7, no. 1 (1965): 66–97, 66.

life."[48] Truman, though, said that the idea of "a continuing and self-perpetuating program of technical assistance to the underdeveloped nations of the world" had been in his mind since the Marshall Plan was launched.[49] While historians of Cold War development are skeptical of this self-explanation, they agree that the fourth point was drawn from existing ideas and projects, not something new.[50]

When Truman's fourth point was turned into overnight headline news by the American media, "the White House and the State Department were taken completely by surprise."[51] Washington reporters saw Point Four as "one of the most ambitious pronouncements on foreign affairs" made by an American president.[52] How Americans of various backgrounds responded to the televised speech is harder to judge, but domestic interest in Point Four did help create an international audience for the speech in a way Truman had not expected. As Jahangir Amuzegar observed, the speech "inspired interest and enthusiasm throughout the world."[53] Over the next few years there was a flurry of publications about Point Four by academics and policymakers. As one of these noted, ordinary people in Latin America were also soon talking "about 'Punta Cuatro', and [...] Iranian farmers about 'Astle Charom'."[54] Rist, in contrast, claimed that Point Four "went almost unnoticed at the time."[55]

Resource Flows

If Truman's inaugural speech initiated significant resource flows for development this would be an indicator of invention and support for the idea that it

---

48 Louis Halle, "On Teaching International Relations," *Virginia Quarterly Review* 40, no. 1 (1964): 11–25, 17.
49 Harry S. Truman, *Memoirs by Harry S. Truman, vol. 2: Years of Trial and Hope* (New York: Doubleday & Company, Inc., 1956), 231 as quoted in McVety, *Enlightened Aid*, 88.
50 David Ekbladh, *The Great American Mission: Modernization and the Construction of an American World Order* (Princeton: Princeton University Press, 2010), 98; Sara Lorenzini, "Truman's Dream: When the Cold War and Development Met," in *Global Development: A Cold War History* (Princeton: Princeton University Press, 2019), Kobo e-book, 14–16/36.
51 Halle, "On Teaching," 17.
52 James Reston, *New York Times*, January 21, 1949 as quoted in McVety, *Enlightened Aid*, 93.
53 Jahangir Amuzegar, "Point Four: Performance and Prospect," *Political Science Quarterly* 73, no. 4 (1958): 530–546, 530. Amuzegar was a member of a politically prominent family in Iran.
54 Jonathan Bingham, "Partisan Politics and Point Four," *Bulletin of the Atomic Scientists* 10, no. 4 (1954): 84–86, 84.
55 Rist, *History of Development*, 5.

was a historical turning point. Given the context for Point Four's inclusion in his speech, this was clearly not Truman's intent. As it also had when the Marshall Plan was announced in 1948, the State Department moved quickly to squelch hopes that the President's speech would mean significant new transfers to countries in Latin America, Asia or Africa.[56] An additional concern with Point Four was whether Truman meant the US government to become a guarantor for American private foreign investment. The answer was no. As with direct spending, officials were keen to quash expectations of a significant new financial role for the government.[57]

Point Four's American supporters emphasized that "*self*-help [was] fundamental" to the Point Four Program, the practical outcome of Truman's speech.[58] Recipient countries had to request assistance, and they were expected to contribute half the resources for the Program's training programs and demonstration projects. Agreements with recipient governments were thus crucial, and each agreement was to be tailored to the recipient country.[59] Drafting agreements and getting experts and supplies into place took time, so it was not until mid-1951 and in some cases early 1952 that the Program was actually operating.[60] By this time it had a Cold War function that went beyond reducing international tensions and wooing citizens of underdeveloped countries through improved living standards. It housed geological surveys that identified deposits of strategic minerals needed by the US[61]

The Eisenhower administration that succeeded Truman's continued to offer international aid, including technical assistance, after 1953 but Point Four was no longer the American aid flagship. With the transfer of development programming to a new International Cooperation Administration in 1955, the Point Four

---

56 Robert Wood, *From Marshall Plan to Debt Crisis: Foreign Aid and Development Choices in the World Economy* (Berkeley: University of California Press, 1986), 45–46.

57 "Possible Questions and Proposed Answers," April 12, 1949, Harry S. Truman Presidential Library & Museum, accessed May 18, 2022, https://www.trumanlibrary.gov/library/research-files/possible-questions-and-suggested-answers-concerning-presidents-technical?documentid=NA&pagenumber=2.

58 Omar Pancoast, Jr., "The 'Point Four' Policy," *Bulletin of the Atomic Scientists* 10, no. 3 (1954): 87–92, 87, emphasis in the original.

59 Rollin Atwood, "The United States Point Four Program—A Bilateral Approach," *Annals of the American Academy of Political and Social Science* 323 (1959): 33–39, 35.

60 Samuel Hayes, "An Appraisal of Point Four," *Proceedings of the Academy of Political Science* 25, no. 3 (1953): 31–46, 31.

61 Megan Black, "Interior's Exterior: The State, Mining Companies, and Resource Ideologies in the Point Four Program," *Diplomatic History* 40, no. 1 (2016): 81–110.

Program disappeared.[62] Ethiopia and Iran are the two recipient countries whose Point Four experiences have so far been examined in depth.[63]

The Point Four Program did not receive Congressional approval until May 1950, the victim of infighting between the White House and State Department as well as partisan differences.[64] The Program was modest, even more so after skeptical Congress members whittled the $45 million requested for its first year down to $35 million.[65] This was a fraction of what the US was then providing in other kinds of international assistance. The Program's outlays were also small in comparison to private American investment, which the Truman administration expected would flow to underdeveloped countries after the Point Four Program catalyzed their economic development.[66] However, the share of American foreign investment directed at Africa, Asia, and Latin America fell between 1940 and 1960, even as the total stock of American investment almost doubled.[67] Truman's inaugural address did not generate significant new American flows of aid or investment for development.

One of the Program's administrators suggested that Point Four's novelty was not the amount of money involved, but the range of its intended recipients—the commitment to provide assistance to "all peace-loving peoples," not just to "allies, satellites, and dependencies."[68] A look at the allocation of Point Four funds between 1952 and 1954, however, shows the majority of them were concentrated on allies and satellites, like Iran, Israel, Jordan, and Formosa, as well as countries whose relationship to US was colonial or quasi-colonial, like the Philippines, Puerto Rico, and Liberia.[69] Although Truman said his bold, new program would replace imperialism, Point Four funds were also allocated to the "Depend-

62 Stephen Macekura, "The Point Four Program and U.S. International Development Policy," *Political Science Quarterly* 128, no. 1 (2013): 127–160, 153–155.

63 McVety, *Enlightened Aid*; Richard Garlitz, *A Mission for Development: Utah Universities and the Point Four Program in Iran* (Logan: Utah State University Press, 2018).

64 Thomas Paterson, "Foreign Aid Under Wraps: The Point Four Program," *Wisconsin Magazine of History* 56, no. 2 (1972–1973): 119–126, 121–122.

65 Macekura, "The Point Four Program," 140; Lorenzini, "Truman's Dream," Kobo e-book, 19/36.

66 Hayes, "An Appraisal of Point Four," 33; Macekura, "The Point Four Program," 140; McVety, *Enlightened Aid*, 97.

67 Michael Twomey, *A Century of Foreign Investment in the Third World* (Abingdon: Routledge, 2000), 33, 38.

68 Bingham, "Partisan Politics," 84.

69 Jonathan Bingham, *Shirt-Sleeve Diplomacy: Point 4 in Action* (Freeport: Books for Libraries Press, 1970 (1953)), 245, 251.

ent Territories" of European allies, meaning their colonies.[70] These were the "most underdeveloped parts of the world," American officials argued. They hoped, though, to associate "colonial people" with "posts of some significance and responsibility" in the Program to avoid accusations of neo-imperialism.[71] In Sub-Saharan Africa "Dependent Territories" were by far the largest recipients of Point Four funds, though in both the Caribbean and Pacific regions they were minor recipients.[72] In this respect the Point Four Program resembled the Marshall Plan, which the US had allowed its allies to use for development projects in their colonies—even to cover the cost of suppressing anti-colonial rebellions.[73] When Rist suggested that Point Four inserted colonies "*into a different problematic*," re-interpreting them as underdeveloped areas, he overstated the degree of historical discontinuity.[74]

Implementation and Institutionalization

Implementation is the final criterion proposed to evaluate the impact of a speech. Like other Post-Developmentalists, Rist downplayed this aspect of innovation, and with respect to the advent of official development assistance he was right to do so.[75] As a range of historical work on European imperialism has pointed out, Britain's 1940 Colonial Development and Welfare Act was a prominent example of pre-1949 official development aid. It named the welfare of colonial subjects as a goal of development, though economic growth remained a primary aim. It also institutionalized planning, as each colony's administration was required to submit a multi-year plan to access money under the Act. In French colonies the 1946 *Plan de modernisation et d'équipement*, modeled after the 1940 British Act, guided post-war reconstruction and development. Its distinctive element was a significant growth in public transfers, both grants and loans, to finance development in the empire.[76] Both the 1940 Act and the 1946 *Plan* had

70 Macekura, "The Point Four Program," 127; Bingham, *Shirt-Sleeve Diplomacy*, 245, 255–256.
71 Advisory Committee on Technical Assistance, "Point Four Program in Relation to Dependent Areas," July 27, 1949 as quoted in McVety, *Enlightened Aid*, 105.
72 Bingham, *Shirt-Sleeve Diplomacy*, 245, 255.
73 Wood, *From Marshall Plan to Debt Crisis*, 43, 55–56.
74 Rist, *History of Development*, 78, emphasis in the original.
75 Rist, *History of Development*, 56.
76 R. E. Wicker, "Colonial Development and Welfare, 1929–1957: The Evolution of a Policy," *Social and Economic Studies* 7, no. 4 (1958): 170–192; Catherine Coquery-Vidrovitch, "Economic Changes in Africa in the World Context," in *UNESCO General History of Africa, vol. VIII: Africa*

precedents in British and French policies following World War One and the inter-war recessions, policies that ensured access to essential raw materials and discouraged unrest. The International Labour Organization's work on nutrition and the League's Mandates Commission were additional inter-war influences on colonial development and aid for it.[77]

Recent scholarship has shown the Point Four Program had important American precursors as well. These included the Export-Import Bank, wartime technical assistance offered through the Institute of Inter-American Affairs, and publicly-funded international relief provided after World War One.[78] Americans were also aware of British colonial development precedents. Critic Henry Hazlitt, for instance, argued Point Four was designed to repeat all the mistakes of Britain's East African Groundnuts Scheme.[79] If Rist had been content to make a much narrower historical argument about development aid as a tool of American foreign policy, he would have been on solid ground. Point Four was the moment when development aid became a permanent part of America's foreign policy tool kit, a point made in several recent histories of Cold War development.[80]

It is worth noting that not all critical scholars shared Post-Development's assertion that Truman invented development in 1949.[81] Some suggested inflection points rather than historic breaks between the "colonial project," the post-World War Two "development project," and the "globalization project" that succeeded it.[82] Some accepted 1949 as a historical turning point, but complained that talk of

since 1935, ed. Ali A. Mazrui (Paris: UNESCO, 1993), 285–316, are examples of the literature (in English) available before Rist wrote his first edition.

77 For an overview see Ruth Rempel, "Colonialism and Development in Africa," in *The Palgrave Handbook of African Colonial and Postcolonial History*, ed. Martin Shanguhiya and Toyin Falola (New York: Palgrave Macmillan, 2018), 576–583.

78 Macekura, "The Point Four Program," 127–129, 131–138; Claude Erb, "Prelude to Point Four: The Institute of Inter-American Affairs," *Diplomatic History* 9, no. 3 (1985): 249–269; Michael Adamson, "'Must We Overlook All Impairment of Our Interests?' Debating the Foreign Aid Role of the Export-Import Bank, 1934–41," *Diplomatic History* 29, no. 4 (2005): 589–623.

79 Henry Hazlitt, *Illusions of Point Four* (Irvington-on-Hudson: Foundation for Economic Education, 1950), 13–16.

80 Erb, "Prelude to Point Four," 249; Nick Cullather, *The Hungry World: America's Cold War Battle against Poverty in Asia* (Cambridge: Harvard University Press, 2010), 212–213; Ekbladh, *Great American Mission*, 98.

81 For example, Fiona Mackenzie, "Selective Silence: A Feminist Encounter with Environmental Discourse in Colonial Africa," in *Power of Development*, ed. Jonathan Crush (London: Routledge, 1995), 100–112; Uma Kothari, "From Colonialism to Development: Reflections of Former Colonial Officers," *Commonwealth and Comparative Politics* 44, no. 1 (2006): 118–136.

82 For example, Philip McMichael and Heloise Weber, *Development and Social Change: A Global Perspective* (Los Angeles: Sage, 2021[7]).

a development project and a globalization project downplayed their shared characteristic—American imperialism.[83] Yet others were bothered by the claim of a "rupture" in development history in the late 1940s, believing that this argument helped "mask the fact that the global political and economic organisation established in the late nineteenth century is still largely intact."[84]

In spite of critical responses and the growing literature on development history from historians and social scientists, Rist extended rather than re-examined his argument in subsequent editions. "When the first French edition of this book appeared," Rist said, "it was possible to think that 'development' was running out of steam."[85] It was not, and Rist added recent examples of development, like the Millennium Development Goals, to his critique, but made no changes to the earlier, history-focused chapters of his book. He evidently felt no need to consult the emerging literature to deepen his understanding of development in the colonial era. Although Escobar noted some of the early research on imperial development in Africa in his first edition, he also did not use more recent histories to update his 1995 observation that "the period between 1920 and 1950 is still ill understood from the vantage point of the overlap between colonial and developmentalist regimes of representation."[86] The unfortunate pattern of updating prefatory material, but not the book's core chapters or the late 1980s and early 1990s research on which they were based, is also evident in the 2019 edition of *The Development Dictionary.* None of these Post-Development classics address histories of development published after 2000. Elsewhere, though, Rist responded to critics who pointed out that Point Four was added to Truman's speech for publicity reasons. Though Truman's "stroke of genius" might have been unintentional, it did not change his speech's historical significance for Rist.[87]

---

83 For example, Henry Veltmeyer, "Development and Globalization as Imperialism," *Canadian Journal of Development Studies* 26, no. 1 (2005): 89–106.

84 April Biccum, "Theorising Continuities between Empire & Development: Toward a New Theory of History," in *Empire, Development & Colonialism: The Past in the Present*, ed. Mark Duffield and Vernon Hewitt (Woodbridge: James Currey, 2009), 146–160, 154.

85 Gilbert Rist, "Preface to the Third Edition," in idem, *History of Development: From Western Origins to Global Faith* (London: Zed Books, 2014^4), xi-xii, xi.

86 Escobar, *Encountering Development*, 27.

87 Gilbert Rist, "Development as a Buzzword," in *Deconstructing Development Discourse: Buzzwords and Fuzzwords*, ed. Andrea Cornwall and Deborah Eade (Oxford: Practical Action and Oxfam GB, 2010), 19–28, 19.

Why Speeches by American Presidents?

Given the lack of evidence for terminological or conceptual innovation, for the intent to create change or for altered resource flows, and the mixed evidence for implementation and institutionalization, the question becomes why Rist and other Post-Developmentalists insist that Truman's speech inaugurated a new historical era. Rist gave three reasons: the prior absence of a concept of development as intentional change, an alteration in historical agency with the end of colonization, and the changed role of the US in international affairs. As we have seen, there is little evidence for the first of these. The second reason depends on viewing imperialism and trusteeship—as well as modernization—as binary relationships where only one side possessed power. This view was being questioned in the early 1990s and is challenged more strongly by recent historical scholarship.[88] Monica van Beusekom's research on the *Office du Niger* is one example of work showing how imperial officials were compelled to take into account the views of African participants in their development projects.[89] Rist's third reason is thus the crucial one: colonization and the mandates system were essential to European history and both "were conducted without the United States."[90] While this is a questionable statement, for Post-Developmentalists the post-war years were an important "historical conjuncture" in which a new world power, the United States, needed a global mission as it faced off against the USSR.[91] Development, as announced in Point Four, became that mission. It "allowed the US to behave as herald of national self-determination while at the same time founding a new type of world-wide domination."[92] With the end of

---

88 For example, Frederick Cooper, "Modernizing Bureaucrats, Backward Africans, and the Development Concept," in *International Development and the Social Sciences: Essays on the History and Politics of Knowledge*, ed. Frederick Cooper and Randall Packard (Berkeley: University of California Press, 1997), 64–92. Cooper's earlier "Conflict and Connection: Rethinking Colonial African History," *American Historical Review* 99, no. 5 (1994): 1516–1545 and his work on labor in French-ruled West Africa made similar points, and were available when Rist wrote his first draft; for example, Frederick Cooper, "From Free Labor to Family Allowances: Labor and African Society in Colonial Discourse," *American Ethnologist* 16, no. 4 (1989): 753–754.

89 Monica van Beusekom, *Negotiating Development: African Farmers and Colonial Experts at the Office du Niger, 1920–1960* (Portsmouth: Heinemann, 2002), 118–146; Monica van Beusekom and Dorothy Hodgson, "Lessons Learned? Development Experiences in the Late Colonial Period," *Journal of African History* 41, no. 1 (2000): 29–33.

90 Rist, *History of Development*, 66.

91 Escobar, *Encountering Development*, 4; Sachs, "On the Archaeology," 42.

92 Wolfgang Sachs, *The Archaeology of the Development Idea: Six Essays* (Montreal: Intercultural Institute of Montreal, 1990), 2.

the Cold War, Post-Developmentalists expected development would lose its ideological fuel and be consigned to "the scrapyard of history."[93]

It is worth asking why the Americans were so central to Post-Developmentalists' conception of development history. The answer may be that the early 1990s, when Rist was writing and the *Development Dictionary* was published, was the end of the Cold War.[94] The US had won and Western liberal democracy and capitalism triumphed, said many.[95] Some saw parallels between the emerging post-Cold War world and American dominance of the global economy after World War Two.[96] Rist certainly saw parallels between intensified support for structural adjustment policies, strongly associated with the US, and the justifications for colonization that had intensified as mid-twentieth century challenges to empire grew.[97] Neoliberalism, the theoretical basis for structural adjustment, reached its apogee in the early 1990s with vociferous supporters combatting an increasing range of critics. In addition, the early 1990s saw significant change in the development aid landscape. Disenchantment with aid and recession in many donor countries, the collapse of Soviet aid, and dramatic reductions in aid from oil-producing countries all played a part. Consequently Western donors, led by the US, were by default supplying the vast majority of the development aid on offer.[98] The only historical parallel for this aid dominance were the early years of the 1950s. This is speculation, but this conjuncture may have led Rist and other Post-Developmentalists to identify the US as the key actor in their historical outline. In addition, work on development by historians at the turn of the millennium was American-centered, which validated the Post-Development interpretation.[99]

Rist's methodology also predisposed him to a particular view of development history. He located "significant episodes" that represented "particular ep-

---

93 Sachs, "Introduction," Kobo e-book, 9/21, 15/21.
94 Hodge, "Writing the History of Development (Part 1)," 434–437.
95 Francis Fukuyama's "The End of History," *The National Interest* 16 (1989): 3–18 is a widely cited example.
96 For example, Justin van der Merwe and Nicole Dodd, *The Political Economy of Underdevelopment in the Global South: The Government-Business-Media Complex* (Cham: Palgrave Macmillan, 2019), 40.
97 Rist, *History of Development*, 58.
98 OECD, "Query Wizard for International Development Statistics," accessed May 18, 2022, https://stats.oecd.org/qwids/.
99 Marc Kunkel, "Writing the History of Development: A Review of the Recent Literature," *Contemporary European History* 20, no. 2 (2011): 215–232, 217; David Engerman and Corinna R. Unger, "Introduction: Towards a Global History of Modernization," *Diplomatic History* 33, no. 3 (2009): 375–385, 377.

ochs" in the long span of history, and within each of whose characteristics were revealed by "great texts."[100] This focus on "great texts" biased his inquiry, and that of Post-Developmentalists who shared his approach to discourse, toward the speech of those powerful enough to be recorded or published and widely circulated. Combining this method with the assumption that development was (and is) the hegemonic product of "the preoccupations of the industrialized countries" made it appropriate to focus on the speech of persons from those countries.[101] In the early 1990s, choosing the speech of an American president to initiate a new historical era was not surprising; neither was the use of another presidential speech to embody the transfer of development to the UN.

Other Speeches and Alternate Histories

Rist's decision to use bits from the 1991 and 1992 UNDP *Human Development Reports* to represent UN development thinking, remarked earlier, inadvertently reveals his omission of a person whose speech should matter in histories of the UN and broader histories of development—Pakistani economist Mahbub ul Haq. Haq was hired by the UNDP in 1989 and led the team that created the annual *Human Development Reports*.[102] The first *Report*, published in 1990, set out the concept of human development and provided an indicator for it, the first to successfully challenge the primacy of national income per capita. Those who worked with Haq used words like "crusade" and "heresy" to talk about this effort to put human well-being rather than economic growth at the center of development.[103] The early *Human Development Reports* embodied a change in thinking. They were initially controversial within the UN and in many member countries.[104] To imply that these *Reports* represented the UN's understanding of development and that its essence had not changed since the early 1960s is inaccurate.[105]

100 Rist, *History of Development*, 2, 4–6.
101 Rist, *History of Development*, 4.
102 Richard Ponzio, "The Advent of the Human Development Report," in *Pioneering the Human Development Revolution: An Intellectual Biography of Mahbub ul Haq*, ed. Khadija Haq and Richard Ponzio (New Delhi: Oxford University Press, 2008), 88–111, 88–89.
103 Oscar Arias Sánchez, "The Legacy of Human Development: A Tribute to Mahbub ul Haq," *Journal of Human Development* 1, no. 1 (2000): 9–16, 10; Amartya Sen, "A Decade of Human Development," *Journal of Human Development* 1, no. 1 (2000): 7–23, 17.
104 Ponzio, "Advent," 104–106.
105 Rist, *History of Development*, 90–91.

The concept of human development also did not appear suddenly in 1990, but rather emerged from work spanning many years. Haq played an important role, but did not invent human development. He did, though, play a notable role in re-thinking development in various UN agencies. In the early 1970s Haq was senior advisor to Robert McNamara, who had been appointed President of the World Bank in 1968. McNamara's speech at the Bank's 1973 annual meeting is arguably a significant one for development history, if the criteria for a speech's impact are conceptual change plus new resource flows that followed from it.[106]

In September 1973 the World Bank's and International Monetary Fund's governors convened in Nairobi, their first meeting outside Washington, DC. There McNamara announced that poverty reduction would become an explicit goal of the World Bank. This was a noteworthy change, one that Martha Finnemore argued soon spread throughout the international development establishment.[107] McNamara also articulated changes in the conceptualization of poverty: it was a characteristic of people, not nations. Further, it was a destabilizing force and an indicator of political failure, not an inevitable or even necessary side effect of economic growth.[108] McNamara also advocated a focus on "absolute poverty," a poverty so extreme that "it degrades the lives of individuals below the minimal norms of human decency."[109] Absolute poverty afflicted about 40 % of the people in developing countries. Some could be found in slums, but the vast majority lived in rural areas. "And it is there—in the countryside—that we must confront

106 Several *Development Dictionary* authors noted this speech but saw it as the start of rural-targeted development and the basic needs approach, which did not change the essence of development. See Ivan Illich, "Needs," in *The Development Dictionary: A Guide to Knowledge as Power*, ed. Wolfgang Sachs (London: Zed Books, 2019), Kobo e-book, 22–23/57; Arturo Escobar, "Planning," in *The Development Dictionary: A Guide to Knowledge as Power*, ed. Wolfgang Sachs (London: Zed Books, 2019), Kobo e-book, 26–28/58. For a history of the basic needs approach available to these authors see Douglas Rimmer, "'Basic Needs' and the Origins of the Development Ethos," *Journal of Developing Areas* 15, no. 2 (1981): 215–238.
107 Martha Finnemore, "Redefining Development at the World Bank," in *International Development and the Social Sciences*, ed. Frederick Cooper and Randall Packard, 203–227, 203–204. The argument that by the end of the 1960s there was a recognizable development establishment in Western countries is made *inter alia* by Cranford Pratt, "From Pearson to Brandt: Evolving Perceptions Concerning International Development," *International Journal* 35, no. 4 (1980): 623–645.
108 Finnemore, "Redefining Development," 208–211.
109 Robert S. McNamara, "Address to the Board of Governors by Robert S. McNamara," September 24, 1973, Presidential Speech Washington, D.C., World Bank Group, accessed May 25, 2022, https://documents.worldbank.org/en/publication/documents-reports/documentdetail/930801468315304694/address-to-the-board-of-governors-by-robert-s-mcnamara.

their poverty," McNamara urged.[110] Eradicating absolute poverty by the end of the twentieth century would require developing country governments to reverse growing inequality within their nations and invest in agriculture, health, and education, an approach later elaborated in the World Bank's *Redistribution With Growth* (1979).

McNamara gave voice and impetus to emerging development ideas in his Nairobi speech, he did not invent them.[111] Increased use of the term absolute poverty started in the late 1960s, and the explosive growth in its use in the early 1970s was associated with rather than initiated by McNamara's speech.[112] McNamara oversaw a substantial increase in World Bank lending, much of which went to countries in Africa, Asia, and Latin America. The share of Bank lending allocated to agriculture and social development also more than doubled.[113] The initiative McNamara and the Bank took on agriculture was particularly significant at a time when fears of a global food crisis were intensifying.[114]

McNamara's speech dropped out of the public eye quickly, as the Yom Kippur War broke out only weeks later, and it was accompanied by Organization of the Petroleum Exporting Countries production cuts to enforce their demand for higher prices plus an embargo by some members against Israel's allies.[115] Real international oil prices quickly doubled, which dramatically changed the global context for development. Although eclipsed in a way that Truman's inauguration address was not, McNamara's Nairobi speech was the point at which "the momentum behind the anti-poverty program snowballed."[116] As Finnemore argued, prior to McNamara's World Bank presidency

> most states and even most development experts did not understand poverty alleviation to be central to the development effort. By 1975, poverty had been moved to center stage. The World Bank was not solely responsible for this change. It did not invent the poverty concern nor was it the only actor promoting a poverty orientation. What the Bank did was to pick up

---

110 McNamara, "Address to the Board of Governors."

111 Devesh Kapur, John Lewis, and Richard Webb, *The World Bank: Its First Half Century,* vol. 1 (Washington, D.C.: Brookings Institution Press, 1997), 16, 18.

112 Google Books Ngram Viewer, s.v. "Absolute Poverty."

113 While lending to the southern continents remained at 87% of the Bank's total lending, the growth in lending doubled resource flows to these regions. Kapur, Lewis, and Webb also establish that the Bank's attention to agriculture did not begin under McNamara; Kapur, Lewis and Webb, *World Bank*, vol. 1, 6, 382–391.

114 For example, Lowell Hardin, "Meetings That Changed the World: Bellagio, 1969: The Green Revolution," *Nature* 455, no. 25 (2008): 470–471, 470. Kapur, Lewis, and Webb, *World Bank*, vol 1, 379.

115 Kapur, Lewis and Webb, *World Bank*, vol. 1, 18.

116 Finnemore, "Redefining Development," 217.

> this new approach to development and institutionalize the poverty focus so that it became a necessary part of development efforts by both states and international development agencies.[117]

Identifying McNamara's 1973 speech as an important one for development history would support the emphasis put on American agency by Post-Developmentalists, since McNamara was US Secretary of Defense prior to his appointment at the World Bank. However, discussing the role Haq played in the Bank's institutional interest in poverty gives the history a different slant, as would looking at the speech that brought him to the World Bank.[118]

In April 1968 Mahbub ul Haq was the youthful chief economist of Pakistan's National Planning Commission. While the country was celebrating a decade of rapid economic growth that Haq helped to engineer, he made a speech at the University of Karachi.[119] In it he pointed out that the benefits of that growth were being appropriated by a few. Twenty-two families "controlled about two-thirds of industrial assets, 80 per cent of banking, and 79 per cent [of] insurance."[120]

> Meanwhile, [...] the real wages of the industrial workers had dropped by a third in less than a decade, the percentage of illiterates was steadily increasing, fifteen times as much had been spent on importing private cars as public buses, and 80 – 90 per cent of private construction work was going into "what can only be called luxury housing".[121]

What worried Haq most, though, was the way the 22 families colluded to control the country's economic decision-making, preventing structural change.[122] Coming from a senior public official, the speech was "a bombshell."[123] Haq left Paki-

117 Finnemore, "Redefining Development," 219.
118 Khadija Haq and Richard Ponzio, "Introduction," in *Pioneering the Human Development Revolution: An Intellectual Biography of Mahbub ul Haq*, ed. Khadija Haq and Richard Ponzio (New Delhi: Oxford University Press, 2008), 1 – 17, 4.
119 M. S. Jillani and Masooda Bano, "From 'Growth' to 'Growth with a Social Conscience': Haq as an Economic Planner in Pakistan," in *Pioneering the Human Development Revolution*, ed. Khadija Haq and Richard, 18 – 40, 23. Some say Haq's speech was given in May 1968.
120 Mahbub ul Haq, "Pakistan's 22 Families," in *Economic Growth with Social Justice: Collected Writings of Mahbub ul Haq*, ed. Khadija Haq (New Delhi: Oxford University Press, 2017), Kobo e-book, 1/10.
121 Mahbub ul Haq as quoted in "Changing the Structure," *New Internationalist*, January 2, 1980, accessed May 18, 2022, https://newint.org/features/1980/01/01.
122 Haq, "Pakistan's 22 Families," Kobo e-book, 5 – 6/10.
123 Haq, "Pakistan's 22 Families," Kobo e-book, 4/10. Unrest caused by the popular perception that Pakistan's growth was "a fraud that a handful of vested interests were perpetrating on so-

stan for the World Bank some months later.[124] Challenges like Haq's speech helped drive a new interest in poverty in the late 1960s, and were rootstock for human development in the early 1990s; they also prepared the ground for contemporaneous Post-Development critiques.

It is worth noting that some Cold War-focused histories of development echo another part of Post-Development's historical outline when they argue the UN's development ideas came from the US David Ekbladh, for example, argued the Tennessee Valley Authority (TVA) was the inspiration for America's modernizing development. Then, "when the UN discussed how modernization might [...] be achieved, the TVA and the liberal development it stood for led the conversation."[125] He highlighted a 1948 UN conference on development where the US presented the TVA to delegates from other countries. Nick Cullather said the "postwar order began with food." The Roosevelt administration's 1943 assembly of 77 national delegations "to institute the first component of a new UN system, the FAO" inaugurated that order.[126] Cullather also suggested the UN's concept of community development was American-inspired, linked to a 1952 rural development program in India in which the Ford Foundation and the Point Four Program were both involved.[127] However, Nicole Sackley, looking at this program's pilot in Uttar Pradesh, argued that an "American-centric story" did not do justice to this complex initiative.[128] Larry Grubb's study of the Americans who helped draft Nigeria's 1962–1968 development plan also provided a more nuanced view of the role of American technical assistance.[129] More recently, Sara Lorenzini's *Global Development* adds Soviet views and initiatives, as well as those of European countries to the Cold War history of development. Lorenzini also makes some space for the leaders and governments of aid receiving countries in her account of development initiatives and UN development debates.[130]

There is no doubt that development became a central issue in the UN system. The question of how and when that happened is one where a choice of speeches—and of events more broadly—yields different possible histories. The

ciety" contributed to the fall of General Ayub Khan's government in 1969; Shahid Javed Burki, "Ayub's Fall: A Socio-Economic Explanation," *Asian Survey* 12, no. 3 (1972): 201–212, 202.

124 Jillani and Bano, "From 'Growth'," 24.

125 Ekbladh, *Great American Mission*, 91.

126 Cullather, *Hungry World*, 34.

127 Cullather, *Hungry World*, 77.

128 Nicole Sackley, "Village Models: Etawah, India, and the Making and Remaking of Development in the Early Cold War," *Diplomatic History* 37, no. 4 (2013): 749–778, 749.

129 Larry Grubb, "Bringing 'the Gospel of Modernization' to Nigeria: American Nation Builders and Development Planning in the 1960s," *Peace and Change* 31, no. 3 (2006): 279–308.

130 Sara Lorenzini, *Global Development*.

International Labour Organization, which the UN inherited from the League of Nations, was a forum for debates about development in the 1940s. In a footnote, Rist acknowledged that an "ILO functionary" used underdeveloped in the Trumanesque sense in 1942, but Rist did not consider this to be history-changing speech because this booklet did not reach a wide audience.[131] Daniel Maul, though, argues that the ILO publicly committed itself to development in its 1944 Declaration of Philadelphia.[132] He also noted that within the ILO it was Latin American and Asian member countries who put "increasing pressure on the ILO" to implement the Declaration and provide practical assistance to nations that wanted "economic and social progress."[133]

This point—that the concept of development and the perceived need for it was not created by the US and transferred to the UN—is made strongly in publications of the UN Intellectual History Project.[134] Books and articles by UN development staff reiterate the same point. Nassau Adams and Digambar Bhouraskar, economists from Jamaica and India respectively, emphasized the role of governments and individuals from Latin America, Asia, Africa, and the Middle East in their histories of development at the UN.[135]

Bhouraskar, for example, described how during the UN General Assembly's first session in 1946 the Lebanese delegation requested that the UN create advisory boards to provide expert advice on economic, social, and cultural development.[136] In making the case for this technical assistance, Lebanon's representative Charles Habib Malik classified countries into four groups: "highly developed countries," "Non-Self-Governing Territories, and the Trusteeship Territories," and between them states that "enjoyed full sovereignty" but "did not have sufficient technical and economic means for development without outside help."[137] While

---

131 Rist, *History of Development*, 72, fn. 5.

132 Daniel Maul, "'Helping Them Move the ILO Way': The International Labor Organization and the Modernization Discourse in the Era of Decolonization and the Cold War," *Diplomatic History* 33, no. 3 (2009): 387–404, 389.

133 Maul, "Helping Them Move," 390.

134 For example, Richard Jolly et al., *UN Contributions to Development Thinking and Practice* (Bloomington: Indiana University Press, 2004).

135 Nassau Adams, *Worlds Apart: The North-South Divide and the International System* (London: Zed Books, 1993); Digambar Bhouraskar, *United Nations Development Aid: A Study in History and Politics* (New Delhi: Academic Foundation, 2007).

136 Bhouraskar, *United Nations Development Aid*, 24–25.

137 UN General Assembly, Joint Second and Third Committee, Tenth Meeting, December 6, 1946, Item 19, A/C.2&3/38, in *Joint Committee of the Second and Third Committees Summary Record of Meetings, 18 November-10 December 1946* (Lake Success: United Nations, 1946), 70. I am indebted to the staff of the Dag Hammarskjöld Library for a scanned copy of this document.

countries in the first group had developmental responsibilities for the territories under their imperial control or trusteeship administration, countries in the last group were in a difficult situation. They needed external assistance but would have to "resort to bilateral agreements" to get it. This threatened their "economic independence" and put them at risk of conflict as aid-providing developed states competed for influence over them. Disinterested technical assistance from the UN would remedy these problems, Malik said.[138] His remarks, made several years before Truman's, contained a division of the world's countries based on their development status, a clear concept of development as intentional change, and a role for international technical assistance in bringing about that change. The diplomats who responded to Malik took issue with some of them but did not react with surprise to the conceptual scheme he put forward, demonstrating that December 6, 1946 was also not the birthday of development.

Histories that include Malik's speech also include another voice that Rist omits, that of W. Arthur Lewis.[139] A St. Lucian economist, Lewis was an advisor to the British government on colonial development policy in the 1940s and the lead author of a 1951 report that many referred to as the UN's primer on development.[140] The story of this report is another illustration of the key role that Latin American, Asian, and African representatives played in putting development on the UN's agenda. In the UN's Economic and Social Council (ECOSOC) and the General Assembly these representatives insisted that prosperity and peace—the industrialized countries' goals—could not be achieved unless the growing gap between developed and underdeveloped countries was addressed.[141] When the experts who wrote a 1949 ECOSOC report on employment only discussed industrialized countries, the UN Secretary General was pushed to appoint another expert group to study the problems of developing ones. The make-up of this group —only one of its five experts came from an industrialized country—was noteworthy.[142] Although the group's formal mandate was employment, informally its members were told to focus on the question Latin American, Asian and African

---

138 All quotes from Joint Second and Third Committee, December 6, 1946, Item 19, in *Summary Record of Meetings*, 71.

139 For example, Olav Stokke, *The UN and Development: From Aid to Cooperation* (Bloomington: Indiana University Press, 2009); Craig Murphy, *The United Nations Development Programme: A Better Way?* (Cambridge: Cambridge University Press, 2006).

140 See Robert Tignor, *W. Arthur Lewis and the Birth of Development Economics* (Princeton: Princeton University Press, 2006).

141 Bhouraskar, *United Nations Development Aid*, 28.

142 John Toye and Richard Toye, "Arthur Lewis and the United Nations." Paper presented at conference *The Lewis Model After Fifty Years*, Manchester University, July 2004, 4–5, accessed May 18, 2022, https://johntoyedotnet.files.wordpress.com/2012/02/arthur-lewis2004.pdf.

delegates were continually posing in UN debates: "what measures are required if development is to be speeded up in underdeveloped countries?"[143] The resulting report, *Measures for the Economic Development of Underdeveloped Countries* (1951), would be a far better text to analyze for emerging concepts of development at the UN than speeches by American presidents.

The omission or minimization of voices like those of Malik, Lewis, and Haq is the symptom of an underlying problem in Post-Development's historical outline: the need to demonstrate that development is Western, that it is monolithic, and that it is unchanging in essence.[144] Post-Developmentalists were not interested in debates about developmentalism in non-Western empires, for example.[145] While some admitted that modernity and the West were neither monolithic nor synonymous, they did not re-visit this working assumption.[146] Histories that focus on the role of American (or European) ideas, actors, and resources in global modernization also present development as Western and homogenous, even if their authors say development was an encounter or an interchange rather than an activity with a unidirectional flow of ideas and causality.[147] If the American or European side of developmental interactions is far better documented and analyzed, readers are left with the impression that Asian participants were objects rather than agents.[148] Since Asia was a Cold War focal point, development histories of the region are essential, but development occurred elsewhere too. The history of development, especially the relationship between imperialism and devel-

---

143 W. Arthur Lewis, "United Nations Primer for Development: Comment," *Quarterly Journal of Economics* 67, no. 2 (1953): 267–275, 267.

144 See Stuart Corbridge, "'Beneath the Pavement Only Soil': The Poverty of Post-Development," *The Journal of Development Studies* 34, no. 6 (1998): 138–148, 144–146; Aram Ziai, "Post-Development 25 Years After 'The Development Dictionary'," *Third World Quarterly* 38, no. 12 (2017): 2547–2558, 2549.

145 For a comparative overview of developmentalism and empire, see Kenneth Pomeranz, "Empire & 'Civilizing Missions', Past & Present," *Daedalus* 134, no. 2 (2005): 34–45.

146 Escobar, for example, acknowledged "non-dominant, peripheral and alternative forms of modernity": Gustavo Esteva and Arturo Escobar, "Post-Development@25: On 'Being Stuck' and Moving Forward, Sideways, Backward and Otherwise," *Third World Quarterly* 38, no. 12 (2017): 2559–2572, 2568.

147 For example, Cullather, *Hungry World*, 6–7; Ekbladh, *Great American Mission*, 6.

148 Compare, for example, Ekbladh, *Great American Mission*, 114–152; Greg Andrew Brazinsky, "Koreanizing Modernization: Modernization Theory and South Korean Intellectuals," in *Staging Growth: Modernization, Development, and the Global Cold War*, ed. David Engerman et al. (Amherst: University of Massachusetts Press, 2003), 251–273.

opment, was different in African countries, for instance.[149] Abiola Irele has argued that discussions of modernity in Africa also had a distinctive character.[150] Others African scholars suggest a different interpretation of post-war development history. Thandika Mkandawire for instance, argued that the African and Asian leaders who met at Bandung in 1955 initiated an emancipatory post-war project of development that differed from the Trumanesque one, and called out Post-Developmentalists for ignoring it.[151]

Conclusion

Speaking of invention draws attention to agency, implying that an identifiable actor (or actors) created something new. With development as an invention, it is natural, even necessary, to identify an inventor, someone like Harry Truman. As Ekbladh observed, it is also satisfying to be able to name a "simple and easily definable takeoff point" for an important historical phenomenon—hence January 20, 1949.[152] The ideological reasons for Post-Development thinkers to assign agency to the United States or "the West" are understandable, if debatable. Their continuing insistence on Truman's speech as the moment of development's invention, after almost 30 years of research on development history, is not.

An interest in how development is spoken about has been an early and continuing feature of development history, and for that speeches are a potential tool. However, a more careful analysis of those speeches than has so far been provided by Post-Developmentalists is necessary. Rist drew attention to the performative aspect of discourse, which is an immediately evident characteristic of a speech, but did not integrate this into discourse analysis. Attention to a speech's context and reception are equally important, as are the speaker's intentions, all things which the Post-Development outline of history did not provide. The implementation of ideas in a speech and the resources committed to that implementation are also crucial. They point to the way that speeches and texts are yoked

149 For example, Emmanuel Akyeampong et al., eds., *Africa's Development in Historical Perspective* (New York: Cambridge University Press, 2014); Bahru Zewde, *Pioneers of Change in Ethiopia: The Reformist Intellectuals of the Early Twentieth Century* (Oxford: James Currey, 2002).
150 Abiola Irele, "Dimensions of African Discourse," *College Literature* 19–20, no. 3 (1992–1993): 45–59, 46, 52.
151 Thandika Mkandawire, "Running While Others Walk: Knowledge and the Challenge of Africa's Development," *Africa Development* 36, no. 2 (2011): 1–36, 7.
152 Ekbladh, *Great American Mission*, 3.

together with heterogenous elements, both physical and social, to give effect to discourse.[153]

Historians of development should also look at different types of speeches, not just ones delivered on special occasions. Workaday speeches by Clare Short, Eveline Herfkens, Hilde Johnson, and Heidemarie Wieczorek-Zeul played an important role in reviving and reforming development aid in the late 1990s, for example.[154] It is also essential to look at a wider range of speakers, not least because this choice implies assumptions about agency in history and positions vis-à-vis development theory. As this paper itself illustrates, it is not easy to move beyond the speeches most easily accessible to historians—those made by powerful men and those made in European languages.

153 See, for example, Giorgio Agamben, "What Is an Apparatus?" in *What Is an Apparatus? and Other Essays*, ed. Werner Hamacher (Stanford: Stanford University Press, 2009), 1–24. Actor-Network Theory, though not without its flaws, uses this approach but has not been much used to study development; see Richard Heeks, "Development Studies Research and Actor-Network Theory" (Working Paper 1, February 18, 2013), accessed May 18, 2022, https://papers.ssrn.com/sol3/papers.cfm?abstract_id=3540083.

154 These four women were cabinet ministers with responsibility for international development in the U.K., the Netherlands, Norway, and Germany respectively. Their work is described in Constantine Michalopoulos, *Ending Global Poverty: Four Women's Noble Conspiracy* (Oxford: Oxford University Press, 2020).

II Measuring Development
(ed. Corinna R. Unger and Jack Loveridge)

Stephen Macekura

The Historiography of Measuring Development

"Statistics must always have a purpose," wrote the Indian planner Prasanta Chandra Mahalanobis in 1965. For the man whose economic models informed India's second Five Year Plan, the purpose was clear. Statistics were the "essential information required to prepare the plans of economic development." They also served tools for "assessing the progress" of those plans, and experts could adjust their strategies based on new data that they collected. In other words, statistics were constitutive of the entire project of India's development, just as they were for all other countries. Because of the centrality of measurement to global development aspirations, Mahalanobis foresaw an "increasing demand for statistics" long into the future to "bring in the new age of peace, prosperity, and progress of the world."[1] Mahalanobis' claims about the power of statistics contain valuable insights for the historian of international development. To study the measurement of development is to study development itself. After all, how can one understand development if it is not measured, quantified, and assessed?

Across the twentieth century world, experts debated how development should be measured. The dominant metrics were those associated with national income accounting, such as Gross National Product (GNP) and later Gross Domestic Product (GDP).[2] This was true for national economic policy and international development. For much of the twentieth century, national leaders and many experts equated economic growth measured by GNP as evidence of development. The German-British economist Hans Singer noted that a belief in the power of GNP growth as an economic cure-all "enabled economists to transfer familiar concepts and familiar modes of thinking to the relatively new but rapidly emerging problems of the Third World," assuming a "trickle-down" effect would be a solvent for political and social strife.[3] Yet there were many thinkers

1 P. C. Mahalanobis, "Statistics for Economic Development," *Sankhyā: The Indian Journal of Statistics Series B (1960–2002)* 27, no. 1–2 (1965): 179–188, 181, 185.

2 GDP is the value of the production within a country, and GNP is that value plus net property income from abroad. From the 1930s through the early 1990s, most countries used GNP. Since the 1990s, GDP has become far more common.

3 H.W. Singer, "Poverty, Income Distribution, and Levels of Living: Thirty Years of Changing Thoughts on Development Problems," in *Reflection on Economic Development and Social Change: Essays in Honour of Professor V.K.R.V. Rao*, ed. C. H. Hanumantha Rao and P.C. Joshi (New Delhi: Allied Publishers Private Ltd., 1979), 29–40, 31.

https://doi.org/10.1515/9783110730234-007

and activists who envisioned alternative ways of quantifying economic development. From heterodox scholars who attempted to create alternative metrics for developmental success – some of which still have some valence today, such as Mahbub ul Haq's Human Development Index – to those that questioned the use of statistics at all, the measurement of development has long been a subject of political contestation.

In recent years, economic measurement has become a subject of historical inquiry. This innovative research follows from the theoretical and empirical work undertaken by political theorists, anthropologists, and historians to historicize the notion of "the national economy" as a social space and the related concept of quantitative "economic growth." This field of research stemmed in part from Timothy Mitchell and Adam Tooze's generative work that placed the rise of the economic growth paradigm in the 1930s and 1940s as a core element of the twentieth century. In countries as different as the United States, United Kingdom, Sudan, and Japan, policymakers embraced economic growth measured by GNP as central to national purpose.[4] The Cold War between the United States and Soviet Union reinforced the centrality of aggregate economic metrics as proxies for developmental success. Both countries defined their goals for foreign aid and measured the viability of national economic strategies in aggregate

4 See, for instance, Timothy Mitchell, *Rule of Experts: Egypt, Techno-Politics, Modernity* (Berkeley: University of California Press, 2002); Timothy Mitchell, "Economists and the Economy in the Twentieth Century," in *The Politics of Method in the Human Sciences: Positivism and Its Epistemological Others*, ed. George Steinmetz (Durham: Duke University Press, 2005), 126–141; Timothy Mitchell, "Economentality: How the Future Entered Government," *Critical Inquiry* 40 (Summer 2014): 479–507; J. Adam Tooze, "Imagining National Economies: National and International Economic Statistics, 1900–1950," in *Imagining Nations*, ed. Geoffrey Cubitt (Manchester: Manchester University Press, 1998), 212–228; Adam Tooze, *Statistics and the German State, 1900–1945: The Making of Modern Economic Knowledge* (Cambridge: Cambridge University Press, 2001). On the United States, see Robert M. Collins, *More: The Politics of Economic Growth in Postwar America* (Oxford University Press, 2000); Andrew L. Yarrow, *Measuring America: How Economic Growth Came to Define American Greatness in the Late Twentieth Century* (Amherst: University of Massachusetts Press, 2010); Timothy Shenk, "Inventing the American Economy" (PhD diss., Columbia University, 2016); Daniel Hirschman, "Inventing the Economy, Or: How We Learned to Stop Worrying and Love the GDP" (PhD diss., University of Michigan, 2016); on the United Kingdom, see Benjamin Mitra-Kahn, "Redefining the Economy: How the 'Economy' Was Invented in 1620, and has Been Redefined Ever Since" (PhD diss., City University London, 2011); on Japan, see Scott O'Bryan, *The Growth Idea: Purpose and Prosperity in Postwar Japan* (Honolulu: University of Hawaii Press, 2009); on Sudan, see Alden Young, *Transforming Sudan: Decolonization, Economic Development, and State Formation* (New York: Cambridge University Press, 2018).

growth rates.[5] Economic growth was a shared language, an object of governance, and a political expectation that transcended the ideological and temporal divisions that too often frame our narratives of the previous century.[6] For these reasons, historians have described the embrace of GNP growth as a significant "ideology," "imperative," and "paradigm."[7] Altogether, these scholars argued that to understand twentieth century global history, one had to comprehend the origins and evolution of how experts and leaders measured development.

Scholars have also studied the politics of numbers. There has long been a focus on how political elites used statistics to make claims about how to use the resources of the state and justify various policy choices.[8] Furthermore, scholars have now analyzed in great detail how economists became especially important figures in this process. Economists supplied influential frameworks and concepts that leaders and lay citizens alike used to make sense of the world. Economic statisticians worked in government to identify standards and practices for collecting data, creating models of national economic activity, and comparing national economies across time and space. As a result of their efforts, economic

5 Nick Cullather, "The Third Race," *Diplomatic History* 33, no. 3 (2009): 507–512.
6 Historian John McNeill, for instance, claims that economic growth was "easily the most important idea of the twentieth century." J. R. McNeill, *Something New Under the Sun: An Environmental History of the Twentieth-Century World* (New York: W.W. Norton & Company, 2000), 336.
7 On growth as ideology, imperative, and paradigm, see Charles S. Maier, "The World Economy and the Cold War in the Middle of the Twentieth Century," in *The Cambridge History of the Cold War*, vol. 1, ed. Melvyn P. Leffler and Odd Arne Westad (Cambridge: Cambridge University Press, 2010), 44–66, 48; Charles S. Maier, "The Politics of Productivity: Foundations of American International Economic Policy after World War II," *International Organization* 31, no. 4 (1977): 607–633; Alan S. Milward, *The European Rescue of the Nation-State* (London: Routledge, 2000), 51–52; Bentley B. Allan, *Scientific Cosmology and International Orders* (New York: Cambridge University Press, 2018).
8 On statistics, aggregation, and accounting in public life, see, for instance, Alfred W. Crosby, *The Measure of Reality: Quantification and Western Society, 1250–1600* (Cambridge: Cambridge University Press, 1997); Sarah E. Igo, *The Averaged American: Surveys, Citizens, and the Making of a Mass Public* (Cambridge, Mass.: Harvard University Press, 2007); Theodore M. Porter, *The Rise of Statistical Thinking, 1820–1920* (Princeton: Princeton University Press, 1986); Thomas A. Stapleford, *The Cost of Living in America: A Political History of Economic Statistics, 1880–2000* (Cambridge: Cambridge University Press, 2009); Michael A. Bernstein, "Numerable Knowledge and its Discontents," *Reviews in American History* 18, no. 2 (1990): 151–164; Caitlin C. Rosenthal, "From Memory to Mastery: Accounting for Control in America: 1750–1880," *Enterprise & Society* 14, no. 4 (2013): 732–748; Jacob Soll, *The Reckoning: Financial Accountability and the Rise and Fall of Nations* (New York: Basic Books, 2014); Judith G. Kelley and Beth A. Simmons, "Politics by Number: Indicators as Social Pressure in International Relations," *American Journal of Political Science* 59, no. 1 (2015): 55–70; Marion Fourcade, "Cents and Sensibility: Economic Valuation and the Nature of 'Nature,'" *American Journal of Sociology* 116, no. 6 (2011): 1721–1777.

statistics such as GNP assumed a privileged role in public life through their use in national planning and through the ways in which they defined popular expectations of what governments can and should do.[9]

In addition to providing historical perspective on economic growth and statistics in policy-making, historians have also analyzed how international development emerged throughout the late nineteenth and twentieth centuries as a fundamental aspect of global politics. Over the last couple of decades, historians have uncovered the intellectual and policy origins of development thought and practice, the material and ecological consequences of international development, and the ways in which development shaped major aspects of international life, from the end of colonialism to the global Cold War through the global War on Terror. This research has placed international development in its rightful role in the international history of the twentieth century world, and not just as another feature of US hegemony and foreign policy priorities. Indeed, some of the most important recent research has de-centered the United States and highlighted the role of non-state actors, social movements, and non-Western intellectuals and activists in shaping the trajectory of development.[10]

In this essay, I analyze this historiography by explicitly exploring the linkages and insights to be found by connecting the new histories' economic growth, statistics, and international development. In particular, I focus on three major themes in the historiography of measuring development. First, I argue that scholars have placed the origins and diffusion of aggregate economic indicators (chiefly Gross National Product, or GNP) as a central theme in the history of in-

9 On the importance of economic statistics to modern policymaking, see Daniel Speich Chassé, "The Use of Global Abstractions: National Income Accounting in the Period of Imperial Decline," *Journal of Global History* 6, no. 1 (2011): 7–28. On economists in governance, see Michael A. Bernstein, *A Perilous Progress: Economists and Public Purpose in Twentieth-Century America* (Princeton: Princeton University Press, 2001); John Markoff and Veronica Montecinos, "The Ubiquitous Rise of Economists," *Journal of Public Policy* 13, no. 1 (1993): 37–68; Marion Fourcade, *Economists and Societies: Discipline and Profession in the United States, Britain, and France, 1890s to 1990s* (Princeton: Princeton University Press, 2009); Stephanie L. Mudge, *Leftism Reinvented: Western Parties from Socialism to Neoliberalism* (Cambridge, Mass.: Harvard University Press, 2018).

10 The literature on international development in the twentieth century is rapidly growing. For recent reviews of this literature, see Stephen J. Macekura and Erez Manela (New York: Cambridge University Press, 2018), "Introduction," in *The Development Century: A Global History*, ed. Stephen J. Macekura and Erez Manela, 1–20; Joseph Morgan Hodge, "Writing the History of Development (Part 1: The First Wave)," *Humanity: An International Journal of Human Rights, Humanitarianism, and Development* 6, no. 3 (2015): 429–463; Joseph Morgan Hodge, "Writing the History of Development (Part 2: Longer, Deeper, Wider)," *Humanity: An International Journal of Human Rights, Humanitarianism, and Development* 7, no. 1 (2016): 125–174.

ternational development. Second, I show how historians of development have used the history of GNP as a lens through which to analyze how development captured important themes of the twentieth century writ large, such as the economic dimensions of territoriality and the meaning and limits of nationhood. Finally, I illuminate how some historians have begun to investigate the history of criticisms of dominant forms of measurement and the flaws in so many historical statistics used in narratives about economic development. I rely on studies of economic measurement that have focused on Western European countries, the United States, and Japan, as well as the growing literature on international development experts and measurement in the Global South. For studies of the socialist world, see the essay by Artemy Kalinovsky in this volume.

The recent scholarship on measuring development has made fruitful connections between the history of economic thought, state formation, and nation-building. Prior to the twentieth century, of course, there had long been attempts by individuals to assess the quantity of national and imperial wealth. What changed during the twentieth century was the extent to which the national economy, defined as a measurable entity that most every capitalist country calculated in similar way, became the shared object of development for national governments and international organizations. The revolutions in national income accounting during the Great Depression and World War Two tied the statistical representation of the economy to the geographical territory of the nation-state. The global spread of national statistical agencies and the standardization of national income accounting reinforced the nationalization of economic statistics and the quantification of economic life.[11]

The widespread use of GNP furnished a way of discussing national economic production and broader discussions of national well-being, too. Economists and statisticians used economic aggregates in historical narratives of national success and failure. In turn, political elites deployed these stories to describe overall national vitality. In popular discourse and policy circles, it was common to claim that countries that experienced high GNP growth had made the right economic choices and held a bright future, whereas those that faced low growth had chosen poorly and faced dimmer prospects. Measuring development became intertwined with international comparisons that depicted countries as monolithically rich or poor, growing or stagnating, or improving or declining.[12]

---

11 See Stephen J. Macekura, *The Mismeasure of Progress: Economic Growth and its Critics* (Chicago: University of Chicago Press, 2020), 13–20, 63–71.

12 Daniel Speich, "Travelling with the GDP through Early Development Economics' History," in *Working Papers on The Nature of Evidence: How Well Do Facts Travel?* 33 (2008), London School

Historians have done well to expose this way of thinking and criticize its implications. Yet more work is necessary on a couple of fronts. For one, we would benefit from further studies that focus less on the intellectual and political history of economic measurement and more on its social implications. In other words, we need more research to investigate how acts of measurement – by national elites, academic experts, local enumerators, and surveyors – shaped the daily experience of people around the world, the extent to which individuals incorporated numerical ways of depicting national life into their own self-perceptions, and how calculative practices reshaped both lives and landscapes in fundamentally material ways. Second, while historians have begun to examine the long history of criticisms of dominant forms of measurement, there is a need for additional inquiries in this vein. What alternative metrics did activists and reformers put forth to challenge GNP? To what extent did they fail? How have recent trends in subnational metrics – especially those created by social scientists for studying subnational developmental outcomes – challenged or reinforced popular measurement practices? More work on the history of alternative approaches would be valuable, to expand on the important foundational work historians have done to uncover the origins and evolution of the most common forms of economic measurement.

The History of Development as the History of GNP

Much of the historiography of measuring developed has focused on GNP. Historians have shown that the efforts to quantify the economic life of the colonial and post-colonial world derived from three interrelated crises. The first crisis was the global crisis of capitalism in the 1930s. The Great Depression exposed how little governments knew about the economic activity that took place in their borders, and it led many leaders to call upon new techniques of measurement to track, manage, and assess their recovery programs. Keynesian economics, which required aggregate economic statistics, took hold in Washington and London. Measuring national economies in terms of national income figures thus became common practice.[13]

---

of Economics, Department of Economic History, September 2008, http://eprints.lse.ac.uk/22501/1/3308Speich.pdf.

13 Shenk, "Inventing the American Economy." See also J. W. Kendrick, "The Historical Development of National-Income Accounts," *History of Political Economy* 2, no. 2 (1970): 284–315; C.S.

The second crisis was the looming crisis facing the British Empire (and indeed, all other empires). The Depression exposed not only the inequalities wrought by capitalism in the metropole, but the brutal and squalid conditions throughout the empire. Imperial authorities turned to aid for development – promising increasing prosperity and improved living conditions – to re-legitimize imperial rule and forestall the possibilities of widespread unrest and radical demands for political change. British economists and statisticians had been especially influential in national income estimates and viewed them as important tools to manage colonial affairs.[14]

The third crisis was one of expert knowledge, particularly economic knowledge. Economists stood poised to exploit both these crises and position themselves in the vanguard of knowledge production. The Depression exposed how little governments actually knew; the late colonial turn towards development revealed a stark dearth of information (let alone knowledge) about the national income of the colonies. Many important economists and statisticians who constructed and advocated for national income estimates, such as British economists Richard Stone and Austin Robinson, worked in research institutes and international organizations that put them in close contact with colonial officials.[15] As a result, there were acutely aware of the similar administrative and intellectual needs for greater information.

Carson, "The History of the United States National Income and Product Accounts: the Development of an Analytical Tool," *The Review of Income and Wealth* 21, no. 2 (1975): 153–181; Michael A. Bernstein, "Economic Knowledge, Professional Authority, and the State: The Case of American Economics During and After World War II," in *What Do Economists Know? New Economics of Knowledge*, ed. Robert F. Garnett, Jr. (London: Routledge, 1999), 103–123.

14 For recent scholarship on the history of international development within imperial governance, see Helen Tilley, *Africa as a Living Laboratory: Empire, Development, and the Problem of Scientific Knowledge* (Chicago: University of Chicago Press, 2011); Charlotte Lydia Riley, "Monstrous Predatory Vampires and Beneficent Fairy-Godmothers: British Post-War Colonial Development in Africa" (Ph.D. diss., University College London, 2013); Suzanne Moon, *Technology and Ethical Idealism: A History of Development in the Netherlands East Indies* (Leiden: CNWS Publications, 2007); Joseph Morgan Hodge, *Triumph of the Expert: Agrarian Doctrines of Development and the Legacies of British Colonialism* (Athens: Ohio University Press, 2007); Monica van Beusekom, *Negotiating Development: African Farmers and Colonial Experts at the Office du Niger, 1920–1960* (Oxford: Oxford University Press, 2002); Benjamin Zachariah, *Developing India: An Intellectual and Social History, c. 1930–50* (New Delhi: Oxford University Press, 2005). On British economists and colonial developmentalism, see Macekura, *The Mismeasure of Progress*, 44–47.

15 Macekura, *The Mismeasure of Progress*, 42–63. This research on colonial economic life later contributed to the field of development economics. On the history of development economics, see Michele Alacevich, "Theory and Practice in Development Economics," *History of Political Economy* 49 (2017): 266–291.

These three crises led Western development thinkers to embrace GNP as a tool in national economic governance and as a component in economic theory building. They did so just as GNP became a central component of national economic policy in the United States, Canada, Western Europe, and Japan. During the 1920s and 1930s, scholars incorporated advanced data collection methods and mathematical calculations to analyze putative economic phenomenon in what became known as econometrics. The growing interest in macroeconomic analysis during the Great Depression – inspired by the British economist John Maynard Keynes and his many acolytes – led many economists to incorporate econometric analysis into national policy. These experts produced detailed statistical depictions of national economic activity that policymakers could use to manage a country's affairs. During World War Two, economists and statisticians entered into government positions and used GNP estimates to guide wartime procurement policy and mobilization planning.[16]

Across Western Europe, the United States, and Japan, leaders and economists drew inspiration from the successful incorporation of these metrics into national budgeting and planning. Policymakers believed that in the post-war world countries needed to boost production, employment, and consumption – aggressively and continuously – to avoid recurrent recessions, minimize class conflict, and support the new national welfare systems. Thus after the war ended, across the capitalist world a "politics of productivity" took hold.[17] Leaders viewed the increase in national GNP as a precondition for economic prosperity and social harmony. GNP provided a common language for economic policymakers to describe the progress of their national economies. It also served as a yardstick leaders used to compare capitalist productivity against that of the Soviet Union in the global Cold War. In this context, international development experts adopted GNP as a way of articulating different levels of development in their international comparisons, which reinforced to policymakers the dangerous state of "underdevelopment" across the so-called "Third World" and helped to justify new foreign aid programs.[18]

While the popularity of GNP among policymakers in the West contributed to development experts' enthusiasm for the metric, there were other important incentives for the post-colonial world to adopt it, as well. The requirements set in place to join new international organizations reinforced the need for national in-

---

16 For an overview of econometrics, see Mary S. Morgan, *The History of Econometric Ideas* (Cambridge: Cambridge University Press, 1990); Francisco Louçã, *The Years of High Econometrics: A Short History of the Generation that Reinvented Economics* (New York: Routledge, 2007).
17 Maier, "The Politics of Productivity."
18 Macekura, *The Mismeasure of Progress*, 34–41, 63–71.

come figures. For example, the United Nations calculated member dues on the basis of national income and the World Bank used estimates of national income as the basis for determining loan repayment rates.[19] During the 1950s and 1960s, then, GNP went global as countries began to pursue GNP growth as their foremost economic goal.

Historians have also demonstrated how the promise of economic growth measured in GNP captivated the minds of leaders and policymakers throughout the Third World. All around the world, leaders spoke the language of growth and adopted GNP by the 1960s. In India, Prasanta Mahalanobis and Jawaharlal Nehru, the country's first post-independence prime minister, embraced GNP growth as the "means to build a modern nation," in David Engerman's words.[20] Daniel Speich Chassé tells a similar story of about post-colonial Kenya. There, Tom Mboya, the country's Minister of Justice and leading development voice, claimed that the goal of his country's economic planning was to "attain higher growth rates of our national income and, therefore, achieve higher living standards for all people."[21] Post-colonial leaders relied upon aggregate economic statistics to set targets and define the parameters of national policymaking.[22] As Alden Young reveals in his book on post-colonial Sudan, national economic planning based on economic metrics was central to post-colonial state building because planning enabled elite bargaining and bureaucratic consensus-building. The "project of governing Sudan," he writes, "was transformed from the management of a collection of distinct populations, each with its own attributes, to the management of a national economy made up of equal individuals, whose preferences policymakers assumed could be aggregated and even maximized."[23] Sudanese leaders "fetishized the 'economy'." Statistical abstractions such as GNP became a "means of representing a successful government." If Sudanese planners met the targets laid out in their plans, they could then earn public legitimacy to justify their continued rule.[24]

In practice, leaders often struggled to manage their economic life and reach the heights promised by the parade of statistics and developmental interventions

---

19 Macekura, *The Mismeasure of Progress*, 59–63.

20 David C. Engerman, "Bernath Lecture: American Knowledge and Global Power," *Diplomatic History* 31, no. 4 (2007): 599–622, 619.

21 Tom Mboya, "African Socialism and its Application to Planning in Kenya," May 4, 1965, in Brack Brown, *The Challenge of Nationhood: A Collection of Speeches and Writings by Tom Mboya* (New York: Praeger Publishers, 1970), 103.

22 Speich Chassé, "The Use of Global Abstractions," 26; Speich, "Travelling with the GDP."

23 Young, *Transforming Sudan*, 14.

24 Young, *Transforming Sudan*, 17.

that came to symbolize the future in the period of global decolonization. And local leaders rarely tried to fit universal models without considerable adaption. Mahalanobis, for instance, adopted Keynesian macroeconomic measures but not Keynesian policies, opting instead for a more concerted central planning approach modeled loosely on the Soviet Union. Moreover, scarcely did local social practices reflect the soaring rhetoric put forth by so many elites. But historians have shown GNP growth became central to national self-representation for nationalist leaders worldwide.[25] Statistical activities such as measuring national income and product "became central to articulating and elaborating decolonial ideas about economic uplift and fairness," as well.[26] As Speich Chassé notes, "In the imagination of the heroes of African independence such as Kwame Nkrumah in Ghana or Tom Mboya in Kenya, political sovereignty necessarily had to be followed by major schemes of statistically rendering the body politic in view of national development goals" and they needed "a stable comparative framework in order to legitimize their claims."[27] Economic statistics such as GNP created the framework that permitted easy international comparison and national expression of future goals, present problems, and past injustices.

The Cold War conflict further reinforced the primacy of GNP growth in the Third World countries and conditioned the way in which the superpowers interpreted and understood the politics of decolonization. The growing consensus among experts in the United States during the late 1940s was that radicalism and communism stemmed from poverty and an absence of economic growth. Economic measurements furnished US policymakers with the tools they used to analyze the Third World. US leaders held up GNP growth rates as indicators of success for their foreign aid programs.[28] Soviet officials likewise made rapid economic growth a promise for their allies, and they sent experts and aid abroad throughout the late 1950s and early 1960s to countries such as India, Egypt, and Ghana. During the Khrushchev era, the Soviet Union nurtured its own field of development economics, with Soviet scholars drawing often on the Soviet experience in Central Asia and emphasizing central planning, mechanization of agriculture, and industrialization (for some, though not all, countries). In all cases, as the historian Alessandro Iandolo shows, the "state was to be the only engine

25 Engerman, "Bernath Lecture," 619 620.
26 Poormina Paidipaty, "Testing Measures: Decolonization and Economic Power in 1960s India," *History of Political Economy* 52, no. 3 (2020): 473–497, 475.
27 Daniel Speich Chassé, "The Roots of the Millennium Development Goals: A Framework for Studying the History of Global Statistics," *Historical Social Research / Historische Sozialforschung* 41, no. 2 (2016): 218–237, 231.
28 Macekura, *The Mismeasure of Progress*, 67–71.

of growth" as the Soviet proposed their own models of national economic growth for the Third World.[29] By the early 1960s, Mao's China also jostled for support among fledgling communist parties throughout the Third World, often inciting conflicts with Soviet-backed communist and nationalist regimes, such as in India and Algeria.[30]

By the early 1960s, growth rhetoric had truly gone global. In late 1961, the UN General Assembly proclaimed the 1960s as the "United Nations Development Decade" (on President Kennedy's urging). To give the phrase meaning, the General Assembly encouraged all developing countries to set GNP growth rate targets of at least five % per year. This target-setting solidified GNP as the dominant discursive framework for conceptualizing national economic life at the international level, in organizations such as the Organization for Economic Cooperation and Development (OECD). In national governments and international organizations alike, economic measurement became part and parcel of international development.[31] Historians of growth and foreign aid have collectively revealed how important the measurement of development was to structuring how countries defined what developmental success actually meant. With GNP used to define independent nation-states' relative levels of development, Daniel Speich Chassé claims that "a new comparative statistical perception of the world became dominant."[32] In other words, GNP defined how leaders conceptualized developmental success.

Economic Measurement, Nationalism, and Developmental Politics

The global diffusion and adoption of GNP had many implications for developmental politics. One important consequence was that economic metrics shaped the nature of post-colonial state-building. Alden Young's study of Sudanese development demonstrates how national income accounting conditioned policymakers to view their economic life in terms of national, territorial boundaries.

29 Alessandro Iandolo, "The Rise and Fall of the 'Soviet Model of Development' in West Africa, 1957–1964," *Cold War History* 12, no. 4 (2012): 683–704, 692.
30 Odd Arne Westad, *The Cold War: A World History* (New York: Basic Books, 2017), 248–249.
31 Matthias Schmelzer, *The Hegemony of Growth: The Making and Remaking of the Economic Growth Paradigm and the OECD, 1948 to 2010* (Cambridge: Cambridge University Press, 2016), 227–238; "Economic Growth in the United States Since the Second World War," 1961. Box 4, Entry UD-UP 734-H, RG 56, National Archives and Records Administration, Maryland, USA, II.
32 Speich Chassé, "The Roots," 233.

But this focus came with unfortunate consequences for life within the country. Young argues that Sudanese plans chose to fund development projects most likely to contribute to GNP, which obscured important regional inequalities.[33] Barbara Weinstein has uncovered an analogous dynamic in mid-century Brazil. Weinstein claims that inter-regional inequalities deepened between urban and rural portions of the country and that broad generalizations about national economic growth obscured the policy choices that worsened spatial disparities. "Representations of São Paulo not just as producing more but as more modern and productive, and of the Nordeste as backward [...] had discernible material consequences that further concentrated resources and exacerbated the process of divergence," she argues.[34] Scholars have identified similar trends in how statistical practices influenced post-colonial state-building choices elsewhere, too, as Poornima Paidipaty has done for India.[35] These case studies show how national economic measurement and territorial state-building became mutually reinforcing, as leaders and policymakers conceived of the object of their development through the lens of the aggregate measurements they used to depict it.

The use of statistical targets influenced the course of post-colonial political legitimacy. For instance, when leaders staked their claims to legitimacy on the promise of economic transformation, insufficiently low growth rates could stand as symbols for the failure to deliver progress. As Brad Simpson argues in his study of Indonesia, Sukarno's revolutionary post-colonial government struggled and ultimately lost power as the country's high inflation and low production hampered the country's economy by the mid-1960s. Yet few leaders deviated from the standard script that placed economic growth measured in aggregate statistics as the cornerstone of national politics. In Indonesia, General Suharto's regime subsequently promised to improve the country's plight once again through a "commitment to modernization and the promise of stability and rapid economic growth."[36] Alden Young likewise notes that throughout the first decade of Sudanese independence a "failure to achieve economic growth," in the eyes of the first post-colonial leadership class, threatened to undermine their claims as the premier nationalist modernizers of the country and "jeopardize the independence of the nation."[37]

33 Young, *Transforming Sudan*, 3, 6, 126.
34 Barbara Weinstein, "Presidential Address: Developing Inequality," *American Historical Review* 113, no. 1 (2008): 1–18, 12.
35 Paidipaty, "Testing Measures."
36 Brad Simpson, "Indonesia's 'Accelerated Modernization' and the Global Discourse of Development," *Diplomatic History* 33, no. 3 (2009): 467–486, 477.
37 Young, *Transforming Sudan*, 94.

This regime of using calculative practices for political ends shaped other aspects of political developments. For instance, Michelle Murphy analyzes how "population" became an important object of government intervention alongside the national economy for post-colonial states. She narrates the relationship between the two – population and economy – as evidence of a broader "economization of life" during the mid-twentieth century. She presents a set of practices that "differentially value and govern life in terms of their ability to foster the macroeconomy of the nation-state," such as how life contributed (or detracted) from gross domestic product (GDP).[38] Whereas income and product accounts marked forms of aggregate economic activity abstracted from labor, "population" marked an aggregation of human lives that could be managed and modeled as a unitary whole. As a category, population conjured a "phantasmagram": population growth, like GDP, was a metric that was "enriched with affect, propagate imaginaries, lure feeling, and hence have supernatural effects in surplus of their rational precepts."[39] Measuring population and economic growth were intertwined. She exposes how American social scientists calculated the value of "averted birth" (humans not born as a result of family practices, calculated in terms of their potential effect on GDP) in countries such Taiwan and South Korea to persuade governments that population control measures would redound to their economic benefit (and all the while assuage the racist fears of elites in the Global North about population growth in the Global South).[40] Similarly, many historians have analyzed how the measurement of population engendered widespread fears and justified a variety of interventions to control its growth. During the 1950s, 1960s, and 1970s, demographers' calculations of future population growth stirred popular anxieties that rapid increases in population would spark Malthusian crises. Matthew Connelly shows that even though these projections rarely occurred as predicted, they were "still taken as irrefutable signs of inevitable doom" that both governments and non-governmental organizations (NGOs) used to justify coercive population control campaigns in the Third World.[41]

Measurement practices also shaped the international politics of development by becoming an important issue around which international cooperation took place. Recent scholarship has highlighted how attempts to create global

38 Michelle Murphy, *The Economization of Life* (Durham: Duke University Press, 2017), 6.
39 Murphy, *Economization*, 24.
40 Murphy, *Economization*, 47–49.
41 Matthew Connelly, *Fatal Misconception: The Struggle to Control World Population* (Cambridge, Mass.: Harvard University Press, 2008), 370–371. See also Alison Bashford, *Global Population: History, Geopolitics, and Life on Earth* (New York: Columbia University Press, 2016).

measurements often influenced the course of international development endeavors in favor of homogenization. In her study of the World Agricultural Census, conducted by the International Institute of Agriculture (the forerunner of the Food and Agricultural Organizations), Amalia Ribi Forclaz details how FAO flattened the diversity of farming practices globally to a set of narrow output targets. The Census "worked as a homogenizing tool in which a wide variety of societies were defined by their agricultural outputs," she writes. Its designers saw it "as a way to create a global picture of worldwide agricultural resources that could be used for a systematic review of the current and prospective state of nationally and regionally defined agricultural practices," which would set the standard for future agricultural development.[42] Yet such projects also served to build consensus among experts over how to view and perceive developmental problems. Perrin Selcer demonstrates how the UN Education, Science, and Cultural Organisation's (UNESCO) attempt to create a "Soil Map of the World" forged transnational community among soil experts and made possible the "construction of a global environment about which it was possible to debate issues of equity and sustainability."[43] Though the map had little direct impact on the development policies of any one country, the act of measuring and classifying varieties of soil and depicting them from a synoptic view point cultivated a community of experts dedicated to using it to define agricultural development and environmental problems in easily understood ways.

Yet standardization of measurement practices was rarely a smooth process, and international standardization unsurprisingly rendered local variation invisible and favored that topics that were more easily constructed through widely available data collection techniques. The standardization of national income and accounting techniques provides a useful illustration. In the early attempts to quantify economic activity in the British colonies, economists noted that the large presence of subsistence production – a process neither monetized nor marketized – conducted by women was very difficult, though not impossible, to estimate. The work of British economist Phyllis Deane over the 1940s and 1950s attested the significance of this putative economic activity and the value of incorporating it into national aggregates. Sir Richard Stone, who guided the UN's creation of a standardized System of National Accounts, ultimately decided against the inclusion of subsistence production and unwaged women's work in

42 Amalia Ribi Forclaz, "Agriculture, American Expertise, and the Quest for Global Data: Leon Estabrook and the First World Agricultural Census of 1930," *Journal of Global History* 11, no. 1 (2016): 44–65, 64.
43 Perrin Selcer, *The Postwar Origins of the Global Environment: How the United Nations Built Spaceship Earth* (New York: Columbia University Press, 2018), 172.

national accounts because of its variation across borders and the difficulty of acquiring data on it.[44] In this instance, standardization narrowed the accepted definition of activities that could be defined as "economic" and codified the gendered politics of statistical representation. Following Deane's work, in later years feminists critics of national income accounting argued that the choice to define waged labor as "productive" and household labor outside the production boundary reinforced a blinkered view of social value and consigned basic elements of social reproduction to the realm of "extraeconomic life" excluded from popular national metrics such as GNP.[45]

The Limits of Economic Measurement in Historical Perspective

Although much of this literature has focused on the consequences of GNP and the calculative practices associated with measurement, historians have also begun to explore alternative narratives of economic measurement in historical perspective. One strand of research focuses on the development of indicators that predated the rise of national income and products accounts or meant to supplement or displace GNP. For instance, in the early twentieth century a loose transnational movement of businessmen, workers, and liberal reformers all attempted various methods to quantify workers' "standard of living" and use it for targeted policymaking – either for raising wages to squash competition or to redress material deprivation.[46] Grace Davie's research reveals how in South Africa, social scientist Edward Batson carried out extensive social surveys of Cape Town to create a "poverty datum line" of minimum needs for households, which reformers used to advocate for the advancement of people from poverty, much as standard of living statistics had been intended to do.[47] Michele Alacevich shows how the World Bank used a range of statistics – including some standard of liv-

44 Luke Messac, "Outside the Economy: Women's Work and Feminist Economics in the Construction of National Income Accounting," *Journal of Imperial and Commonwealth History* 46, no. 3 (2018): 552–578, 563, 572, ft. 58.

45 Murphy, *Economization*, 33. For more on feminist criticisms of national income accounting, see Messac, "Outside the Economy."

46 Michele Alacevich, "The World Bank and the Politics of Productivity: The Debate on Economic Growth, Poverty, and Living Standards in the 1950s," *Journal of Global History* 6, no. 1 (2011): 53–74.

47 Grace Davie, *Poverty Knowledge in South Africa: A Social History of the Human Science, 1855–2005* (New York: Cambridge University Press, 2015), 103–141.

ing figures – in its early years before GNP took over. In these cases, scholars have highlighted how socially-oriented statistics often directed attention away from abstract national economies and towards specific groups or communities with often more redistributive goals in mind.

In addition, scholars have detailed attempts by reformers to challenge the hegemony of GNP directly. For example, Maria Bach and Mary Morgan study shifting poverty metrics within the UNDP as the organization attempted to refashion its policy priorities away from national progress and towards poverty alleviation. They argue that the shift to poverty alleviation and accompanying poverty metrics "had a two-fold power base: *informationally*, it was built into choices of measuring instruments because new notions of development required different kinds of poverty index numbers, but for intervention purposes—even though it invited local actions—it was still largely operated by those who had made those choices (for example, to privilege poverty reduction over growth and fiscal rectitude)."[48] The objects of development changed along with the new metrics. Morgan and Bach argue that the UNDP shifted "from measuring averages of the national level to measuring differences at the national and subnational level including specific subgroups of the population."[49] But the new shift towards bespoke and subnational metrics exposed ongoing problems with data collection. The UNDP's sophisticated "Multidimensional Poverty Index," which incorporated ten different variables, was only available for just over a hundred countries (even the Human Development Index, by comparison, was available for almost every country in the world.[50] There was an important continuity between this era of debate and the rise of GNP. As Morgan and Bach note, "Poverty action required one definition, goal, and target that could create a consensus, an 'umbrella' that could cover the work at the UNDP, IMF, and World Bank."[51] The use of new poverty metrics did not displace the broader technocratic impulse that governed development policymaking. The very act of setting quantitative targets still conditioned how policymakers mobilized resources and political will for concrete actions.

In general, studies of attempts to displace GNP with alternative metrics often featured similarity to the targets of their reforms. Often the alternative statistics rested on similar assumptions about the value of ranking and comparing nation-

48 Maria Bach and Mary S. Morgan, "Measuring Difference? The United Nations' Shift from Progress to Poverty," *History of Political Economy* 52, no. 3 (2020): 539–560, 540. Emphasis in the original.
49 Bach and Morgan, "Measuring Difference?," 547.
50 Bach and Morgan, "Measuring Difference?," 549.
51 Bach and Morgan, "Measuring Difference?," 551.

states as a coherent whole. Daniel Speich Chassé suggests in his study of the Millennium Development Goals that the MDGs, for example, "still stuck to this methodological nationalism by imagining a global developmental ranking of nations."[52] I have argued elsewhere in a study of multiple attempts to displace GNP over the 1970s and 1980s that new statistics reflected an underlying technocratic impulse that placed too much faith in the capacity for new numbers to generate political change and too often played down the role of political mobilization and mass politics in reshaping development policies.[53]

Along with alternative metrics, historians have also analyzed how new categories of economic measurement have shaped international development. One major new concept that emerged during the 1960s was the "informal sector." Originally named by British anthropologist Keith Hart in his study of migrant workers in Ghana, by the early 1970s the informal sector became a distinct object of inquiry for development organizations and experts. Historian Aaron Benanav reveals that the informal sector emerged as a subject of interest as development experts grappled with the limitations of conventional categories of employment to capture accurately all the forms of labor that did not often involve formalized wages. Attempts by economists within the International Labour Organisation (ILO) during the early 1960s to construct a measure of global unemployment had not succeeded because of the inability to price and quantify labor that did not involve reliable wages. Instead, the ILO adopted informality as a way to try and categorize labor that defied existing employment classification schemes. Though this marked an attempt in the "global disarticulation of GNP measurement from an orientation towards full employment," it also once again highlighted the challenges and value judgments inherent in economic measurement.[54]

Historians have also noted that international development experts were often the most skeptical and vociferous critics of dominant metrics. Across the world during the 1960s and 1970s, historians have recently uncovered a variety of reform movements to challenge the use of GNP in policymaking. To capture the social aspects of life left invisible by economic accounts and the persistent poverty and inequality within countries, a transnational movement of experts sought to introduce "social indicators" in public policy. There was also renewed interest in quantifying aspects of labor and economic activity that was unwaged and not expressed in market relations, such as "informal" labor and women's

52 Speich Chassé, "The Roots," 231.
53 Macekura, *The Mismeasure of Progress*, 138–165.
54 Aaron Benanav, "The Origins of Informality: The ILO at the Limit of the Concept of Unemployment," *Journal of Global History* 14, no. 1 (2019): 107–125, 125.

household work. Environmental critics sought to redress the ecological crises by pricing environmental externalities and constructing alternative models and metaphors for economic activity that linked economic and biophysical systems into a cohesive whole. These alternatives all drew widespread international attention, reflected the most prominent arguments among critics of economic growth, and revealed the range of debate over the meaning and measurement of international development.[55] During this era, economists such as Simon Kuznets and Irma Adelman also challenged the empirical basis that had undergirded the intellectual justifications for dominant foreign aid programs by arguing that growth policies had often "worsened equity, poverty, and stability around the globe" and called for better data to promote new development approaches, such as satisfying basic human needs.[56]

Historians have taken these criticisms a step further by identifying fundamental problems with the underlying data used to make claims about international development in the first place. Morten Jerven's vast exploration of the limited data on poverty in Africa offers a valuable starting point for questioning the reliability of the "stylized facts" of African development. Jerven's 2013 book *Poor Numbers* uncovers the startling details about how many African countries' statistical departments lacked effective data collection capacity and only irregularly produced national income and product measurements.[57] Economists' and development experts' common refrains about structural low growth among sub-Saharan African and chronic poverty likewise lacked a sufficient evidentiary basis. The World Bank's World Development Indicators dataset, for instance, only contains data starting in 1960, and systemic coverage of GNP estimates only began in the mid-to-late 1960s. As a result, most economic claims about persistent low growth and poverty rest on data only for a few decades in the late twentieth century.[58] Recent work by economic historians paints a different picture. Reconstructions

55 Macekura, *The Mismeasure of Progress*, 89 – 102.

56 Michael Gubser, "The Presentist Bias: Ahistoricism, Equity, and International Development in the 1970s," *The Journal of Development Studies* 48, no. 12 (2012): 1799 – 1812, 1803.

57 Morton Jerven, *Poor Numbers: How We Are Misled by African Development Statistics and What to Do About It* (Ithaca: Cornell University Press, 2013).

58 Morten Jerven, "The History of African Poverty by the Numbers: Evidence and Vantage Points," *Journal of African History* 59, no. 3 (2018): 449 – 461. See also Morten Jerven, "An Unlevel Playing Field: National Income Estimates and Reciprocal Comparison in Global Economic History," *Journal of Global History* 7, no. 1 (2012): 107 – 128. In the case of demographic statistics, some post-colonial governments went as far as to launch education campaigns to build public trust in data collection to try and ensure reliability of census estimates. See Gerardo Serra, "'Hail the Census Night': Trust and Political Imagination in the 1960 Population Census of Ghana," *Comparative Studies in Society and History* 60, no. 3 (2018): 659 – 687.

of real wages series of eight British African colonies from 1880 to 1940 indicate that real wages exceeded subsistence levels throughout the period and surpassed those in major Asian cities.[59] Moreover, assessments of African poverty often relied on statistics whose meanings evolved far beyond their initial use. Vincent Bonnecase argues that statistics on nutrition and French colonial Africa only became evidence of widespread poverty decades after their initial compilation.[60] This line of research shows that developmental claims about the supposedly objective state of relative development have been based on flawed data and a process of commensuration that was both "technical and political."[61]

The issues with reliable data were not lost on contemporary observers, either. In her path-breaking estimates of national income in the British colony of Northern Rhodesia during the late 1930s and early 1940s, Phyllis Deane noted that the absence of basic economic data made the estimates nearly impossible. The "great dearth of information," she wrote, was a "serious obstacle" to producing a "comprehensive picture of the economy." Given how little information was actually available, she added that she had to resort to "pure guesswork" in her estimates.[62] Unable to convince the Colonial Office to make the collection of macroeconomic statistics a government task, Deane struggled to construct reliable income estimates despite numerous attempts into the 1950s.[63] Researchers who embarked on similar endeavors to calculate national income during the late colonial and early post-colonial reported also noted that the absence of reliable data undermined the strength of their estimates from the British West Indes to Nigeria.[64]

The recent historiography on alternative metrics to GNP and the flaws in calculating GNP has important implications for historical inquiry. Narratives of post-war international development tend to follow from empire, with international expert governance viewed as a coherent and cohesive form of hegemonic knowledge. Economists often appear as omniscient and excessively confident

---

59 Jerven, "African Poverty," 455; Ewout Frankema and Marlous van Waijenburg, "African Real Wages in Historical Perspective, 1880–1940," *Center for Global Economic History Working Paper Series*, Working Paper 2 (2011), https://www.cgeh.nl/sites/default/files/CGEH.WP_.No2_.FrankemavanWaijenburg.jan2011.pdf.
60 Vincent Bonnecase, "When Numbers Represented Poverty: The Changing Meaning of the Food Ration in French Colonial Africa," *Journal of African History* 59, no. 3 (2018): 463–481.
61 Bonnecase, "When Numbers," 481.
62 Phyllis Deane, "The Construction of National Income Tables for Colonial Territories," 2 (paper draft), August 6, 1944, CO 852/554/2, National Archives of the United Kingdom, Kew Gardens, UK. See also Macekura, *The Mismeasure of Progress*, 47–55.
63 Speich Chassé, "The Use of Global Abstractions," 13–14.
64 Macekura, *The Mismeasure of Progress*, 52–53.

in their aspirations. The power of expertise in government is taken as a granted. But stories of critiques, debates, and reforms suggests something different: just how difficult it was to divine and manage the numbers of contemporary economic development; how uncertain development economists were in their methods and their application; how subsequent policymaking rested on a shaky foundation. Only by looking at the actual accounting practices does this become clear. The recent studies that described the difficulties inherent in calculating post-colonial economies attest to this. For governments to generate and maintain high levels of economic growth, they first had to measure the economic activity within their territory that could be used as a basis for charting growth over time. For this, economists first had to agree upon a standard calculation process for measuring an economy. What did it mean for the future of development if the boundaries, size, and scope of the economy – that "useful fiction" – could not be agreed upon? In the 1940s, at least, that question produced more confusion and anxiety than clear and confident answers.

Within the larger history of international development, these struggles over how best to measure national income and whether it should form the basis for policy interventions point to persistent challenges about the object – the national economy – so often assumed as a stable and meaningful entity in development rhetoric and policy. How a country measures its development goes a long way toward shaping how it pursues development. Official measurements reflect what leaders value in society, and analyzing the history of statistical constructs reveals the cultural sensibilities and ideological predilections that shaped the numbers in the first place. Yet the recent historiography demonstrates a long-standing debate over how best to measure a society, and also how to select, even more basically, what to measure. For just as long as GNP stood in for national well-being and economic growth measured in terms of GNP symbolized developmental success, intellectuals and activists have questioned the usefulness of these numbers. Not only did they wonder about how well their measurement techniques traveled and ponder the meaning of the limitations of their data, but many put forth alternative metrics – from social indicators to ecologically specific ones – that expressed a differing definition of what it meant for a country to develop, how policymakers should be assessed, and how a society would express its core values. In other words, the debates over economic measurement were not an aberration. They are a core component in the longer history of international development from its inception to the present day.

Conclusion

The new histories of international development that explore the place of economic measurement have enriched our understanding of modern global history. They have analyzed how statistics influenced state-building, the trajectory of decolonization and Cold War foreign aid, the role of expertise in public policy, and how varying regimes of valuation have fallen in and out of public favor. This research thus illuminates the power and limits of technocratic governance at the national level and within the modern international system, how numerical knowledge reshaped popular expectations of governments the world over, and the ideological and experiential similarities and differences that conditioned how leaders and policymakers viewed their subject populations.

There remains more to be done, of course. Historians have only begun to explore the histories of contestation and debate over alternative metrics, the role of target-setting and its consequences for the implementation of development industry within the aid industry, the technologies of everyday development – from project reports to grant applications to research surveys – that followed from such target-setting, and the relationship between economic measurement and ecological devastation. Much of the historiography on development has homed in on the role of measurement within international organizations and national governments. There has been comparatively less focus, for instance, on how foreign aid agencies embraced target-setting and measurement techniques that shaped the conduct of actual development interventions. Along these lines, historians should explore how measurement and assessment practices shaped the social history of individuals and communities and how they influenced the environmental history of the past century. Similarly, there is more research to do to understand the recent surge of interest in sub-national metrics of development success. This research will only strengthen the valuable contributions the scholars discussed in this essay have made.

The historians of development and measurement have pointed us in a fruitful direction, as they have begun to historicize notions of developmental "success." What, after all, did it mean for a development intervention to succeed or fail? In part, the answer to that question depended on measurement choices: projects that met a certain timeline, or boosted production by a certain quota, or contributed some specified amount to GNP growth. Likewise, for a development project to fail required developers to justify such an assessment by recourse to numerical reasoning and statistical expression. Historian Nick Cullather proposes that scholars should analyze development as a “narrative strategy.”[65] By investigating how developers used statistics to tell stories about what development meant and what it did or did not accomplish, the new histories of development and measurement have done just that. As Prasanta Mahalanobis recognized decades ago, to tell stories about a country’s development requires statistics, just as the construction of statistics is inextricably bound up with the process of economic and social change.

65 Nick Cullather, *The Hungry World: America’s Cold War Battle Against Poverty in Asia* (Cambridge, Mass.: Harvard University Press, 2010), 183.

Artemy M. Kalinovsky

Numbers in Space: Measuring Living Standards and Regional Inequality in the Soviet Union

In his 1964 textbook *Ekonomicheskaia Geographia* (Economic Geography), Petr Lavrischev extolled the economic transformation of Soviet republics that had once been colonies of the Russian empire.[1] The Soviet Union covered a vast territory roughly matching the borders of the Russian empire that had collapsed in 1917, but reorganized into national sovereign republics. The tenth congress of the Bolsheviks in 1921 had made equalizing levels of development one of the party's priorities. These priorities were largely forgotten as the Soviet Union under Joseph Stalin chose crash industrialization in anticipation of a major conflict. By the time Lavrischev published his textbook in 1964, the Soviet Union was a very different place than it had been 40 years earlier. But Lavrischev's textbook glossed over the enormous discrepancies that remained. Major cities like Moscow and Leningrad were recovering from the war, growing rapidly, and had the best schools, doctors, public transportation, and the most well-stocked stores. To the east and north, in the Ural mountains and beyond, the earth contained enormous resources of hydrocarbons and precious metals, but long, dark winters made life difficult. Further south were the Central Asian republics and the Caucasus, conquered by the Russian empire over the course of the eighteenth and nineteenth centuries. With the exception of larger cities like Baku in Azerbaijan or Tashkent in Uzbekistan, these regions had seen very little industrialization; indeed, the priorities of Stalin's crash industrialization program essentially condemned these regions to becoming commodity producers for the rest of the USSR.

Even as Lavrischev was writing his textbook, Soviet planners were trying to confront these disparities. By the mid-1950s, with Stalin dead and a new leader-

Note: The author would like to thank Julia Chernyavskaya, Alessandro Iandolo, and Eva Rogaar for assistance with archival materials, and Vanni Pettina, Yakov Feygin, Isaac Scarborough, Corinna R. Unger, and Jack Loveridge for their comments on earlier drafts. This article was prepared as part of the ERC project *Building a Better Tomorrow: Development Knowledge and Practice in Central Asia and Beyond, 1970–2010,* which is based at the University of Amsterdam (ERC 865898).

1 A.N. Lavrischev, *Ekonomicheskaia Geografia SSSR* (Moscow: Ekonomika, 1964), 175–177.

https://doi.org/10.1515/9783110730234-008

ship trying to revitalize the Soviet project and compete with the United States for the allegiance of the decolonizing world, questions of equality and standards of living once again came to the fore. Yet how should planners measure equality, let alone achieve it, across a land as large and diverse as the USSR? What kind of indicators would reveal how the Soviet Union was doing? What really counted in building a developed socialist society? Was it levels of industrialization? The percentage of the labor force employed in industry? Access to education, cultural institutions, and consumer goods? Participation of women in the workforce? These questions occupied Soviet politicians, planners, and scholars, as well as observers of the USSR in the west. What became clear in the 1950s, however, was that to understand equality in the USSR, Soviet planners would have to get better at understanding how its population lived; as they tried to do so, they also engaged in debates about what really mattered. Discussions about how and what to measure inevitably became discussions about what development and equality were really about.

This article investigates the history of measurement in the USSR from the perspective of the Council on Productive Forces (SOPS), a research institute attached to the main Soviet State Planning organ (GOSPLAN) for most of the post-war period.[2] There are several reasons that SOPS provides a useful window for thinking about measurement of development in the USSR. First, it was intimately tied to planning: SOPS had an expansive research program, but its main function was producing long term plans for the territorial placement of industry that would serve as guides for GOSPLAN's five-year plans.[3] Second, SOPS' remit meant that its researchers had to toggle between (and redefine) different under-

2 In this article I draw primarily on the SOPS materials from the Russian State Archive of the Economy (RGAE), fond 399, the Archive of the Russian Academy of Sciences (ARAN) (especially Nikolai Nekrasov's papers in fond 1825 and the social science section, fond 1731), as well as publications in economics and planning journals from Moscow and the republics. The SOPS collection and those of the Academy of Sciences are particularly valuable because they contain not only studies and reports, but also discussions of those reports and ongoing research projects.
3 Despite this, SOPS has received very little attention in accounts of Soviet planning, including books focused on regional issues. See, for example, Michael Ellman, *Socialist Planning* (Cambridge: Cambridge University Press, 2014); Peter Rutland, *The Politics of Economic Stagnation in the Soviet Union: The Role of Local Party Organs in Economic Management* (Cambridge: Cambridge University Press, 1993). The organization gets one mention in Jan Ake Dellenbrant, *The Soviet Regional Dilemma: Planning, People and Natural Resources* (New York: Routledge, 2017), 68. The "spatial turn" in Russian and Soviet history has thus far largely bypassed the history of Soviet spatial planning. For an exception, see Marina Loskutova, "Regionalization, Imperial Legacy and the Soviet Geographical Tradition," in *Empire De/Centered: New Spatial Histories of Russia and the Soviet Union*, ed. Maxim Waldstein and Sanna Turoma (London: Routledge, 2013), 135–158.

standings of space. Finally, SOPS did not do this work alone, but coordinated the research of hundreds of research institutes across the USSR. Tracking the development of measurement through this organization is thus particularly fruitful for understanding the importance of these issues for the USSR as a whole. By tracing the way that SOPS dealt with issues of territorial planning, migration, and equality in living standards across the USSR, we can better understand the particular challenges of measurement created by Soviet planning practices and ideological commitments.

The article proceeds in the following manner: first, it provides an overview of changing Soviet development priorities from the 1930s through the post-war decades. It then presents the history of SOPS and its changing research agenda over the course of the 1960s and 1970s, with particular reference to migration and living standards. For most of the period under discussion, SOPS was led by Nikolai Nekrasov, and the history of the institution is inseparable from Nekrasov's attempt to articulate a new "science," regional economics, that would allow Soviet planners to make sense of their diverse country.[4] Without abandoning SOPS' original grounding in physical geography, Nekrasov sought to establish a multi-disciplinary research program which could incorporate demography, sociology, ecology, and economics, and incorporate research from those fields into Soviet planning. The political implications of what SOPS was doing is further highlighted in the third section, which deals with the controversies over Nekrasov's book *Regional Economics* and his wider research program. Nekrasov's opponents felt that his program not only undermined the effectiveness of the planning system but the professionalism of the disciplines he sought to integrate. They also found his focus on regional inequality politically dangerous. The story of Nekrasov's bureaucratic struggles highlights the fraught nature of what SOPS was expected to do. But although Nekrasov ultimately left SOPS to focus on more academic research work within the Academy of Sciences, his colleagues at SOPS continued the research tradition begun under his leadership. The final section traces some of this research and the debates it engendered, paying particular attention to the limits of measurement confronted by researchers involved in these efforts.

The anthropologist Sally Merry Engle argued that quantification – the use of numerical indicators – in the fields of global governance and social reform has a

---

4 I find quite helpful Egle Rindzeviciute's statement that "Research on Soviet technocracy, therefore, should focus on the links between the production of formal knowledge, informal social relations, and decision processes as a matter of elaborate discursive construction." Egle Rindzeviciute, *The Power of Systems: How Policy Sciences Opened up the Cold War World* (Ithaca: Cornell University Press, 2018), 18.

knowledge effect and a governance effect. The former produces a "world knowable without context or history"; the latter reflects the role these measurements play in decision-making, legitimation, and thus power.[5] Indicators are seemingly objective but reflect the "theories and values" of their authors; they can serve the causes of reform as well as control.[6] SOPS' research was both technocratic and highly political. The question of living standards and equality was in and of itself highly political, insofar as it reflected Soviet ideological commitments, the way the USSR presented itself to the world, and the way the Soviet state presented itself to its own citizens. SOPS was charged with making political issues technocratic by identifying problems and providing planners with the tools to address them in a way consistent with ideological commitments and economic interests. Further, it was supposed to act as a counterweight to regional politics and lobbying by rationalizing decisions about placement and investment. But the research conducted and coordinated by SOPS was only partially successful in making these questions technocratic. Lobbying continued to play a large role in planning decisions. More importantly, the work on inequality and standards of living forced politicians, planners, and researchers to broaden and deepen their understanding of these problems. The definition of living standards changed over time, in part as a result of this work. The research on living standards, developed in a technocratic setting, ultimately contributed to heated debates about inequality in the USSR in the late 1980s. Finally, the search for new methods and techniques to gain an ever more intimate view of the population ultimately undermined the rationale for planning.

Changing Development Priorities

The Soviet Union was arguably the world's most ambitious developmental state. In the 1930s, it undertook collectivization of agriculture and a crash industrialization campaign that led to the death of millions of peasants in Ukraine, as well as parts of Russia and the North Caucasus, and some 1.8 million Kazakhs. Simultaneously, the Soviet state tried to centralize production through a system of directive planning, effectively eliminating private enterprise and trade. The So-

5 Sally Engle Merry, "Measuring the World: Indicators, Human Rights, and Global Governance," *Current Anthropology* 52, no. 3 (2011): 584–585.

6 Sally Engle Merry, "Measuring the World", 585. Also see Morten Jerven, *Poor Numbers: How We are Misled by African Development Statistics and What to do About It* (Ithaca: Cornell University Press, 2013), 5–6; Sally Engle Merry, *The Seductions of Quantification: Measuring Human Rights, Gender Violence, and Sex Trafficking* (Chicago: University of Chicago Press, 2016).

viet leadership under Joseph Stalin achieved its goal of industrializing the country and preparing it for world war. Not only was the human and ecological cost of crash industrialization enormous, however, but this approach to development left the economy with serious disproportions. The Soviet economy was oriented towards producer industries, with few resources dedicated to consumer production; agricultural production proved sufficient to support the industrialized workforce, but only barely.[7] Industry was concentrated in European cities and newly developed sites in the Urals and Siberia, like Magnitogorsk.[8] Large parts of Central Asia were supposed to focus on cotton production, in essence (re)creating a colonial dynamic.

After Stalin's death in 1953, his successors tried to overcome some of these disproportions without, however, giving up on the planning system. Nikita Khrushchev, who beat out his rivals to become the General Secretary of the Communist Party of the Soviet Union and eventually Chairman of the Council of Ministers, promised that the Soviet Union would "catch up and overtake" the United States in agricultural production. At the same time, Khrushchev also sought to undo some of the regional disproportions caused by Stalinist development: while Central Asia would remain a cotton producer, it would also get resources for industrialization and to raise standards of living to the union average.[9] Both of these shifts had domestic as well as Cold War priorities. The Soviet Union was beginning to present itself as a supporter of decolonizing states in Asia, Africa, and the Middle East; Central Asia, a region colonized in the nineteenth century by the Russian empire, was supposed to serve as proof that the USSR had overcome its imperial origins. More broadly, rising standards of living were to demonstrate that Soviet socialism was a better developmental model than western capitalism. The measurement of living standards became one element of "peaceful coexistence," Khrushchev's attempt to compete with capitalism without military confrontation.[10]

---

7 Robert C. Allen, *Farm to Factory: A Reinterpretation of the Soviet Industrial Revolution* (Princeton: Princeton University Press, 2003); Jenny Leigh Smith, *Works in Progress: Plans and Realities on Soviet Farms, 1930–1963* (New Haven: Yale University Press, 2014).

8 Stephen Kotkin, *Magnetic Mountain: Stalinism as Civilization* (Berkeley: University of California Press, 1995).

9 Artemy M. Kalinovsky, *Laboratory of Socialist Development: Cold War Politics and Decolonization in Soviet Tajikistan* (Ithaca: Cornell University Press, 2018).

10 S. A. Bakanov and A. A. Fokin. "A pri kommunizme vse budet: gosudarstvennoe planirovanie urovnia zhizni Sovetskogo cheloveka," *Noveischaia istoria Rossii* 9, no. 2 (2019): 420–436. As Yakov Feygin points out, the numbers that Khruschev produced in his speeches were not based on any serious calculations. Yakov Feygin, *Building a Ruin: Economic Thought and the International Politics of Soviet Reform* (Cambridge, Mass.: Harvard University Press, forthcoming 2023).

The shift in priorities did not mean the abandonment of planning. The planning system expanded, drawing on expertise from economists, sociologists, demographers, geographers, and other specialists. All of these fields had been either eliminated as "bourgeois science" in the 1930s or had been marginalized, but were revived in the 1950s. Working in semi-autonomous institutes within the Academy of Sciences or directly for the main state planning organ (GOSPLAN), specialists in these fields refined techniques for studying resources and needs and predicting behavior to perfect planning. The group of people involved in planning also became more diverse as it expanded. While agencies located in Moscow might still have recruited primarily from the European parts of the USSR, every republic expanded its own planning bodies and research institutes, and these recruited primarily from the republic's titular population.

Finding better data for models was one motivation for expanding research into socio-economic questions, but there were at least two others: managing migration and mitigating regional inequality. Following Stalin's death, the USSR abandoned mass incarceration and repression, and thus also the practice of forced relocation for agricultural and industrial development. After the chaos of the Virgin Lands Campaign, when thousands of poorly prepared urbanites descended on the steppes of Kazakhstan to help grow wheat, the Soviet Union gradually de-emphasized mobilization as well. Instead, as planners sought to develop industries in resource-rich parts of Siberia or labor-rich Central Asia, they were forced to pay more attention to the conditions that would make people come and stay in these new locations. As the Khrushchev era gave way to what historians now call "late socialism," commitment to raising living standards across the USSR only increased; the Communist Party de-emphasized reaching full communism and focused instead on improving conditions under "real existing socialism."[11] Although nominal equality was easily achieved by limiting the range of formal incomes paid across professions and regions, actual equality of living standards was another matter. But understanding how people lived – and what people thought of as good living across a land as large and diverse as the USSR – required planners to expand their toolkit and set up institutional collaborations allowing them to get a closer look at life in Central Asian villages, Siberian cities, and collective farms in the Caucasus. This, in turn, raised the profile of social scientists and planners from those areas, expanding their ranks and

---

11 See James R. Millar, "The Little Deal: Brezhnev's Contribution to Acquisitive Socialism," *Slavic Review* 44, no. 4 (1985): 694–706; Artemy M. Kalinovsky and Dina Fainberg, *Reconsidering Stagnation in the Brezhnev Era: Ideology and Exchange* (Lanham: Lexington Books, 2016); Natalya Chernyshova, *Soviet Consumer Culture in the Brezhnev Era* (London: Routledge, 2013).

drawing them into the planning process within their own republics and even in Moscow.[12]

Soviet debates about measuring domestic development paralleled (and were informed by) global discussions.[13] As Stephen Macekura notes in *The Mismeasure of Progress: Economic Growth and its Critics*, dissatisfaction with the limits of Gross Domestic Product as an indicator of welfare – led academics, governments, and international organizations to look for new measures that could better capture how people lived and devise policies to address problems such indicators highlighted. The UN Statistical Commission sought to help governments "develop social statistics which relate directly and immediately to social concerns of the general public and political authorities."[14] Economists designed new indicators like the Physical Quality of Life Index that captured things like infant mortality, life expectancy, and literacy.[15] Not all of the new measurements impacted policy directly, but together they drew the attention of governments, NGOs, and development organizations to realities they had previously ignored, contributing to the emergence of such paradigms as "Basic Needs" in the World Bank and the Women in Development initiative promoted through the United Nations.[16] As we will see, while Soviet planners never quite settled on the "right" mix of indicators, the search for those indicators contributed to changing conceptions of living standards and equality.

---

12 Artemy M. Kalinovsky, "Central Planning, Local Knowledge? Labor, Population, and the 'Tajik School of Economics'," *Kritika: Explorations in Russian and Eurasian History* 17, no. 3 (2016): 585–620.

13 Alden Young, "Measuring the Sudanese Economy: A Focus on National Growth Rates and Regional Inequality, 1959–1964," *Canadian Journal of Development Studies / Revue Canadienne d'études Du Développement* 35, no. 1 (2014): 44–60; Stephen Macekura, *The Mismeasure of Progress: Economic Growth and Its Critics* (Chicago: University of Chicago Press, 2020); Michele Alacevich, "The World Bank and the Politics of Productivity: The Debate on Economic Growth, Poverty, and Living Standards in the 1950s," *Journal of Global History* 6, no. 1 (2011): 53–74.

14 Macekura, *Mismeasure of Progress*, 142.

15 Macekura, *Mismeasure of Progress*, 144–150.

16 Martha Finnemore, "Redefining Development at the World Bank," in *International Development and the Social Sciences: Essays on the History and Politics of Knowledge*, ed. Frederick Cooper and Randall Packard (Berkeley: California University Press, 1997), 203–227.

Spatial Planning: From Physical Geography to Human Behavior

The Council on Productive Forces was not the most obvious Soviet institution to study inequality. The council had its roots in the Committee for the Study of Productive Forces, established within the Imperial Academy of Science in 1915 under the leadership of the legendary scientist V. I. Vernadsky. The committee's immediate purpose was to help compile and coordinate information about the empire's natural resources so that they could be better mobilized for the war effort.[17] The committee survived the 1917 revolutions along with the rest of the Academy, and its importance only grew with the Soviet government's adoption of rapid industrialization and planning at the end of the 1920s. The committee was reorganized into the Council of Productive Forces in 1930, and, still within the (now USSR) Academy of Sciences, became the central body responsible for mapping out the country's natural resources by carrying out "complex expeditions" staffed by geologists, chemists, and other scientists. SOPS carried out some 40 to 50 expeditions a year. Branches of SOPS were opened in almost every Soviet republic as well as many autonomous republics.[18] As with many aspects of the USSR, the imperial legacy of SOPS proved durable; it was only in the 1960s that SOPS would make the transition from an institution that focused primarily on identifying resources for the union's economic needs (the council's original purpose in the last years of the Tsarist empire) to one that produced research meant to promote equality across the USSR – though it never abandoned its initial function.

In 1960, SOPS was transferred to the USSR's State Planning Committee (GOSPLAN), a move that should be understood in the context of earlier problems with Khrushchev's economic reforms. The need for expert involvement was brought home after Khrushchev's initial push for increasing living standards led to falsification as regional and republican officials scrambled to meet targets set in the center.[19] Expertise was supposed to help overcome the kind of "voluntarism" among local officials that led to disproportions or, worse, outright fraud. But a stronger embedding of territorial planning could also help overcome the tension

---

17 Loskutova, "Regionalization, Imperial Legacy."

18 Alexander G. Granberg, "Izuchenie proizvditel'nykh sil Rossii," *Vsetnik Rossiyskoy Akademii Nauk* 66, no. 7 (1996): 579–584.

19 Oleg Khlevniuk, "The Economy of Illusions: The Phenomenon of Data Inflation in the Khrushchev Era," in *Khrushchev in the Kremlin: Policy and Government in the Soviet Union, 1953–1964*, ed. Jeremy Smith and Melania Ilic (London: Routledge, 2011), 171–189.

between sectoral organization of production and regional development. Khrushchev had also tried to replace the sectoral ministries, which undermined planning by lobbying and hoarding resources for their own industries, with regional economic councils (*Sovnarkhoz*) that would coordinate economic activity, including the development of social infrastructure. The elimination of the councils after 1962 put decision-making power back in the hands of sectoral ministries, while also increasing the need for coordination of industrial placement, social infrastructure, and labor resources.[20]

From that point on, SOPS would be more directly involved in planning by helping to "rationalize" the placement of industry; its research and calculations were supposed to diminish the role of lobbying by offering instead complex analysis of all factors of production in a given space.[21] Among SOPS' tasks was the creation of long-term pre-planning studies for the placement of industry, which in turn were supposed to guide the investment decisions of the main planning organs.[22] Increasingly, it was also called upon to provide advice not just on the available natural resources, but more complex assessments on the viability of investment in a given territory. That meant, among other things, studying labor resources. SOPS began to cooperate and coordinate its work with research institutes across the USSR, including those focused on issues of labor and demography.[23] In all, SOPS coordinated the work of 400 to 500 institutes and government agencies, including institutes of labor, demography, and geography in Moscow and at the republic level.[24]

SOPS' ambitions and research in this period highlighted a tension within Soviet economics between mathematically inclined modeling and research more rooted in political economy. Indeed, SOPS' initial foray into studying research into labor, consumption, and related issues may have been motivated by the need for better data for models that could be employed in decisions about industrial placement. These models were supposed to help planners consistently pre-

---

20 Peter Rutland, *The Politics of Economic Stagnation*, 95.

21 Khrushchev in a way exacerbated the problem of lobbying by raising the profile of republican and regional leaders as he built up his own political base after Stalin's death. He complained about the wasteful "parallelism" that resulted from regional and republican leaders' insistence on building industrial plants on their territory. *Nikita Sergeevich Khrushchev: Dva tsveta vremeni*, ed. N. G. Tomilina et al. (Moscow: Demokratiia, 2009), 686–687. See also Rutland, *The Politics of Economic Stagnation*, 93–96.

22 N. Batova, "Novoe v razmeschenie proizvoditel'nykh sil," *Voprosy ekonomiki* 11 (1967): 159–160; RGAE, Fond 399, opis 1, delo 1036.

23 Granberg, "Izuchenie."

24 The first figure is from 1963, in RGAE, F. 399, op. 1 d. 1036, 33; the second from 1968, in RGAE, F. 399, op. 1 d. 1686, 18. See also Batova, "Novoe v razmeschenie."

dict the effectiveness of placing an industry in a given area – taking into account the cost of infrastructure, availability of raw materials, transport costs, and labor.

Throughout the 1950s SOPS had been led by V. I. Nemchinov, who, unlike his predecessors, was an economist, and one of the pioneers of adopting input-output analysis to the Soviet planned economy. Input-Output tables had been developed by Wassily Leontieff, a Soviet émigré who had spent most of his career abroad, first in Germany and then in the US. Input-Output analysis allows the study of inter-industry relationships, and the effect of increasing or decreasing production of intermediate goods. Input-Output tables could also be expanded to account for transportation or, for that matter, labor.[25] Nemchinov had overseen experiments with input-output tables from his perch at the Laboratory for Economic-Mathematical Methods at the USSR Academy of Sciences.

The quality and usefulness of any input-output table, or of any model for that matter, depends on the information provided. And here the information available from Soviet statistics came up short. As V. S. Kossov, then one of Nemchinov's deputies, explained: "The emphasis [in government statistics] is not on the detailed analysis of the structure of expenditures – no matter how necessary this analysis is for the construction of an input-output table." The solution was to conduct detailed investigations of enterprises to decipher categories such as "cost of raw materials, components, fuel, energy, wages, amortization."[26] But such studies were only practical for large enterprises; they left out smaller enterprises, as well as "individual non-socialized economic units which produce a still appreciable part of the agricultural output. This single exception, when its operation is on a large scale, requires that selective investigations be made of the budgets of the families of collective farmers (kolkhozniks), workers and servants."[27] While input-output analysis only played a limited role in Soviet planning, the methodological problems raised by Kossov continued to occupy SOPS researchers over decades that followed.[28]

The decision to develop sparsely inhabited northern regions created a problem that was both technical and ideological. Regional plans were supposed to guarantee a "roughly identical standard of living in every region."[29] How was the government supposed to convince people to move to regions where sub-

25 Wassily Leontieff, *Input-Output Economics* (New York: Oxford University Press, 1986).
26 V. V. Kossov, "Regional Input-Output Analysis in the U.S.S.R.," *Papers in Regional Science* 14, no. 1 (1964): 175–181, 176.
27 Kossov, "Regional Input-output," 176.
28 Murat Albegov and Alexander Granberg, "Regional and Multiregional Modelling in the U.S.S.R.," *Papers in Regional Science* 66, no. 1 (1989): 77–86.
29 Kossov, "Regional Input-Output," 175.

zero temperatures dominated for much of the year and there was no sun during the winter months? Or, for that matter, to work in areas where the daytime temperatures in the summer months were above 40 degrees Celsius? The big agricultural and infrastructure projects of the Khrushchev era showed that mobilization and enthusiasm was still enough to get people to move to the Virgin Lands or the large dams being built at Bratsk in Siberia or Nurek in Tajikistan, but not enough to keep them there.[30] More broadly, demographic analysis clearly showed that people tended to leave Siberia even as government propaganda celebrated the movement of people to "new lands."[31] Finally, intra-republic and intra-regional migration patterns also defied expectations. In the Central Asian republics especially, local planners and party leaders had successfully lobbied for industrial investment, arguing that the region's booming population, mostly occupied in the countryside, would flock to new factories. Instead, the rural population seemed to stay put, and the new factories ended up recruiting workers from the European parts of the USSR or Siberia. The demographer Boris Urlanis explained the stakes of getting incentives right: "the existence of migration patterns that contradict the economic goals of the country, shows that the population will quickly react to any errors made by our planning and economic organs. Equal pay with differing costs of living are the main source of individual migration in an undesirable direction."[32] In other words, if planners wanted to get people to move and stay in areas where they needed labor, they needed to think in a more comprehensive way about what people needed to live an acceptable life.

Soviet planners had not ignored these questions before. Even during the crash industrialization of the 1930s, party leaders and managers were expected to provide workers with schools, health clinics, stores, and cultural institutions.[33] Party officials and inspectors were expected to report back on the construction of such facilities at new industrial sites. But the new conditions created by the turn away from mass mobilization and forced resettlement on the one hand, and the greater role assigned to economists and other social scientists in the planning process on the other, changed how these problems were studied

---

30 Especially in the early years of construction, when as many workers arrived as left in a given year. Even at the end of the decade Nekrasov complained that planners had gotten Nurek wrong by failing to plan for the transformation of a construction site into a long-term industrial complex. Kalinovsky, *Laboratory of Socialist Development*, 91–116.

31 Interview with demographer Zhanna Zaionchkovskaia, accessed January 11, 2021, https://www.samddn.ru/eto-interesno/kak_izuchali_migratsiju/?type=pda.

32 ARAN, F. 1877, op. 8, d. 519.

33 Kotkin, *Magnetic Mountain.*

and how they could be factored into planning. SOPS and its partners had to find new methods to make sense of these developments.

From the 1960s onwards, labor and population questions gained increasing prominence within SOPS as well as within its republican branches.[34] Researchers working in Moscow had unparalleled information about population trends, migration flows, salaries, costs of living, and access to services and consumer goods collected around the USSR. But Nikolai Nekrasov, who took over as chairman in 1964, also recognized that material gathered in Moscow was insufficient, and that effective planning required partnering with local institutions to get more granular detail. One had to be able to zoom in and out to make sense of how people lived across the USSR. At a meeting at the Academy of Sciences in June 1968 he used the example of demographic patterns to illustrate this point: from far away, it looked like Central Asia and the Caucasus had very similar demographic patterns. But when one looked at more closely, it became clear that there were big differences not just within the regions, but even within the individual republics. "If you take Kirgizstan," Nekrasov said, "you see the same processes in the rural regions, connected to growing birth rates. But if you take the city of Frunze, the situation is completely different." The only way to take this into account was to tackle these questions "together with sociological research" and bring in scholars active in the republics themselves.[35]

Under Nekrasov, SOPS increasingly engaged in studies bridging geography, economics, sociology, and demographic research. These studies tried to make sense of the exceptions identified by Kossov – the kind of units and activity not captured in official statistics. But they also went further. Working with partner institutions, SOPS carried out large scale surveys to identify why people chose to stay or move, their desired family size, and life choices more broadly.[36] Over the course of the 1970s, as we will see below, SOPS and its various partner institutions carried out increasingly detailed analysis of how people lived, supplementing official statistics with survey work, to compare living standards using an array of categories.

The transformation of SOPS' research agenda proceeded alongside – and informed – a larger discussion about defining and measuring development in the USSR. To an extent, Soviet agencies and many economists continued to use national income produced (NIP) and national income utilized (NIU) to calculate production and consumption in the USSR and in individual republics. Yet this

34 ARAN, F. 591, op. 2, d. 2527.
35 ARAN, F. 1731, op. 1, d. 96, 56–58.
36 R. Galetskaia, "Demograficheskaia situatsiia i trudovye resursy SSSR," *Voprosy Ekonomiki* 10 (1973): 155–159.

included only the net value added in production, and did not include services or government.[37] Attempts by Soviet scholars to measure equality relied on dividing this income by the size of a population of a given republic or economic region.[38] As the reviewer of one such effort noted in 1972, such calculations could help compare industrial production and national income, but said little about living standards. More broadly, the reviewer noted, "the concept of 'economic development' is much broader than the contents of 'productive forces,' if only by the size of the service sector."[39] In other words, national income was a decent indicator of living standards only if you assumed that levels of industrial production reflected people's access to living space, amenities, pre-schools, healthcare, food, consumer products, and so on. Insofar as investments in these areas were indeed driven by industrial ministries (that might build pre-schools or health clinics for their workers, for example), such indicators were not useless, but they obscured enormous intra-regional differences. Moreover, the policy implication was that only industrial placement would raise standards of living. Yet, as we have already seen, people were not moving in the way that models had predicted they moved, forcing planners to revisit their assumptions.

The Soviet effort to find the right indicators and methods to understand the well-being of their population took place in parallel to developments in industrialized capitalist countries and among international development experts. SOPS in particular was actively studying the approach of foreign countries to regional planning, producing reports on the methods used in countries like Japan, France, and elsewhere. Nekrasov was an active participant if not a driver of this process. Nekrasov, both as head of SOPS and as the Chair of the Committee for International Research Ties, frequently traveled and received visitors. In 1971 alone, Nekrasov went to Poland, Hungary, and Japan to lecture on Soviet experience of regional planning, as well as to lecture the Japanese about the twenty-fourth party congress and Soviet development in Siberia and the far East."[40] That same year he led a delegation from SOPS to a UN organized meeting in Warsaw on the preparation of planning cadres.[41] The archival record makes it difficult to track the actual influence of these interactions, because (in this and other cases) while it provides plenty of evidence of Soviet officials and scholars keenly ob-

37 I. S. Koropeckyj, "Equalization of Regional Development in Socialist Countries: An Empirical Study," *Economic Development and Cultural Change* 21, no. 1 (1972): 68–86.
38 M. Bakhrakh, "L.N. Telekop, Urovni Ekonomicheskogo Razvitia Raionov SSSR (Ekonomoika, 1971)," *Voprosy Ekonomiki* 8 (1972): 143–145.
39 Bakhrakh, "Telekop," 143.
40 RGAE, F. 399, op. 1, d. 1259, 11.
41 RGAE, F. 399, op. 1, d. 1257.

serving and analyzing the work of their counterparts, those same individuals were less keen on admitting the influence of foreigners on their own work. As we will see, moreoever, Nekrasov had good reason to avoid highlighting his interest in foreign methods too much. Even as such cooperation was encouraged in the 1960s and 1970s, the charge of copying "bourgeois" models could get one into much trouble.

Regional Economics and Economic Geography

Nikolai Nekrasov was nothing if not ambitious for what SOPS could accomplish; not surprisingly, he made enemies. While the conflicts that preceded Nekrasov's retirement from SOPS in 1979 were rooted in academic and bureaucratic politics, they also revealed SOPS' limitations in providing technocratic solutions to the problems of regional inequality, as well as the controversies of studying inequality.

Soon after taking over as head of the organization he told the institute's research committee: "the problem of industrial placements are not just ones that can help solve economic problems of the population's employment, or the use of labor resources, but many social problems as well."[42] Yet he found Soviet scholars woefully unprepared for this task. He complained to the head of personnel at GOSPLAN that neither Soviet economists nor economic geographers were properly trained to carry out the work that SOPS was being asked to do. One way to solve this issue, as we saw, was by collaborating with hundreds of institutes across the USSR. But even then, Nekrasov complained, one had to rely on people who learned about industrial placement on the job. SOPS was effectively forced to train its own specialists through its' in-house graduate program. Nekrasov was particularly critical about the USSR's Economic Geographers, who he felt lacked technical skills and were mostly suited for teaching high school. One way to overcome this deficiency was to change the training of economists and economic geographers, a request Nekrasov wanted passed on to the Ministry of Education. Another was to found a new field entirely.

In the 1970s Nekrasov set about writing an introduction to a new field he called "Regional Economics," which he claimed was distinct from Economic Geography as well as from Economics. The idea of a new field had been discussed

42 RGAE, F. 399, op. 1, d. 1068.

within SOPS at least as far back as 1972.[43] Nekrasov's monograph came out in 1976, with a second edition following in 1978. While not a detailed handbook, it set out the parameters of his proposed new field, which Nekrasov argued could help systematically even out standards of living, account for cultural differences among the USSR's various nationalities, regulate the distribution of people across the USSR, and provide the scientific basis for plans to protect natural resources and the environment.[44]

One of the more innovative (and ultimately, more controversial) aspects of the book was the use of term "region" (регион) alongside that of "district" (район). The "raion" in Soviet planning was a space delineated by planners; the problem was that the activities of people within that space, or the region's ecology, did not always correspond to what planners had in mind when they first marked out a raion (raion could also denote an administrative district, but this is not the way that spatial planners used the term). The term "region" allowed Nekrasov and SOPS to think about the USSR as consisting of overlapping spaces of various scales, from three "macroregions" (the European part of the USSR, the Caucasus and Central Asia, and Siberia) to microregions within republics.[45] Only by understanding space in a way that preceded the plan could SOPS hope to improve territorial planning.

Nekrasov's book was warmly received in Kazakhstan and Tajikistan, where Nekrasov's republic-level counterparts organized roundtables to discuss the book.[46] It also received a positive response from specialists organized by the leading Soviet party journal, *Kommunist*, where the economist and academician Anatoly Rumiantsev hailed the emergence of a new science[47] (Rumiantsev, it should be noted, had helped found the Institute of Concrete Sociological Research, and thus did much to promote the rebirth of sociology in the Soviet Union. The institute was reorganized when party authorities found its orientation to be too "liberal"). *Kommunist* also published an overview of letters from specialists across the USSR, almost all of them positive. The journal's readers hailed

43 O. A. Konstantinov, "Economic Geography and Regional Economics," *Soviet Geography* 17, no. 1 (1976): 28–37.

44 Nikolai Nekrasov, *Regional'naia Ekonomika: Teoriia, Problem, Metody* (Moscow: Ekonomika, 1965), 32.

45 Nekrasov, *Regional'naia Ekonomika*, 34–35. For more on the overlapping terminologies used by Soviet planners: Denis J. B. Shaw "Regional Planning in the USSR," *Soviet Geography* 27, no. 7 (1986): 469–484.

46 M. Ismailova, "Regional'naia Ekonomika i Ee Problemy," *Izvestiia Akademii Nauk Tadzhikskoi SSR* 1 (1976): 95–99.

47 A. Rumiantsev, "Vazhnoe Napravlenie v Ekonomicheskikh Issledovaniiakh," *Kommunist* 1 (1976): 48–52.

the emergence of a new field, and especially its promises for applying mathematical models and systems analysis to the problem of regional development.[48]

Yet not everyone was happy with this new terminology, which Nekrasov had begun using even before writing the textbook. V. F. Pavlenko, who was the head of territorial planning within GOSPLAN at the time, rejected the use of the term "region" as simply introducing confusion and creating a superficial similarity between regional planning in capitalist countries and territorial planning in the USSR.[49] But the appearance of *Regional Economics* inspired nothing less than a campaign against Nekrasov from some of the country's leading Economic Geographers, led by A. N. Lavrischev, a Professor at the All-Soviet Distance-learning Financial and Economic Institute (VZFEI).[50] At a three day conference organized at Lavrischev's institute, economic geographers from around the USSR gathered to attack Nekrasov's book and his approach to studying regional issues.[51] One delegate from Leningrad found the very term "region" to have a "dangerous meaning."[52] In a follow-up letter to the Central Committee of the CPSU, Lavrischev, himself the author of a textbook on Economic Geography, accused Nekrasov of many sins, among them that Nekrasov was trying to claim the founding of a new discipline when he was just cannibalizing the work of Economic Geographers.

The letter, whose signatories also included two of Nekrasov's subordinates from SOPS, raised more substantive points that were clearly intended to get the attention of senior party functionaries. One was that in using terms like "regional science" Nekrasov was copying bourgeois scholarship. Nekrasov was accused of being influenced by bourgeois economists, and in particular Walter Isard, whose textbook *Methods of Regional Analysis: an Introduction to Regional*

48 L. Golovanov, "Vazhnoe Napravlenie v Ekonomicheskikh Issledovaniiakh: Obzor Pisem," *Kommunist* 10 (1976): 60 – 64.

49 V. F. Pavlenko, *Territorial'noe Planirovanie v SSSR* (Moscow: Ekonomika, 1975), 45 – 47. By contrast, demographers seemed to be more comfortable not only using the term "region" but also introducing other terms like "macrozones," analogous to Nekrasov's macro-regions. B. S. Khorev, *Razmeschenie Naselenie v SSSR* (Moscow: Mysl', 1986).

50 Lavrischev largely echoes criticisms published in the form of a "letter to the editor" that appeared in *Planovoe khoziastvo* and signed by several economists and economic-geographers. See V. Vasiutin et al., "Pis'mo v Redaktstsiu," *Planovoe Khoziastvo* 3 (1977): 156 – 158. But Lavrischev goes farther by criticizing not just the book but also Nekrasov's career and management of SOPS.

51 ARAN F. 1825, op. 1, d. 39.

52 ARAN F. 1825, op. 1, d. 39, 9.

Science was translated into Russian and published in the USSR in 1966.[53] A second charge was that Nekrasov's interest in inequality would provide the "economic foundations" for "localism" and "bourgeois nationalism" and "contradicts the further coming together of socialist nations." Nekrasov was mistaken to point out that the USSR had "economically poorly developed districts," Lavrischev continued,[54] since "every economic geographer and economist knows that in our country there are no poorly developed districts or agricultural districts. Every large economic district is a developed industrial-agricultural district."[55] Finally, Lavrischev attacked Nekrasov's record as head of SOPS. For all of its 600 employees and 560 partner organizations, Lavrischev claimed the council repeatedly failed to produce analyses that would resolve the issues that confronted Soviet planners: new cities with inadequate transportation, new factories without sufficient housing, and so on.[56]

Lavrischev certainly had a point, in so far as these problems bedeviled Soviet planning until the end, as did the issue of inequality. Yet this was hardly the fault of Nekrasov, or of SOPS. Rather, there were two issues that are in themselves quite revealing about the Soviet planning system and its limitations. The first, as we have seen, was that the increasing complexity that SOPS uncovered in its research was difficult to translate into planning documentation. How, exactly, did one incorporate "national" traditions into a planning document? Or all of the informal economic activity that SOPS researchers knew was going on, but couldn't quantify? The second was that planning was never a simply technocratic process, with policy made on the basis of research and information, but a result of lobbying and negotiation. Such lobbying undermined the efforts of SOPS to take ecology or human needs into account in planning recommenda-

53 Walter Isard, *Methods of Regional Analysis: An Introduction to Regional Science* (Cambridge, Mass.: Technology Press of the Massachusetts Institute of Technology, 1960); У. Изард, *Методы регионального анализа: введение в науку о регионах* (Москва: Прогресс, 1966). The Russian edition included a generally positive assessment from the economic geographer A. E. Probst, who stated that Isard's techniques, including his application of input-output analysis, would be of use to Soviet planners, provided they broadened out the range of indicators. Lavrischev ignores this assessment, as well as the fact that Isard was a student of Soviet émigré Vassily Leontieff and subsequently worked with the Polish socialist economist Oskar Lange. Whether Nekrasov was really inspired by Isard, or whether Isard's terminology simply proved useful for articulating something Nekrasov was trying to do anyway, is impossible to say. See also David Boyce, "A Short History of the Field of Regional Science," *Papers in Regional Science* 83, no. 1 (2004): 31–57.

54 Nekrasov, *Regional'naia Ekonomika*, 129.

55 ARAN, F. 1849, op. 1, d. 269, 124.

56 ARAN, F. 1849, op. 1, d. 269, 125.

tions, or even override calculations about the economic rationality behind a given project. This was a frequent complaint not only of Nekrasov but of his counterparts in other institutions.[57] Aleksandr Granberg, who eventually succeeded Nekrasov as head of SOPS, wrote that the power of different lobbies was a "shared misfortune of all regionalists." Many recommendations about complex development, placement of industry, or inter-regional ties faced resistance from "ministries and agencies that had enormous power, and sometimes, ambitious local managers."[58]

On their own, Lavrischev's complaints did little harm to Nekrasov.[59] Asked to evaluate the complaints of the letter writers, the head of the republic-level SOPS' in Ukraine, A.N. Alimov, rejected their arguments point by point.[60] More problematic for Nekrasov was the criticism from colleagues in GOSPLAN, especially the head of the sector for territorial planning, V.F. Pavlenko.[61] Pavlenko had criticized some of SOPS work in public, but apparently was leading a full blown campaign against Nekrasov and SOPS behind the scenes, writing letters to the Central Committee and to the head of GOSPLAN.[62] Nekrasov was under pressure to retire, and urged A.N. Kosygin, the Chairman of the Council of Ministers, to move SOPS back to the Academy, lest the organization end up liquidated under pressure from Pavlenko and others.[63] In the end, Nekrasov left his post at SOPS, heading up a new Committee on the Study of Productive Forces and

57 See the complaints of Fedorenko about Ukrainian politicians securing funding for a chemical plant despite warnings from SOPS that such a plant would be harmful ecologically and not justifiable economically, at a discussion of the general scheme up to 1980. RGAE, F. 399, op. 1, d. 1702.

58 Granberg, "Izuchenie," 582–583. See also A. Adamesku and V. Kistanov, "Razmeschenie Proizvoditel'nykh Sil i Eazvitie Narodnogo Khoziastvo," *Planovoe Khoziastvo* 6 (1990): 109–114. See also Nooa Nykänen, "Competing Institutional Logics in Soviet Industrial Location Policy," *Eurasian Geography and Economics* 59, no. 3–4 (2018): 314–339.

59 Lavrischev had requested that *Kommunist* publish an article containing his critiques of Nekrasov. In 1979 *Kommunist* did publish an article by Lavrischev defending Economic Geography, but it did not mention Nekrasov or Nekrasov's book. It did, however, include a broadside against input-output analysis. A. Lavrishchev, "O Predmete Ekonomicheskoi Geografii SSSR," *Kommunist* 15 (1979): 91–99.

60 ARAN, F. 1849, op. 1, d. 269, 130–138.

61 It should be noted that Pavlenko, like Lavrischev, was the author of a textbook on regional planning. See fn. 40 above.

62 Nekrasov's letter to A. Ia. Pel'she, head of the Party Control Commission, ARAN, F. 1825, op 1, d. 48. Pavlenko is named as one of the people raising criticism of SOPS' work in: V. F. Pavlenko, "V Gosplane SSSR," *Planovoe Khoziastvo* 4 (1977): 156–157.

63 Nekrasov's letter to Kosygin, ARAN, F. 1825, op. 1, d. 49.

Natural Resources within the Academy of Sciences, where he remained until his death in 1984.[64]

The letters and articles in praise of Nekrasov's book also underlined, perhaps inadvertently, some of the methodological difficulties faced by regional planning. Regional economics promised to go beyond economic geography as it existed in the Soviet Union by utilizing mathematical models for regional planning, and thus addressing questions of individual behavior, mobility, and consumption patterns that affected the viability of a given project or long-term plan. But these models needed data about people's real incomes, needs, desires, and abilities. The textbook said little about how the new field would get this data, but research on these questions within SOPS continued to expand, and ultimately showed the limits of what Soviet social science could accomplish in the service of planning.

The Limits of Measurement

The kind of research Nekrasov promoted continued without him. In fact, SOPS and its partners deepened their analysis, trying to incorporate insights from field studies and observable reality into their analysis and recommendations. The research undertaken by SOPS and its partners reflected state priorities, but by making visible the gap between claims and ambitions on the one hand and apparent reality on the other they also forced state leaders to reformulate their claims. What had started as a way to provide better data for models ultimately ended up showing the limitations of those models and ultimately of Soviet planning.

The relationship between claims and measures was dialectic. SOPS' research revealed regional inequality and was encouraged to further its research by GOSPLAN and other organizations.[65] By the early 1980s, Soviet economists had iden-

---

64 Aleksey Chichkin, a former SOPS employee, believes that Nekrasov's ouster had to do with his opposition to the policy of exporting natural gas instead of developing a more balanced economy, as well as his support for local decision-making, which Soviet officials thought too reminiscent of the Yugoslav model. Unfortunately, Chichkin provides no evidence for this. Aleksey Chichkin, "Ekonomisty Milost'iu Bozhey: Nikolay Nekrasov," *File-Rf*, May 15, 2014, accessed October 15, 2020, http://file-rf.ru/analitics/580; Aleksey Chichkin, "Vo Izbezhanie 'Odnobokosti' Ekonomiki'," *RitmEurasia*, April 12, 2015, accessed October 15, 2020, https://www.ritmeurasia.org/news-2015-04-12-vo-izbezhanie-odnobokosti-ekonomiki-vspominaja-akademika-nekrasova-17496.

65 Pavlenko, "V Gosplane SSSR," 156–157.

tified over a hundred indicators that they could use to evaluate the level of socio-economic development of cities and other territorial units.[66] Soviet leaders were now talking not just about "standards of living" but also "level of socialist civilization." At the twenty-sixth CPSU congress in 1982, the party resolved to pay particular attention to "evening out social differences on a territorial level."[67] Commenting on CPSU General Secretary Yuri Andropov's statement at the June 1983 plenum that the concept of living standards could not be reduced to salaries, a member of SOPS' research council commented that "In working on economic issues we have not been paying enough attention to social problems. Our work needs to permeated with the investigation of living standards. That's up to all of SOPS [...] and we have to agree what we mean by 'standard of living.' In essence this is about the quality of life [...]"[68] Again, the idea of "socialist civilization" was not new – what was new in this era was the commitment to quantifying this concept, and the way quantification helped drive redefinition of the concept.

The drive to get closer to on the ground developments was most clearly evident in SOPS' approach to Central Asia. As SOPS researcher Margarita Mazanova pointed out at a meeting on methodology, "One of the most difficult problems is the paradox of Central Asia, where everything is bad with housing, and income, and so on, but people seem to be rushing to live there. We need to find the key to solving this problem."[69] Mazanova was speaking tongue-in-cheek; in fact, people were no longer flocking to Central Asia; the major industrial projects that had drawn a large European population in the 1960s were nearing completion, and the non-Central Asian population was actually declining from the 1970s.[70] But the local population was still booming and showing little interest in moving around the USSR or even within the republics.

The "puzzle" was why people refused to move, and the effort to make sense of that problem drove some of the more intense methodological discussions within the organization as it tried to identify what "living standards" meant and how the state could go about raising them. As SOPS researcher Sergey Khvatov noted in 1978, "The living standards of a population is a multi-dimensional category, which excludes the possibility of expressing it in one synthetic indica-

66 O. Nekrasov, V. Rutgayzer, and N. Kovaleva, "Territorial'noe Planirovanie Sotsial'nogo Razvitie," *Voprosy Ekonomiki* 5 (1982): 24–34.
67 Nekrasov, "Territorial'noe," 24.
68 RGAE, F. 399, op. 1, d. 2054.
69 RGAE, F. 399, op. 1, d. 2054.
70 Sebastien Peyrouse, "The Russian Minority in Central Asia: Migration, Politics, and Language," *Woodrow Wilson International Center for Scholars Working Paper* 297 (2008).

tor."[71] To make sense of this, researchers tried to supplement statistics gathered from organizations with household surveys. Such surveys had been used since the 1950s to study the way families used their time and income, and, importantly, to predict consumer needs.[72] Crucially, the surveys tried to measure not just incomes and prices, but also distance from stores and time spent getting consumer goods. Yet as the economist A. Levin pointed out in a 1974 article in *Voprosy Ekonomiki*, even these surveys had a number of problems: first, they were conducted by sector of employment for the head of household, they did a poor job of capturing regional differences; many parts of the USSR were not surveyed at all.[73] Second, they usually failed to capture how much rural residents received in income or in kind from their personal plots.[74] Third, they were difficult to compare with food prices outside of the state sector, because markets (where peasants could sell produce from their own plots and set prices) were very poorly surveyed.[75] Levin advocated a number of methodological changes to surveys and data gathering more generally, which included comparing residents not just by social class (workers and peasants) but also according to whether they were rural or urban, and carrying out budget surveys that were more representative of the demographic distribution of the USSR.[76]

In fact, by the early 1970s the kind of complex methodology advocated by Levin was being developed by Tatiana Zaslavskaya and her team at the Novosibirsk branch of the Academy of Sciences for their study of villages in western Siberia.[77] By the end of the decade these recommendations seem to have been adopted by SOPS as it continued its study of living standards across the USSR. Scholarship that compared population growth to formal employment opportunities found a large and growing number of "unemployed" in Central Asia; many studies treated all such people as dependents of wage earners.[78] Closer observation revealed that many of these people were engaged in some combination of seasonal labor on collective farms, work on personal agricultural plots, or

---

71 RGAE, F. 399, op. 3 d. 1534, 19.

72 See, for example, Kristy Ironside, *A Full Value Ruble: The Promise of Prosperity in the Soviet Union* (Cambridge, Mass.: Harvard University Press, 2021), 54–88.

73 A. Levin, "Izuchenia Sprosa Naselenia i Problem Informatsii," *Voprosy Ekonomiki* 8 (1974): 34–45, 35, 39.

74 Levin, "Izuchenia," 43.

75 According to Levin, surveys of markets captured only 20% of markets in the USSR, and primarily in large cities at that. Levin, "Izuchenia," 40.

76 Levin, "Izuchenia," 44–45.

77 T. I. Zaslavskaia, "K Metodologii Sistemnogo Izucheniia Derevni," *Sotsiologicheskie Issledovaniia* 3 (1975): 31–44.

78 For example, RGAE, F. 399, op. 3, d. 1534, 10–11.

other kinds of activity oriented around the home. A report completed by the Research Institute of Labor (NII Truda) in 1979 noted that 19.4 % of Central Asians were involved in "personal labor," double the Union average, while the number engaged in home or own-plot labor had grown by 795,000 between 1971 and 1977.[79] Crucially, income from these activities was notoriously hard to track.

In trying to evaluate living standards within Central Asia, Khvatov and his team compared cross-sections of income (including salaries and welfare payments), the structure and volume of consumption, and the level of development of social infrastructure."[80] Khvatov noted that per capita income was lowest in the Central Asian republics, but if you compared families rather than individuals the picture was different. Turkmenistan moved to the top of the rankings from near the bottom and Uzbekistan's collective farmers from twelfth to fourth place.[81] In other words, large families had multiple earners; if they pooled their resources the extended family was much better off than the nuclear family. Moreover, Khvatov found that rural Central Asians tended to combine income from the collective farm with other forms of income much more than others in the USSR. That combined income was 179.7 % of the union average for Tajikistan, 161.8 % for Uzbekistan, and 233.5 % for Turkmenistan. Such economic analysis certainly helped shed light on why people preferred to stay in large extended families in the countryside rather than move to the city. According to these calculations, rural Central Asians were less well off than urban Russians, but they were better off than urban, working class Central Asians and not so far behind the better off peasants elsewhere in the USSR. But these studies led to further questions. For example, income from personal plots appeared to be among the lowest in the USSR, as did size of land plots.[82] Other studies noted that that poorer families relied on personal plots for up to 90 % of their income in Tajikistan, but richer families much less so.[83] Yet rather than pushing people to seek employment in the state sector, or move to cities, lack of land seemed to reinforce the tendency to stay put.

These studies helped uncover economic rationales for immobility that sociological and ethnographic research at the time attributed primarily to cultural factors. Still, such studies – carried out in cooperation with local institutes – could not account for informal or semi-formal activity – what Sovietologists called the

79 GARF, f. 9595, op. 1, d. 635, 122.
80 RGAE, f. 399, op. 3, d. 1534, 19.
81 RGAE, f. 399, op. 3, d. 1534, 21.
82 RGAE, f. 399, op. 3, d. 1534.
83 RGAE, f. 399, op. 3, d. 1498, 40441.

"second economy."[84] For example, personal plots in Central Asia were often used for fruits, including citrus fruits, that took up less space than potatoes or vegetables but were in high demand throughout the USSR. By the 1970s informal middlemen brought such fruits to markets as far away as Moscow and Leningrad.[85] Income from such sales were hard to track. Even the timing of surveys could significantly affect outcomes, since growing seasons varied enormously across the USSR. With growing seasons generally longer, some farmers even managed to use collective farm lands to plant their own crops after the main cash crop had been harvested.[86]

Similarly, planners knew that many individuals, especially women, were involved in producing handicrafts (including clothing and bedsheets) that they sold through the market or informal channels. But understanding the importance of such activity to the household budget was difficult, since people were rarely honest about such income even in household surveys. As a result, studies attempting to determine standards of living seemed to show that life in Central Asian cities was better, as (formal) urban employment provided a higher income than (formal) employment in rural areas.[87] Yet on the ground observations seemed to undermine these findings.[88] As D. I. Ziuzin, a senior researcher at the Research Institute on Labor, pointed out at a meeting organized by SOPS, his "visual observation" during a tour of the region suggested that quality of

84 The term comes from Gregory Grossman, "The Second Economy of the USSR," *Problems of Communism* 26, no. 5 (1977): 25–40. Soviet officials did not study the second economy, leaving its control to law enforcement. See Vladimir Treml and Mikhail Alexeev, "The Second Economy and the Destabilizing Effect of its Growth on the State Economy of the Soviet Union, 1965–1989," *Berkeley-Duke Occasional Papers on the Second Economy of the USSR* 36, no. 6–9 (1993) on the methodological problems of estimating activities in the second economy, even with access to archival data. See also Nancy Lubin, *Labour and Nationality in Soviet Central Asia* (London: Macmillan, 1984).

85 Jeff Sahadeo, *Voices from the Soviet Edge Southern Migrants in Leningrad in Moscow* (Ithaca: Cornell University Press, 2019); Beate Giehler, "Maksim Gorki and the Islamic Revolution in the Southern Tajik Cotton Plain: The Failure of Soviet Integration in the Countryside," in *Allah's Kolkhozes: Migration, de-Stalinization, Privatization and the New Muslim Congregations in the Soviet Realm (1950s-2000s)*, ed. St. Dudoignon and Ch. Noack (Berlin: Klaus Schwarz Verlag, 2014), 123–147.

86 One study that found lower income from personal plots among Central Asians noted that carrying out the survey in September inevitably led to underestimating the income of Central Asian families, since the survey would not have actually captured the results of the harvest. RGAE, F. 399, op. 3, d. 1498, 18.

87 For example, RGAE, F. 399, op. 3, d. 1534, 17–18.

88 See, for example, another part of the report cited above, which notes the generally higher standard of living; GARF, F. 9595, op. 1, d. 635, 313.

life in the rural regions of Central Asia was better, because people benefited from their personal plots and other income that was not registered in official statistics. Life in the countryside also entailed a return to "patriarchal traditions," he went on, but again, he didn't have statistics to back this up, "because such research cannot be signified in numbers." Still, he said "our observations are important for drawing certain conclusions."[89]

Ziuzin's comments reflected a point made by other Soviet academics and planners, sometimes almost casually, that what kept Central Asians in the villages was "tradition," or, in common Soviet parlance, "survivals of the past." The economist and academician Tigran Khachaturov explained at a meeting in 1969 that Central Asia needed special attention because there "they have not rid themselves of the remnants of Sharia, or of pre-capitalist relations, and where there are still particular [...] relations of production."[90] Khachaturov used a vague understanding of religious tradition to explain behavior that did not fit economic models. Sociological studies conducted by local scholars over the course of the 1970s had helped bring nuance to these concepts, asking concrete questions about people's preferences for family size, location, and profession. Ziuzin similarly argued against uncritically using concepts like "tradition [...] as if tradition was not supported by the social-economic conditions of life. The larger the family, the wealthier, and parents have no reason to let children leave."[91] The studies done by Khvatov and his colleagues at SOPS partially demystified what was particular about Central Asia. Although they missed much informal activity, they showed that there were concrete economic reasons for people to maintain extended families, ones actually reinforced by the political economy of the Soviet countryside. Khachaturov suggested that the problem was not with the model but with the people, who were an exception to the rule; research done by SOPS and its partners suggested the model itself might fail to account for the diversity of economic behavior within the USSR.

By the early 1980s, such research had begun to transform Moscow's approach to welfare and placement in the region. Gradually, Soviet planning organs became more supportive of distributing industrial plants through rural areas, so that rural residents could be engaged in industrial labor without moving to large cities. Detailed studies of time use and amenities in different locations contributed to the push for developing "social infrastructure" in rural

89 RGAE, F. 399, op. 1 d. 1989, 76, 78.
90 RGAE, F. 399, op. 1, d. 1702.
91 RGAE, F. 399, op. 1, d. 1989.

areas.[92] Recognizing that women could and did contribute to the family budget while working from home, planners began to encourage the use of cottage labor, pushing factories to engage women with large families to produce piece-work at home.[93] But it took Mikhail Gorbachev's reforms under *perestroika* for more radical changes to take place. In the latter half of the 1980s, Moscow began to encourage not just cottage labor but individual labor, family sub-contracting on the farm, and the further expansion of private plots. The rationale for many of these changes had been built up over many years through the research done by SOPS and its partners. But that research also helped demonstrate the limits of measurement and planning. Even the most detailed studies left planners unable to make sense in a concrete way of a range of activities. It was not until the last year of the USSR's existence that planning was abandoned in favor of a transition to a market economy; but even before that point planners were pulling back from areas that research showed were beyond their capacity to manage effectively. More generally, such research – showing as it did the difficulty of planning and managing a country as diverse as the USSR – contributed to the call for greater economic autonomy within the USSR, as well as for regional integration.[94]

Finally, though there is little space to discuss these issues in detail, the research into regional inequality carried out by SOPS and its partner institutions inadvertently contributed to the more strident critiques of the USSR that emerged in the late 1980s. While work on inequality had not been top secret in previous years, most publications on these issues were confined to specialist journals and rarely included detailed numbers. After 1985, with the policy of *glasnost* (openness), the press began to feature these questions much more prominently, drawing on research produced by specialists. Intended to further the course of reform, such research also provided a source base for activists arguing for greater local control, and, eventually, independence. In a sense, Lavrischev's claim that *Regional Economics* would lead to nationalism was proved correct.

---

92 S. Kasimov, "Nekotorye Regional'nye Aspekty Uskoreniia Sotsial'noi Infrastruktury," *Obschestvenyi Nauki Uzbekistana* 12 (1976): 10–15.

93 GARF, F. 9593, op. 1, d. 4143.

94 Adamesku and Kistanov, "Razmeschenie Proizvoditel-nykh Sil i Razvitie Narodnogo Khoziaystvo"; Sh. Mirsaidov, "Sotsial'no-ekonomicheskoe Razvitie Soiuznoy Respubliki v Sovremennykh Usloviakh," *Planovoe Khoziaystvo* 1 (1990): 1–15; K. N. Bedrintsev, "Regional'nye Problem Razvitiia Ekonomiki UzSSR v Nadrodokhoziaystvennom Komplekse Sredney Azii," *Obschestvennye Nauki Uzbekistana* 3 (1987): 5–14.

Conclusion

Walter Isard, the American regional economist whose textbook had been translated in the USSR and inspired a generation of specialists, made a distinction between material and non-material factors of regional development. The latter included solidarity, security, respect for individuals, and so on. While the latter could not be quantified, Isard argued that they had to be taken into account for any serious consideration of development and total welfare: "in doing so, we include in resources not only the coal, air, personal labor, accumulated machinery, factory buildings, and other goods that we possess, but also the spiritual and other nonmaterial goods that we have at our command. That is, we include our total culture."[95] Isard was writing at a time when social scientists around the world were trying to expand what "counted" in economic analysis to move beyond growth and include broader measures of well-being, as well as economic activity that could not be easily captured in official statistics.[96] As we have seen, Soviet planners and social scientists wrestled with similar problems. Even as their understanding of the material aspects of social welfare expanded, they were also forced to confront the importance of factors, both material and intangible that they could not easily capture.

A decade after Nekrasov was forced out of his position at SOPS, the term "region" gained much wider use. Whereas Nekrasov had used the term to think simultaneously at different scales, in the late Soviet era the term often appeared to cement the idea of the Union divided into three large regions with very different problems and prospects. A report prepared by SOPS in 1989 spoke of Central Asia and Kazakhstan as one "region" with shared characteristics, but also urged that moving forward republics formulate their own internal "regional" plans for social and economic development, rather than relying on central organs.[97] In a 1990 article in the journal *Planovoe Khoziaistvo* two demographers, Aleksandr Avdeev and Irina Troitskaia, spoke of a Central Asian "region" characterized by high birth rates, ecological problems, rising nationalism, and growing unemployment and poverty, which would eventually lead to large-scale migra-

95 Dellenbrant, *Soviet Regional Dilemma*, 21; Walter Isard, *Introduction to Regional Science* (Englewood Cliffs: Prentice Hall, 1975), 377.
96 Douglas Rimmer, *Measuring Social Well-Being: A Progress Report on the Development of Social Indicators* (Paris: OECD, 1976).
97 RGAE, F. 399, op. 1, d. 2217.

tion to the European region, characterized by high levels of industrialization but low birth rates.[98]

Such reports and publications also reflected a sense that territorial economic and social planning had remained one of the weak points of the Soviet planning system. As we have seen, this was not for lack of attention: the Council on Productive Forces was a massive organization, its tentacles extending seemingly to every corner of the USSR, and providing detailed information to planners. Over the course of the 1960s, 1970s, and 1980s, it stimulated new research and helped refine techniques for understanding how people lived and what they wanted. And it made visible inequality across the USSR, forcing policymakers to confront the issue. But it also contributed to a vision of the union as firmly divided between a modern, developed, "north," and a "south" that seemed to be perpetually a source of problems; instead of a union of equally developed regions and peoples united by a common task, the USSR had become, as Avdeev and Troitskaya put, a "scale model of the contemporary world."[99]

---

98 A. Avdeev and I. Troitskaia, "Demograficheskiy Aspekt Razvitia Ekonomiki Na Rubezhe 21 Veka," *Planovoe Jhoziastvo,* no. 12 (1990): 87–92.
99 Avdeev and Troitskaia, "Demograficheskiy," 87.

Verena Kröss

Profitability Through Quantification: The World Bank and Rural Development in the 1970s

Introduction

Both critics and researchers of the World Bank have long pointed to the large gap between its rhetoric and its practice.[1] This article connects to the wide body of literature that emphasizes this discrepancy by going back to its origins: the 1970s. Before the 1970s, the World Bank mostly operated as a rather small, cautious, and specialized investment bank for development. In most cases, the Bank did not pretend to be doing anything beyond its basic remit – financing infrastructure projects with a focus on an adequate economic rate of returns.

It was only during the 1970s, by multiplying its lending and borrowing volume over the decade, that the World Bank transformed into the powerful and influential development finance organization which we know it as today.[2] One important aspect of this institutional transformation was the introduction of several new techniques of quantification in the World Bank's business. Another important element was the rhetorical embrace of a new moral mission: the alleviation of world poverty and a focus on small farmers and rural development.[3]

Many researchers have looked at the Bank's turn towards poverty during the 1970s with a focus on discourses and policy discussions. The World Bank's policy announcements and its contributions to the development discourse certainly matter because they were augmented by the Bank's lending resources and through the wide circulation of its reports. Nevertheless, it is pertinent to also

---

1 With a focus on the 1990s see, for example, Catherine Weaver, *Hypocrisy Trap: The World Bank and the Poverty of Reform* (Princeton: Princeton University Press, 2008); Jonathan Pincus, "The Post-Washington Consensus and Lending Operations in Agriculture: New Rhetoric and Old Operational Realities," in *Development Policy in the Twenty-first Century: Beyond the Post-Washington Consensus*, ed. Ben Fine, Costas Lapavitsas, and Jonathan Pincus (London: Routledge, 2001), 182–218.

2 Patrick Sharma, *Robert McNamara's Other War: The World Bank and International Development* (Philadelphia: University of Pennsylvania Press, 2017), 30–42.

3 Robert McNamara, "To the Board of Governors, Nairobi, Kenya, September 24, 1973," in idem, *The McNamara Years at the World Bank: Major Policy Addresses of Robert S. McNamara 1968–1981* (Baltimore: John Hopkins University Press, 1981), 231–263.

https://doi.org/10.1515/9783110730234-009

go beyond the discursive and rhetorical level in order to investigate what the Bank's new focus on poverty and rural development entailed as a lending practice.[4] This article analyzes the internal difficulties and contradictions the World Bank encountered in its attempt to translate the new moral mission for poverty alleviation and the focus on rural development into a practical lending approach and bankable projects.

The main argument is thus that the gap between Bank rhetoric and practice with regards to its rural development program in the 1970s cannot be understood as a problem of good intentions gone awry. Instead, this gulf was systematically connected to the profit-orientation and quantifying procedures of the World Bank as both a financial institution and as a technocratic organization.

The article loosely builds upon a wide body of literature that emphasizes the technocratic elements of development, analyzing and criticizing the larger development endeavor as a "politics of techno-science"[5] which was rooted in a "high modernist ideology."[6] In the case of the World Bank, its firm orientation on profits and the wide application of generalizing and quantifying procedures are key characteristics that make it a technocratic organization. Both shaped the way in which the World Bank attempted to translate intricate problems of rural poverty into problems of agricultural productivity and into bankable projects that could be implemented with technocratic confidence.

The article adds a new perspective to this literature through the focus on the internal workings and debates within the World Bank in the second half of the 1970s. It charts some of the internal disagreements of Bank staff regarding the quantifying technocratic approach towards rural development that the organization developed throughout the 1970s. These contestations show that the World Bank was not a monolithic actor and that some Bank staff were aware of the complexity of addressing poverty. Nevertheless, a technocratic approach and quantifying logic towards rural development projects prevailed because they were systematically connected to entrenched World Bank procedures and institutional requirements that focused on quantification and profitability.

4 The most insightful older study in this regard is Robert Ayres, *Banking on the Poor: The World Bank and World Poverty* (Cambridge, Mass.: MIT Press, 1983).
5 Timothy Mitchell, *Rule of Experts: Egypt, Techno-Politics, Modernity* (Berkeley: University of California Press, 2002), 15.
6 James Scott, *Seeing Like a State: How Certain Schemes to Improve the Human Condition Have Failed* (New Haven: Yale University Press, 1998), 4.

The Old and the New Bank

The World Bank, in the form of the International Bank for Reconstruction and Development (IBRD), was founded together with the International Monetary Fund (IMF) at the Bretton Woods Conference in July 1944.[7] As one of the central pillars for the postwar international financial order, the Bank was supposed to provide long-term credits for the enormous reconstruction and development needs after the Second World War. While the importance of the World Bank in financing European reconstruction measures was sidelined by the launch of the US – sponsored Marshall Plan in 1948, the World Bank lending portfolio encompassed a wide range of countries during the 1950s, from comparatively high-income countries directly to European colonial powers for their late colonial development schemes, and independent developing countries.[8]

Many of the institutional practices, rules, and norms of the World Bank developed with an eye to Wall Street over the course of the 1950s. On the one hand, this was based on the external resource dependency on Wall Street because IBRD received its funds from bond sales at financial markets. On the other hand, the orientation towards Wall Street and an investment-banker approach to development were also internalized within the organization through the selection of its top personnel. Eugene Black and George Woods, IBRD's presidents from 1949 until 1968, as well as other top personnel, came directly from the New York financial community. They were not development economists who dreamed about a "big push" of large investments and capital transfers for developing countries or about the possibilities of state planning for industrialization. Instead, they came to the World Bank with a cautious and conservative investment-banker mindset and experience that focused on the virtues of private business and was preoccupied with the soundness of investments.[9]

7 For an analysis with a focus on the World Bank and on development issues see Eric Helleiner, *Forgotten Foundations of Bretton Woods: International Development and the Making of the Postwar Order* (Ithaca: Cornell University Press, 2014).

8 High-income countries and European colonial powers accounted for almost half of all lending by the IBRD between 1947 and 1960. Their share subsequently declined over the course of the 1960s, see Verena Kröss, "The World Bank and Agricultural and Rural Development in the 1960s and 1970s" (PhD diss., Jacobs University Bremen, 2021), 29.

9 Devesh Kapur, John Lewis, and Richard Webb, *The World Bank: Its First Half Century. Vol. I* (Washington, D.C.: Brookings Institution Press, 1997), 92, 125. Michele Alacevich's historical work on the Bank has demonstrated that this investment banker approach to development was not unanimous in the IBRD before 1952 but that it ultimately prevailed. See Michele Alace-

Throughout the 1950s and 1960s, the World Bank mostly operated as a rather small and cautious special investment bank for development. Lending levels remained modest, and the loans came on conditions that reflected market terms.[10] The IBRD mostly financed the foreign exchange costs of "productive" infrastructure projects, particularly in the transportation and power sector but also for large irrigation schemes.[11] The projects were based on the calculation of an economic rate of return, and credit was bound to the import of discrete capital equipment.

There were several small deviations from this logic of operations of the World Bank as purely a special investment bank for development throughout the 1960s, from the establishment of the International Development Association (IDA) as a soft loan affiliate within the World Bank[12] to increased attention for financing agricultural projects.[13] The World Bank was also grappling with the effects of decolonization and a rapidly growing membership of newly independent countries, particularly from Africa, and as such was ill-prepared for offering quick investments to their new members.[14]

Nonetheless, it is fair to say that the basic orientation and institutional logic of the World Bank did not change fundamentally from the 1950s until 1968. With regards to the rest of this section, two aspects are important to stress: the alleviation of poverty was largely not an explicit concern of the World Bank during that period.[15] Furthermore, the World Bank generally continued to conduct its lending operations in an "ad hoc style" in which countries came with loan requests to the Bank which were evaluated "on a case-by-case basis."[16]

---

vich, *The Political Economy of the World Bank: The Early Years* (Stanford: Stanford University Press, 2009).

10 Kapur, Lewis and Webb, *The World Bank Vol. I*, 90–91.

11 Over 80% of Bank lending to developing countries between 1948 and 1961 was for the transportation and power sector: Kapur, Lewis, and Webb, *The World Bank Vol. I*, 109. Between 1961 and 1968 it was still over 60%: Kapur, Lewis and Webb, *The World Bank Vol. I*, 141.

12 The establishment of IDA in the World Bank in 1960 should be analyzed as a deflection of the demands of developing countries to establish a special fund for development within the United Nations system. See Kapur, Lewis, and Webb, *The World Bank Vol. I*, 154–156; John Toye and Richard Toye, *The UN and Global Political Economy: Trade, Finance, and Development* (Bloomington: Indiana University Press, 2004), 172–174.

13 Kröss, "The World Bank," 51–85, 86–124.

14 Kröss, "The World Bank," 51–85.

15 See Rob Konkel, "The Monetization of Global Poverty: The Concept of Poverty in World Bank History, 1944–90," *Journal of Global History* 9, no. 2 (2014): 276–300.

16 Sharma, *McNamara's Other War*, 44–45.

Most analysts agree that it was over the course of the 1970s under the presidency of Robert McNamara that the World Bank turned from being a rather small, specialized investment bank for development into the powerful and influential development finance organization which we know it as today.[17] The World Bank rapidly expanded and multiplied its entire lending and borrowing volume, along with its staff and the number of reports it produced.[18] Concurrently, the Bank also expanded its fields of engagement by embracing a rhetoric of poverty alleviation and by experimenting with new poverty-oriented lending fields such as rural development which, for a long time, had been considered the domestic affairs of borrowing countries.[19] Both aspects of the institutional transformation of the World Bank during the 1970s were closely bound up with the introduction of new quantitative management, programming, and accounting techniques at the Bank that fundamentally transformed how it was conducting its business.[20]

Robert McNamara arrived in April 1968 as the new Bank President, directly from his post as Secretary of Defense of the United States, in which he had been one of the people primely responsible for the escalation of the Vietnam War during the 1960s. McNamara came to the Bank with a broad understanding of development as a large-scale process of modernization which was widely held in the Kennedy and Johnson administrations and notably differed from the investment-banker perspective of Bank presidents before him. Development was not merely a limited and profitable investment project but was connected to Cold War strategy, security concerns, and a broad liberal vision of modernization.[21] McNamara also brought with him his faith in modern management techniques and his obsession with quantification.[22]

While McNamara played a crucial role in steering the Bank's rapid expansion over the course of the 1970s, his success was ultimately predicated upon broader shifts in the foreign aid regime and the globalization of financial mar-

---

17 Sharma, *McNamara's Other War*, 5; Kapur, Lewis, and Webb, *The World Bank Vol. I*, 215–216.

18 Kapur, Lewis, and Webb, *The World Bank Vol. I*, 1182; Sharma, *McNamara's Other War*, 30–43.

19 See Escott Reid, "McNamara's World Bank," *Foreign Affairs* 51, no. 4 (1973): 794–810, 795.

20 For more details on the introduction of these techniques see Sharma, *McNamara's Other War*, chapter 2.

21 For the connection between modernization thinking and the war in Vietnam see, for example, David Ekbladh, *The Great American Mission: Modernization and Construction of an American World Order* (Princeton: Princeton University Press, 2010), 190–225.

22 On this point see especially Sharma, *McNamara's Other War*, chapter 2; see also Guy Fiti Sinclair, *To Reform the World: International Organizations and the Making of Modern States* (Oxford: Oxford University Press, 2017), 241–245.

kets.[23] A similar analysis can also be made for the embrace of the poverty theme and the introduction of quantitative programming and management techniques in the World Bank. While the former was clearly linked to wider international discussions about the crisis of development at the end of the 1960s,[24] new techniques of quantification had been on the rise for a while and became widespread from business to academia and government throughout the 1970s.[25]

One of the most fundamental changes that took place at the World Bank at the end of the 1960s was the introduction of a new operational logic into how it managed its lending program. When McNamara arrived at the Bank, he ordered his staff to prepare a five-year lending program from 1969 to 1973 under the assumption that there was no shortage of funds[26] and he announced that he intended to double Bank lending across the period compared to the previous five years.[27] The request to prepare a five-year lending program fundamentally diverted from the way the Bank had been conducting its business. Instead of the traditional qualitative approach in which Bank staff were evaluating each incoming loan request in an "ad hoc style," the new system ingrained a quantitative future-planning logic into the World Bank.[28] Bank staff had previously been involved in project design and economic reports. But a five-year quantitative program with actual lending targets and estimates for all regions, and pressure on staff to meet them, introduced a new operational logic into the Bank's lending program. It was this quantitative planning which made the rapid expansionary drive of the World Bank throughout the 1970s possible.

The programmatic rhetorical embracing of a new moral mission to fight "absolute poverty" as "a condition of life so degraded by disease, illiteracy, malnutrition, and squalor as to deny its victims' basic human necessities" was an-

23 The World Bank made use of the globalization of financial markets and of the internationalization of the aid regime over the course of the 1970s. It became less exclusively dependent on borrowing from the United States and increased its borrowing from West Germany, Japan, and Switzerland as well as from oil-exporting states in the Middle East: Kapur, Lewis, and Webb, *The World Bank Vol. I*, 961–974, 1137.

24 Kröss, "The World Bank," 125–158.

25 Richard Rottenburg et al., eds., *The World of Indicators: The Making of Governmental Knowledge through Quantification* (Cambridge: Cambridge University Press, 2015).

26 President Council (PC), "Draft – Review of 5-Year Country Programs," June 1, 1968, Records of President Robert McNamara (RPRM), World Bank Group Archive (WBGA), folder 1770814, 1.

27 Robert McNamara, "To the Board of Governors, Washington D.C., September 30, 1968," in idem, *The McNamara Years*, 6.

28 Sharma, *McNamara's Other War*, 45.

nounced at McNamara's annual meeting speech in Nairobi in 1973.[29] At the heart of the new focus on "absolute poverty" was the small farmer and a strategy for rural development as McNamara observed that "the vast bulk" of the poor lived in rural areas and that "it is there – in the countryside – that we must confront their poverty."[30]

Yet the moral urgency and pressing critique of the persistence of poverty that McNamara portrayed in many of his speeches were not met with a fundamental transformation of the Bank's business. While a concern for poverty entered the Bank's language and reports, projects that attempted to address the poor directly never accounted for more than 30% of the World Bank's lending during the second half of the 1970s – with rural development accounting for about half of this.[31] It was one thing for McNamara to embrace the small farmer in his speeches, it was quite another to actually integrate this new agenda into the operational logic of the World Bank, which at its core remained a financial institution.

Rural Development as a Financial Institution: Quantity versus Quality

As a highly centralized financial institution, the World Bank was neither particularly well suited nor experienced for carrying out complex programs involving thousands of smallholders that required detailed knowledge about local agricultural, social, and economic aspects. Bank management recognized the fact that rural development did not fit the Bank's traditional focus on channeling capital. McNamara emphasized that it was the "organizational structure" that posed the biggest challenge for rural development[32] and the Bank's sector policy paper on rural development observed that "finance alone is not the limiting factor in bringing about a sustained increase in output among small-scale producers, fre-

29 Robert McNamara, "To the Board of Governors, Nairobi, Kenya, September 24, 1973," in idem, *The McNamara Years*, 238–239.
30 McNamara, *The McNamara Years*, 259.
31 See Table 2 in World Bank, *Focus on Poverty: A Report by a Task Force of the World Bank* (Washington, D.C.: World Bank Group, 1985), 6. Such documents can be accessed through the World Bank website for Documents and Reports, accessed April 19, 2021, http://documents-worldbank.org.
32 McNamara, *The McNamara Years*, 249.

quently technological, organizational, procedural, and manpower difficulties limit the effective use of additional investment."[33]

Bank staff also perceived many of the Bank's traditional standards and policies as an "obstacle" for the implementation of a rural development program: the Bank's standards for international competitive bidding for procurement, the focus on foreign exchange, restrictions on financing recurrent costs, and the difficulty of disbursing money for small items.[34]

The most crucial obstacle to the practical implementation of a rural development lending program at the Bank during the mid-1970s was, however, the "conflict between quantity and quality in lending targets."[35] This conflict was, in fact, a contradiction and tension that was at the core of the operational logic of the World Bank under McNamara during this period.

Bank staff clearly perceived the qualitative objective to design new experimental rural development projects as conflicting with the quantitative lending targets discussed in the previous section: "Rural development projects are difficult to prepare and implement and consume large amounts of time and staff. This conflicts with the strong Management push for meeting quantitative lending targets. Management must choose what it wants."[36] Another Bank official also warned McNamara that the quantitative lending goals were much more dominant in the Bank than the goal to implement an experimental rural development program:

> Your stated quantitative objectives come through the organization loud and clear. The gospel of new ideas does not transpire as easily. The upper and middle levels of management have not been convinced or capable enough to transmit the inspiration, and we have not yet found a good way to "indoctrinate". Hence the accusations for quantitative emphasis.[37]

Other management officials also pointed out that the tension between a qualitative shift and a quantitative expansion of the Bank's lending program was "compounded by the fact that any bureaucracy has a tendency to reward maximum

---

33 World Bank, *Rural Development Sector Policy Paper* (Washington, D.C.: World Bank Group, 1975), 63–64.

34 See the extensive list "Bank Policies and Procedures: Real and Imaginary Obstacles to Rural Poverty Programs," which is the Annex E to the following document: Warren Baum and Ernest Stern to Robert McNamara, "Plan of Action to Implement the Nairobi Speech," November 27, 1973, Robert S. McNamara Papers, Library of Congress (LC), part I, box 36, folder 4, 1–3.

35 Baum and Stern to McNamara, "Plan of Action," Annex E, 6–7.

36 Baum and Stern to McNamara, "Plan of Action," Annex E, 6.

37 AL [?] to Robert McNamara, "Gaining Commitment to the Poverty Program," October 16, 1973, Robert S. McNamara Papers, LC, part I, box 36, folder 4.

output rather than to provide incentives (including the time to do so) for innovative or difficult work."[38]

Pushing out growing amounts of loans, maintaining an efficient Bank budget by keeping staff increases to a necessary limit, and experimenting with the new rural development agenda that required carefully designed pilot projects did not go well together. We will come back to this tension and how these contradictory demands played out in the Bank at the end of this article.

The tension between quality and quantity was also mirrored in the ambivalent Bank understanding and definition of rural development. There was an implicit qualitative understanding among Bank staff that connected it to the broader ambitions of a poverty-focused development approach. This qualitative notion focused on multi-sectoral area development projects in which project components that focused on raising production were combined with social components which concentrated on education, nutrition, health, and rural water supply.[39]

However, for quantitative monitoring purposes, the World Bank developed its own precise but oddly technical definition of rural development. The World Bank classified all lending to the agricultural sector as rural development provided that at least 50% of the intended benefits went to beneficiaries within its poverty target group.[40] This quantitative definition introduced a logic of head counting into the Bank's project design and was oblivious to a project's content and design. If the Bank's project appraisal report estimated that half of the benefits went to poor people in rural areas, then it was classified as rural development, even if most of the loan financed the construction of a rural road, for example, which was something that the Bank had already been financing since the 1950s. Later Bank evaluation reports thus also pointed out that "there was clearly a degree of tokenism in relabeling the conventional project pipeline to conform with the RD [rural development] project definition."[41] This was particularly true for Bank lending to South and East Asia in which tra-

---

38 Warren Baum and Ernest Stern to Robert McNamara, "Plan of Action to Implement the Nairobi Speech," November 27, 1973, Robert S. McNamara Papers, LC, part I, box 36, folder 4, Annex E, 1.

39 World Bank, *Rural Development Sector Policy Paper*, 14–17; World Bank, Operations Evaluation Department (OED), *Rural Development: World Bank Experience, 1965–86* (Washington, D.C.: World Bank, 1988), xiv, 4–6.

40 World Bank, OED, *Rural Development: World Bank Experience*, 4; World Bank, *Focus on Poverty*, 5–6.

41 World Bank, OED, *Rural Development: World Bank Experience*, xiv.

ditional infrastructure investments remained high within rural development projects.[42]

From Rural Poverty to Bankable Projects

It is important to point out that Bank staff generally recognized that there was no quick fix or simple technological solution to rural poverty. For some staff, it was precisely the intricacy of the problem of rural poverty which made Bank lending for it difficult:

> Significant progress in rural areas requires what amounts to a social revolution. Radical changes in the social/economic structure, such as an effective land reform, is likely to be disruptive during the period of transition and thus to slow down economic growth in the short run and worsen the country's creditworthiness. In view of poor performance, the Bank then reduces its lending to the country.[43]

On an analytical level, Bank management was also quite aware of the high requirements for establishing a viable rural development program during the mid-1970s. They recognized the importance of finding the right organizational set-up, the need for political commitment, and participation by smallholding farmers.[44] They also discussed the difficulty of finding locally tested agricultural packages that worked for small farmers[45] and mentioned the need for land reforms.

This analytical knowledge about the complexity of rural development, however, conflicted sharply with the operational logic and reality of the World Bank. Beyond the lofty discussions in speeches and policy papers, the Bank aimed at converting the idea of rural development into a practical lending program during the mid-1970s. This implied that intricate problems of rural poverty needed to be translated into bankable projects. In its operational approach, the Bank abstracted from the complexities involved and found a general form of rural development that it could handle, and which fit the policies of the World Bank. This general form centered on the assumption of productivity and production increases, around which all rural development projects were built and designed.

---

42 World Bank, OED, *Rural Development: World Bank Experience*, 19.

43 Baum and Stern to McNamara, "Plan of Action," Annex E, 6.

44 World Bank, *Rural Development Sector Policy Paper*, 33–38.

45 World Bank, *Rural Development Sector Policy Paper*, 32; see also the discussion of Bank high management with the Mexican team from the Puebla project AL [?] "The Puebla Project," December 17, 1973, Memoranda for the Record, RPRM, WBGA, folder 1771494.

While the World Bank participated in international discussions about "basic needs" at the end of the 1970s,[46] it is important to understand that with regard to lending the Bank did not adopt a "basic needs" approach to development that understood their fulfillment as a right or entitlement. The Bank focused on making investments in the poor in order to increase their productivity and, subsequently, their income, integrating these people into a wider process of economic growth.[47]

The World Bank paid attention to the economics involved, to cost recovery schemes, and the necessary measures to ensure low-enough costs to make social services economically sound. It was the promise of increased production levels which made rural development projects appropriate for Bank financing and which fit traditional Bank standards that promised a high rate of cost recovery and that assessed projects through the calculation of an economic rate of returns. All of this was the attempt of fitting the new agenda of rural development into the procedures and logic of a banking institution in the second half of the 1970s.

As a lending approach, rural development at the World Bank was deeply rooted in a top-down and technocratic approach to development. Rural development projects were built around extremely optimistic expectations for rapid production increases that were estimated at project appraisal. In many cases, it was still unclear how exactly the agricultural production of small farmers could be increased, especially in arid and mountainous regions. Nevertheless, World Bank-project design over the course of the 1970s was inspired by technocratic confidence and by an untested belief in finding technological solutions along the way of project implementation.

The top-down logic also applied to other aspects in the design of rural development projects. The project appraisal report estimated the number of beneficiaries, the expected increase of production, and which component of social infrastructure was to be financed through the project. Robert Ayres has aptly summarized the top-down rationale of this approach through the logic of "targeting," the way of thinking and terminology with which the Bank approached the rural poor, as a "target population" for their projects: "This assumed, to con-

46 On the general turn to basic needs, see Sara Lorenzini, *Global Development: A Cold War History* (Princeton: Princeton University Press, 2019), 144–145 and 155–159; Corinna R. Unger, *International Development: A Postwar History* (London: Bloomsbury Academic, 2018), 137–141.
47 See also Ayres, *Banking on the Poor*, 83–91; Hollis Chenery, "Transcript of Interview with Robert Asher, January 27, 1983," World Bank Group Archives Oral History Project (WBGA OH), 11–12, accessed April 27, 2021, https://oralhistory.worldbank.org/.

tinue the analogy, that the target could be readily identified and that, once identified, it could be 'hit' with the intended benefits."[48]

Thus far we have seen how the World Bank tried to make rural development fit into the logic of the Bank as a financial institution. The integration of rural development into the Bank involved several procedures of quantification: from the calculation of the economic rate of returns to the identification of "target groups" and estimates of the "beneficiaries" in project appraisal reports. The difficulties and limits of these processes of quantification will be analyzed in the next section.

The Limits of Quantification

According to Montague Yudelman, Director of the World Bank's Agricultural and Rural Development Department, the insistence on quantifying the benefits of the rural development program came straight from McNamara: "McNamara, of course, wanted to cite numbers, so I insisted that on every project the staff should tell me how many people benefited from it. So, it may have been like the body count in Vietnam; they may have manufactured numbers, but I had to trust them."[49] High-level managers at the Bank noted that data and information problems made it very difficult to quantify how much money would be reaching the poorest 40% in a country. They observed that any such analysis "must be treated with considerable caution and be seen as giving only rough orders of magnitude" but they still produced the required numbers and estimates.[50] Robert Ayres, who conducted interviews with Bank staff in the late 1970s, also reports that many staff members did not see the utility of monitoring rural development projects through quantitatively measured benefits and that "some admitted that they cooked up the data requested."[51] In many cases, the World Bank staff could not rely on trustworthy data sources but the Bank's headquarters requested the data regardless.

The Division Chief for rural development at the Bank's headquarters, for example, complained to the East Africa Division that most of the early project in-

48 Ayres, *Banking on the Poor*, 103.
49 Montague Yudelman, "Transcript of Interview with Robert Oliver, July 18, 1986," WBGA OH, 9.
50 Warren Baum and Ernest Stern to Robert McNamara, "Status Report on Implementing your Nairobi Speech," April 25, 1974, Robert S. McNamara Papers, LC, part I, box 36, folder 4, Annex F, 7.
51 Ayres, *Banking on the Poor*, 108.

formation briefs were missing the necessary data and that regarding this data the "most important problem is the reluctance of project staff to make estimates."[52] Some staff indeed seemed to have been hesitant in making certain estimates. An economist working in East Africa reluctantly transmitted income guidelines for rural poverty groups but only upon pointing out that they had to be used with "extreme caution," that there was no national account of this income data, and that the methodologies for coming up with the data included "pure guesses."[53]

The problem was not confined to income data alone but involved most data in project appraisal. Staff also expressed "serious reservations" about calculating the precise economic rate of returns for rural development projects which required data on all production-related project aspects. Staff observed that base data contained "enormous margins of error" and that they were able to "produce almost any desired rate of return."[54] Staff defended rural development as an experiment in achieving larger structural reforms with unclear outcomes – but that made the calculation of an exact economic rate of return impossible.[55]

These quantification efforts, especially the "body count" of how many poor people were profiting from World Bank projects, produced a sense of frustration in Bank staff who produced the data: "I accept the fact that we have to try and do some poverty analysis, but I feel that we must be careful that we do not take too seriously the figures we are producing [...]. We should not ignore the cynicism that our own staff have about the poverty figures they produce and some of the cynicism from outside the Bank about our figures these days."[56]

These examples of staff questioning the quantification approach towards rural development came from the East and West Africa Regional Departments, where the lack of trustworthy data sources was likely more severe than elsewhere. Still, it was a great challenge for all project appraisal missions to determine the exact "target group," estimate local rural income data, and calculate

---

52 Leif E. Christoffersen to James Hendry, "Monitoring System of Agriculture and Rural Development Projects Preparation of Quarterly Report," September 18, 1975, East Africa Agricultural Record, WBGA, folder 1411392.

53 Michel Del Buono to Ted J. Davis, "Monitoring Project Information: Rural Poverty Income Guidelines," August 6, 1975, East Africa Agricultural Record, WBGA, folder 1411392.

54 Hans A. Adler to Willi A. Wapenhans, "Rural Development Projects in Eastern Africa," May 1, 1978, East Africa Agricultural Record, WBGA, folder 30339854, 2.

55 Adler to Wapenhans, "Rural Development Projects," 2.

56 J. K. Peberdy to K. Berg, "Poverty Impact Analysis in Appraisal Reporting for Agricultural Projects," February 21, 1980, West Africa Agricultural Record, WBGA, folder 1420582.

the precise economic rate of return based on assumptions of how small farmer production would respond to not yet established agricultural innovations.

Besides the frustration these quantification efforts aroused in Bank staff, it is important to keep in mind that the questionable nature of the data disappeared when it entered World Bank reports. Once established, such data and projections became important project facts.[57]

When the World Bank announced at the end of the decade that it had assisted millions of poor people and was lifting thousands out of poverty, these numbers were the estimates of what the Bank thought would be the effect of their projects before the projects started.[58] They were rarely related to the actual results of projects because there was a considerable lag in the completion review and assessment of projects.

In the World Bank's own evaluation reports on its rural development projects, it dutifully noticed the limitations of the economic rate of return calculations for the assessment of projects that focused on small farmers. Yet it continued the analysis by comparing the rate of return of rural development projects as a whole with the lending to other sectors in order to assess successes and failures.[59]

The Problems with Profitability

By the end of the 1970s, it was clear that it had been impossible to integrate the new agenda for rural development effectively into the operational logic of the World Bank as a financial institution. The World Bank was experiencing a severe crisis of its overall operational approach at the end of the decade.[60] At its core, this crisis revealed the tension that existed in the World Bank between the insti-

---

57 Peberdy to Berg, "Poverty Impact Analysis."

58 See for example Table 3 in World Bank, *Focus on Poverty*, 7 that lists "poor beneficiaries" in million families "at appraisal."

59 World Bank, OED, *Rural Development: World Bank Experience*, 25; World Bank, OED, *Rural Development Projects: A Retrospective View of Bank Experience in Sub-Saharan Africa* (Washington, D.C.: World Bank Group, 1978), 3–6.

60 Patrick Sharma provides a very useful and detailed discussion of this crisis; see Sharma, *McNamara's Other War*, chapter 7; Patrick Sharma, "Bureaucratic Imperatives and Policy Outcomes: The Origins of World Bank Structural Adjustment Lending," *Review of International Political Economy* 20, no. 4 (2013): 667–686. However, I disagree with his strong focus on this crisis as an explanation for the rise of structural adjustment lending; see Verena Kröss, "The North-South Conflict in the World Bank: Understanding the Bank's Turn to Structural Adjustment Lending," *Rivista Italiana di Storia Internazionale* 3, no. 2 (2020): 247–268.

tutional requirements of being both a financial institution and a development organization. Several different problems and elements converged during this crisis: problems with the slow disbursement of funds, the imperative of budget maximization, and diminished staff morale. The crisis was a general one and went far beyond rural development, but the problems of the integration of rural development into Bank procedures represented a powerful indicator of the crisis and of the contradictions within the World Bank.

At the end of the 1970s, a possible negative net disbursement rate was a looming danger to the Bank's image as a development institution that actively channeled capital from its richer member states to its borrowing countries.[61] World Bank management discussed the problem of a slow disbursement rate on several occasions.[62] Numerous aspects could delay the implementation of (rural) development projects, ranging from problems of finding adequate staff and a lack of counterpart funds by the government to complex processes of coordination in multi-sectoral projects, as well as difficulties in finding agricultural packages. When World Bank management looked at the organization's actual resource transfers, meaning the use and disbursement of funds and not just their commitment on paper, all of these difficulties translated into the problem of a "slow disbursement rate." Rural development in particular was simply not an adequate lending endeavor to quickly channel large amounts of capital.

Another aspect of the crisis of the Bank's operational approach was the imperative of budget maximization which demanded high lending levels while keeping administrative and staff costs to a necessary minimum. This imperative focused on the profitability of the organization and was rooted in the institutional character of the World Bank as a financial body. In the second half of the 1970s, the Bank's management regularly debated about how they could cut the yearly budget demands of the various regions because the Bank's Board of Executive Directors, which represents the member states, would not allow too high of a budget increase for administrative expenses.[63] This budgetary pressure was discussed in the regional departments as something that limited the number

61 Robert Wood, *From Marshall Plan to Debt Crisis: Foreign Aid and Development Choices in the World Economy* (Berkeley: University of California Press, 1986), 235–239.
62 PC, February 13 and May 1, 1978, RPRM, WBGA, folder 1770829; PC, June 20, September 26, and December 18, 1978, RPRM, WBGA, folder 1770830. See also Sharma, "Bureaucratic Imperatives."
63 PC, May 10, 1976, RPRM, WBGA, folder 1770827; PC, January 2, 1980, RPRM, WBGA, folder 1770833; Munir Benjenk to Robert McNamara, "Perspective 1983," November 30, 1977, Robert S. McNamara Papers, LC, Part I, Box 28, folder 1, 2.

of well-prepared projects available.[64] It also worked as a constrain on discussing difficulties: "You have in a sense, opened a Pandora's box of complications which, in these days of budgetary constraints on 'non-operational' activities, lending by target, and a thin pipeline of projects could well result in a less than welcoming reception in several areas."[65] The problem was not confined to rural development but it was an illustrative example of a field of lending that required much more staff time and could not be truly reconciled with the imperative of budget maximization.

Another aspect of the crisis of the World Bank's operational approach at the end of the 1970s was discussed internally by the management as "staff morale problems."[66] While some of the problems had to do with compensation issues, other concerns that staff raised were much more directly related to their perception of a declining project quality and to problems with over-control from management and pressure on staff rooted in the introduction of quantitative lending targets and the need to push out money.[67] Hollis Chenery, Vice President of Development Policy, suggested that "quality versus growth issues" were plaguing staff at the Bank and were at the root of some of their concerns.[68] Nevertheless, McNamara obstinately refused to consider any tension or trade-off between quality and quantity at the World Bank.[69] However, this was not the shared perception of Bank staff, especially with regards to rural development which represented the major qualitative shift in lending that McNamara had endorsed.

The Failure of Rural Development

The sheer volume of Bank rural development projects makes any overall assessment that pays attention to details notoriously difficult.[70] Nevertheless, several case studies indicate that the World Bank was not very successful in reaching

---

64 C. Walton to Hans Adler, "Agriculture Projects Programming," July 16, 1976, East Africa Agricultural Record, WBGA, folder 30339853.

65 Pickering to Graham Donaldson, "Farm Technology Issues Paper – Revised Draft," March 9, 1977, East Africa Agricultural Record, WBGA, folder 30339854.

66 PC, April 17, 1978, RPRM, WBGA, folder 1770829; PC, July 5, 1978, RPRM, WBGA, folder 1770830.

67 PC, January 31, 1977, RPRM, WBGA, folder 1770828. See also Sharma, *McNamara's Other War*, 141–143.

68 PC, April 30, 1979, RPRM, WBGA, folder 1770831.

69 PC, April 30, 1979.

70 Between 1974 and 1981 the World Bank financed over 300 rural development projects in dozens of different countries, see World Bank, *Focus on Poverty*, 7.

and benefitting the rural poor with its projects during the 1970s.[71] While using different criteria and perspectives, the World Bank's own retrospective evaluation of rural development projects was unmistakably clear in its assessment that, at the very least, area development projects, which represented "the heart of the rural development experience as originally proposed,"[72] largely failed, especially (but not only) "the many Sub-Saharan African ones, only a minority of which succeeded to some degree."[73]

While a great deal of the Bank's internal discussions focused on the failure of rural development projects in Africa, disillusionment with the rural development agenda was not confined to the continent, though it was strongest there. In 1982, one Bank official summarized the Bank's "disappointment" with rural development projects on general terms and independently from any specific region: "(1) They have reached the poor much less than was hoped; (2) they have taken longer to design, negotiate and execute than was expected; (3) they have had difficulty in building and leaving behind institutions that are able to function on their own and actually deliver services to the poor."[74]

In 1978, the World Bank's Operation Evaluation Department published a sweeping critique of past experiences with rural development in Africa.[75] The report reviewed projects that had been appraised before the new rural development agenda was embraced in 1973 and which were only retrospectively classified as rural development. It was clear in the discussion, however, that many of the problems it identified were similar in recent Bank projects, which was demonstrated by the next Bank evaluation report that was published in 1988.[76]

It is important to emphasize that the assessment of the failure of rural development discussed here refers to the perspective of the World Bank which, to a large degree, focused on the achievement of quantitative goals that were set at appraisal. Other standards and criteria for the assessment of "failures" are both possible and desirable. The Bank's evaluation reports are not a good

---

71 See the discussion in Ayres, *Banking on the Poor*, chapter 6; Sharma, *McNamara's Other War*, 115–124; Geoffrey Traugh, "Yielding Trouble: Development Dilemmas and the Political Uses of Bad Data in Malawi, 1964–1978," *Journal of Southern African Studies* 46, no. 2 (2020): 229–245; Bruce Rich, *Mortgaging the Earth: The World Bank, Environmental Impoverishment and the Crisis of Development* (London: Earthscan, 1994), 86–99, among many others.

72 World Bank, OED, *Rural Development: World Bank Experience*, xiv-xv.

73 World Bank, OED, *Rural Development: World Bank Experience*, xvi.

74 Judith Tendler, *World Bank Staff Working Papers, Rural Projects Through Urban Eyes: An Interpretation of the World Bank's New Style Rural Development Projects* (Washington, D.C.: World Bank, 1982), i.

75 World Bank, OED, *Rural Development Projects: A Retrospective View.*

76 World Bank, OED, *Rural Development: World Bank Experience.*

means to trace and understand possible deflections of benefits and investments or their appropriations and alternative uses by people on the ground, for example. The Bank's own assessment, however, reveals serious structural flaws in project design and major deficiencies in the institutional setup. It shows that the World Bank itself was deeply implicated in the failure of its rural (area) development projects, particularly in several African countries.

The central problem of the Bank's rural development projects was that it often did not have any viable and locally-tested agricultural approaches and technologies through which they could reasonably expect the increase in agricultural productivity that the projects were designed to achieve.[77] The Bank compensated through technocratic confidence and a leap of faith in coming up with a viable agricultural package during project implementation which in most cases was not successful.

The Bank's evaluation reports were quite clear that the focus on increasing agricultural production had proven to be unsuccessful in areas without irrigation in which the Green Revolution package was not an answer.[78] The evaluation report of 1988 observed in this regard that "the experience from audited projects suggests that in general there was a pattern of overoptimism and sometimes even plain error with regard to agricultural technology. Only in a few rare cases was there sufficient caution on the technology issue."[79]

A second problem and source of failure of rural development projects was rooted in the lack of attention the World Bank paid to institution-building. In some cases, the complexity of area development projects simply overburdened the administrative capacity in borrowing countries. Tanzania and the Bank's financing of *ujamaa* in the middle of the 1970s was the most prominent example that was analyzed along these lines in the World Bank.[80]

It should not be forgotten, however, that the Tanzanian case was not typical for the Bank's mode of implementation of rural development projects on the continent. In many other African countries, the World Bank worked through so-called autonomous project units that were separated from existing administra-

77 World Bank, OED, *Rural Development: World Bank Experience*, 30.
78 World Bank, OED, *Rural Development: World Bank Experience*, 30; World Bank, OED, *Rural Development Projects: A Retrospective View*, 14–20.
79 World Bank, OED, *Rural Development: World Bank Experience*, 29.
80 World Bank, OED, *Project Performance Audit Report. Tanzania Kigoma Rural Development Project* (Washington, D.C.: World Bank Group), 5–7, 11; Sean Delehanty, "From Modernization to Villagization: The World Bank and Ujamaa," *Diplomatic History* 44, no. 2 (2020): 289–314, 312.

tive and government structures in borrowing countries.[81] In the eyes of the Bank, autonomous project units promised a quick implementation of projects by helping to bypass inefficiencies and a lack of trained staff in the existing government administrations. But they were detrimental to institution-building.[82] In many African area development projects, the hindrance of institution-building was further exacerbated by the fact that the Bank made extensive use of "foreign experts" as a form of "technical assistance."[83] This model of implementing rural development projects was criticized on several occasions and from different angles as a costly endeavor that kept countries in a dependent position and disregarded the view of local administrators.[84] Nevertheless, the World Bank strongly relied upon ex-colonial civil servants from the United Kingdom, France, and the Netherlands for staffing these autonomous project units because they constituted the "'traditional' market for expatriate agricultural expertise."[85]

Conclusion

The article set out to explore the gap between rhetoric and practice at the World Bank with a focus on its rural development agenda in the 1970s. The analysis focused on the difficulties the Bank encountered in its attempt to integrate the new agenda for rural development into the operational logic of the Bank as a financial institution. The article analyzed the generalizing procedures the Bank employed to make rural development fit the context. These procedures translated complex problems of rural poverty into problems of agricultural productivity and into bankable projects which the Bank designed with technocratic confidence.

---

81 On these different ways of project implementation see Uma Lele, *The Design of Rural Development: Lessons from Africa* (Baltimore: John Hopkins University Press, 1975), chapters 8 and 9.
82 See the Bank discussion on Malawi and Nigeria in World Bank, OED, *Rural Development: World Bank Experience*, 74–79, 85.
83 World Bank, OED, *Rural Development: World Bank Experience*, 33–34.
84 Statement of Mwai Kibaki, Minister of Finance and Governor of the Fund and Bank for Kenya, Annual Meeting 1970, cited in World Bank, OED, *Project Performance Audit Report. Kenya First Livestock Development Project* (Washington, D.C.: World Bank Group, 1976), 6; Lele, *The Design of Rural Development*, 176–178.
85 J. B. Hendry and F. van Gigch to Willy Wapenhans and W. P. Thalwitz, "Technical Assistance for Agriculture in Sub-Saharan Africa," March 28, 1980, West Africa Agricultural Record, WBGA, folder 1420256, 1. See also Joseph Hodge, "British Colonial Expertise: Post-Colonial Careering and the Early History of International Development," *Journal of Modern European History* 8, no. 1 (2010): 24–46.

The most important argument is that the huge gap between rhetoric and practice with regards to rural development in the 1970s could not be understood as a problem of good intentions that went awry. The discrepancy was instead systematically connected to the profit-orientation and the quantifying procedures that were at the core of the World Bank as a financial and technocratic organization. They fundamentally shaped the way in which the new moral agenda for poverty alleviation and rural development was translated into bankable projects. By the end of the 1970s, it was clear that it had been impossible to truly integrate rural development into the operational logic and requirements of the Bank as a financial institution. Many Bank projects were experiencing major problems, particularly in achieving the main goal with which they set out: increasing the agricultural production of small farmers.

The article has provided first insights into the limits and problems of quantification and of the profit-orientation at the World Bank, substantiating the critique of technocratic elements of development through a historic analysis and focus on the internal workings of the World Bank. Future research in this direction could, in my perspective, take up two important focuses that are already discussed in recent literature that should be connected to a close analysis of the World Bank.

First, it is important to consider that the World Bank was and is a crucial site in the production of economic data, particularly with regard to development. In recent decades, historical analyses have taken up some of the insights of the science of technology approaches and have paid increasing attention to the processes and conditions under which economic data was being produced – treating it as a specific product and construction rather than as simply a collection of facts.[86] Economic data and statistics have a dual character in these analyses: "On the one hand, statistics of society and the economy are self-consciously and very overtly the products of a labor of construction. On the other hand, once established, they become objective facts, mere passive reflections of an ex-

86 With regards to development, analysis has focused on the evolution of the growth paradigm, the emergence of the economy as an object of knowledge and on the construction of national income statistics, see for example Timothy Mitchell, "Economentality: How the Future Entered Government," *Critical Inquiry* 40, no. 4 (2014): 479–507, 484; Daniel Speich, "The Use of Global Abstractions: National Income Accounting in the Period of Imperial Decline," *Journal of Global History* 6, no. 1 (2011): 7–28; Morten Jerven, *Economic Growth and Measurement Reconsidered in Botswana, Kenya, Tanzania, and Zambia, 1965–1995* (Oxford: Oxford University Press, 2014).

ternal economic or social reality."[87] The World Bank's role in the creation of economic data and "facts" increased substantially during the 1970s, particularly with the creation of the *World Development Indicators* which were published as an annex to the Bank's flagship publication *World Development Report* that started in 1978. Analysts have already pointed to the fact that these tables full of data and ranking indicators changed the discussion about development which henceforth had "to be backed by numbers."[88] Others have also emphasized that these Bank indicators are not neutral but an expression of specific theories about development.[89] Yet a detailed and wide-ranging analysis of the processes and history of "fact" and data production at the World Bank is ripe for further research.[90]

Second, a close analysis of the Bank in the 1970s and 1980s should be connected to recent discussions that contest existing narratives and chronologies of the "failure of development" in different African countries which the World Bank took a big part in helping to shape in the first place.[91] At the beginning of the 1980s, the World Bank cast aside its own deep implication in the failure of rural development projects in favor of an analysis that almost exclusively blamed African governments and wrong macroeconomic policies for the existing problems.[92] The ominous so-called Berg report advertised a "focus on smallholders" and on "a growth-oriented rural development strategy" with an unbroken authority as if this had not been precisely what the World Bank had been trying to do throughout the 1970s without much success and with numerous contradictions involved in its approach and project design.[93] At the beginning of the 1980s, the World Bank's technocratic solution to rural poverty was scaled up from the (overly) optimistic technocratic belief in agricultural productivity in-

87 Adam Tooze, "Trouble with Numbers: Statistics, Politics, and History in the Construction of Weimar's Trade Balance, 1918–1924," *The American Historical Review* 113, no. 3 (2008): 678–700, 691.

88 Shahid Yusuf et al., *Development Economics Through the Decades: A Critical Look at 30 Years of the World Development Report* (Washington, D.C.: World Bank, 2009), 20.

89 María Angélica Prada Uribe, "The Quest for Measuring Development: The Role of the Indicator Bank," in *The Quiet Power of Indicators: Measuring Governance, Corruption, and the Rule of Law*, ed. Sally Engle Merry, Kevin E. Davis, and Benedict Kingsbury (Cambridge: Cambridge University Press, 2015), 133–155.

90 For a start see the insightful case study on the World Bank and Malawi with a focus on project related data in Traugh, "Yielding Trouble."

91 See Morten Jerven, *Africa: Why Economists Get It Wrong* (London: Zed Books, 2015).

92 World Bank, *Accelerated Development in Sub-Saharan Africa: An Agenda for Action* (Washington, D.C.: World Bank Group, 1981).

93 World Bank, *Accelerated Development*, 50.

creases of the 1970s to finding the right technocratic fix at the macroeconomic policy level, at which devaluation and economic liberalization were supposed to create the right price incentives for farmers who would ideally respond with increased production.

Rohan D'Souza

Was the Large Dam a "Modern Temple"? Taking Stock of India's Development Tryst with the *Bhakra-Nangal*

Is a large dam a technological artefact or a political object?[1] After many debates stretching over decades, the view that seems to have won the day, for now at least, is that the large dam is best grasped as a weave between technical arrangements and ideological motivations.[2] Put differently, holding flows within massive reservoirs and producing hydro-electricity while irrigating crops involves more than the ingenuity of the expert engineer. Rather, putting a river on tap necessarily acknowledges the work of political and economic imaginations.

De-centering the heroic world of the engineer in this way, however, does not de-materialize the large dam.[3] If anything, the ecological and economic impacts, in terms of costs and benefits from damming rivers, continues to be the source for intense social and political contests and fuels many a protest. Disagreements over the actual benefits achieved and whether they contributed to grand ambitions such as progress, development, and economic growth became particularly loud during a frenzied period of dam construction between the 1950s to the 1990s, when, in an oft quoted estimate, close to 45,000 dams were built across rivers the world over.[4] Amidst the construction boom and the enthusiasm, however, troubling questions repeatedly emerged over what could be listed as a benefit of a large dam and how to give measure to them while also discounting for

1 Rohan D'Souza, "Framing India's Hydraulic Crises: Politics of the Modern Large Dam," *Monthly Review Press* 60, no. 3 (July-August 2008): 112–124. Also see the pioneering essay by Langdon Winner, "Do Artifacts have Politics?" *Daedalus* 109, no. 1 (Winter 1980): 121–136.

2 Two recent studies that explore the interweave between the technical and the political would be: Daniel Klingensmith, *'One Valley and a Thousand': Dams, Nationalism and Development* (New Delhi: Oxford University Press, 2007); and Christopher Sneddon, *Concrete Revolution: Large Dams, Cold War Geopolitics, and the US Bureau of Reclamation* (Chicago: University of Chicago Press, 2015). See also Timothy Mitchell, *Rule of Experts: Egypt, Techno-Politics, Modernity* (Berkeley: University of California, 2002), 19–53.

3 According to the World Commission on Dams, a large dam is defined as one that is 15 or more meters high, when measured from its foundation. A smaller dam, too, but with a reservoir volume of more than three million cubic meters can also be considered to be equivalent in terms of its impact to that of a large dam.

4 Patrick McCully, *Silenced Rivers: The Ecology and Politics of Large Dams* (London: Zed Books, 2001, 1996[1]), xxvi.

https://doi.org/10.1515/9783110730234-010

the costs. Could the costs from the forced displacement of communities, for example, be meaningfully compensated through rehabilitation efforts? Did existing methodologies to enumerate forest loss and damage to fisheries ably capture qualitative ecological loss? And, inevitably, could a cost-benefit ratio make a compelling case for constructing a dam?[5]

By the 1990s, intense popular critiques aimed at the official and expert claims about the quantitative and qualitative impacts of the large dam seemed headed for a decisive showdown. The need to effectively resolve what was clearly becoming an ever widening impasse — the benefits and costs conundrum — led to the organization of a workshop in April of 1997 in Switzerland by a slew of global organizations, comprising the International Union for the Conservation of Nature and Natural Resources (IUCN), the World Conservation Union (WCU), and the World Bank. The workshop not only included governments, funding bodies, and engineering companies but across the very same table were also invited several critical voices, who had, through the course of the 1990s, spearheaded some of the most dramatic resistance movements and stunning challenges to dam building projects. In effect, the meeting was aimed to set up a meaningful conversation between the two main protagonists of the large dam story: pro-dam lobbies and anti-dam campaigners. What followed from the vigorous debate between the various adherents of competing perspectives was the setting up of the World Commission on Dams (WCD). The newly instituted WCD, in the main, comprised 12 Commissioners whose role was to oversee and assess the evidence that was to be presented to them by representatives from civil society organizations, government, academia, and industry. These Commissioners, moreover, were to be assisted by a technical secretariat that was to be based in Cape Town (South Africa). While the exercise was chiefly expected to review the working of several large dams it also aimed to bake-in new standards and guidelines that could then re-set an altogether fresh direction for the beleaguered large dam industry. In November of 2000, the WCD finally released its much awaited findings as a report, blandly titled *Dams and Development*.

The *Dams and Development* report cut both ways and received bouquets and brickbats. While several called the entire exercise a sham for not being objective enough, there were many, on the other hand, who argued the opposite: that the WCD had made remarkable gains, specially by offering guidelines on risks and

5 On the emergence of cost-benefit analysis as a style and tool for countering political judgment see Theodore M. Porter, *Trust in Numbers: The Pursuit of Objectivity in Science and Public Life* (Princeton: Princeton University Press, 1995), 148–190.

rights and setting up protocols for participatory decision-making.[6] It was also pointed out that given how the representation and diverse interests were stacked within the WCD process, it was but inevitable that the effort had to aim for a draw, by, at best, offering a credible summary of the arguments made by the pro and anti-dam groupings. Nonetheless, even though the WCD failed to generate a consensus on dam building, it did produce the possibility, intended or otherwise, for debating dams afresh with different criteria: notably, the good dam in contrast to the bad dam. While the good dam meaningfully addressed social and environmental costs, by advancing development goals, the bad dam caused the reverse: leaving people and places worse off after the completion of the project. The WCD exercise, in effect, offered fresh grounds for revisiting the large dam debate by calling attention to actual outcomes and urging for a closer scrutiny of the technical challenges, even as it failed to close the divide between the enthusiasts and the skeptics. Moreover, by collating, authenticating, and summing up the vast number of studies that were presented before the WCD, the large dam question was moved much beyond the previous singular emphasis on displacement and resettlement.

It is in keeping the backdrop of the WCD exercise in mind that this essay will rehearse and give context to two studies that were published in India. Both of these little heralded studies took up as their key theme a post-project review of one of the country's most celebrated and iconic multi-purpose river valley development project — the famed Bhakra-Nangal Project (BNP). These studies, as I will suggest, appeared novel for not only focusing on the "afterlife" of the BNP — the post-project scrutiny of promise, performance, and outcomes — but, critically as well, the authors reconsidered the BNP project without necessarily sharing the earlier exuberance nor the unquestioning belief that dams brought about development. In several ways, the studies of Shripad Dharmadhikary and R. Rangachari, published in 2005 and 2006 respectively, argued for a perceptible shift within the large dam discourse in India. Unlike the previous focus on evaluating the dam within the anti-versus-pro viewpoints, the post-construction outcomes of the BNP was assessed instead within the WCD inspired good versus bad dam frameworks.

6 For a comprehensive discussion on the various interpretations of the WCD report see Christopher Schulz and William M. Adams, "Debating dams: The World Commission on Dams 20 years on," *WIREs Water* (2019): 1–19.

Re-situating the BNP

The construction of the BNP was completed in 1963, within the opening decades of India's independence from British colonial rule in 1947. Planned and designed as a multi-purpose river valley project, the BNP comprised several dams, barrages, a vast canal network, and hydro-electric power houses. Added to this were equally complicated arrangements to carry out inter-basin water transfers. The centerpiece of the whole project, however, was undoubtedly the imposing 740 feet high Bhakra dam that was built across the Sutlej river, one amongst five of the huge watery arms of the sprawling Indus river system.

Though Prime Minister Nehru (1950 – 1964) visited the BNP on several occasions, two speeches given during ceremonies at the site proved to be particularly telling of how India's post-colonial leadership sought to convey the significance of the large dam. Besides inserting dam construction within the grand quests for progress and development, Nehru also purposefully sought to evoke a kind of secular religiosity around the BNP. At the opening of the Nangal canal in 1954, he likened the project to being but the "biggest temple and mosque and gurdwara" that furthermore had turned "holier" after thousands of men had "shed their blood and sweat and laid down their lives as well."[7] At Bhakra, during the dedication ceremony in 1963, Nehru chose to, once again, evocatively reiterate that the dam was the "temple, mosque and gurudwara of modern India."[8] The large dam, thus, in postcolonial India was not only woven into themes about nation-making but was also assiduously overlain with political and spiritual capital. For the historian Daniel Klingensmith, however, in this early phase of India's decolonization, rather than "dams granting legitimacy to the state, the state had to work to legitimize them."[9] That is, as a form of "spectacular development," dams, Klingensmith argues, mostly appealed to the "professional, urban middle classes" and their views about nation making rather than to the vast underclass of "peasants, tribals and workers."[10] Clearly, the imagery surrounding the BNP was shaped as much by discourses about nation-making, generating legitimacy for the post-colonial Indian state and feeding into the

---

7 Jawaharlal Nehru, "Temple of the New Age," July 3, 1954 in *Jawaharlal Nehru Speeches, vol 3. (March 1953-August 1957)*, pub. Ministry of Information and Broadcasting (Calcutta: The Publication Division, GOI, Sree Saraswaty Press, n.d.), 1 – 4. Translated from Hindi.

8 Madhavan K. Palat, ed., *Selected Works of Jawaharlal Nehru, Second Series 83 [1st August-31st October 1963]* (New Delhi: Jawaharlal Nehru Memorial Fund, 2019), 484 – 485. Translated from Hindi.

9 Klingensmith, *'One Valley and a Thousand'*, 255.

10 Klingensmith, *'One Valley and a Thousand'*, 271.

developmental expectations of the urban middle classes, than as being exclusively devoted to celebrating benefits such as hydro-electricity, irrigation, and flood control. The plot, in other words, was meant to be an elaborate one with the BNP aiming at weaving heroic engineering into the making of a post-colonial nationalism that in turn rested on claims for the acquisition of material and productive capacity.

The studies by Dharmadhikary and Rangachari, on the other hand, take stock of the BNP essentially only in terms of its performance as a technical artefact, perhaps driven by the belief that the only the technical could be coldly and objectively calculated. Nonetheless, the BNP as a political object haunts their analyses and assessments. Though again, it must be underlined that Dharmadhikary and Rangachari approach the question of politics and power with starkly dissimilar perspectives, linked not so much by their educational training as by the attitudinal chasm that usually runs between an activist and a technocrat.

Educated with a BE in civil engineering, Rangachari achieved considerable standing as a technocrat and remained widely engaged with the world of policy making. In the course of his long professional career, he served as a member of the Central Water Commission – the Indian government's premier technical organization for harnessing water – and as additional secretary in the Ministry of Water Resources of the Government of India. Dharmadhikary, despite having trained as a mechanical engineer at the prestigious Indian Institute of Technology (Bombay), decided to pursue an unconventional path involving activism and community mobilisation. Over the years, Dharmadhikary has not only been part of a number of popular campaigns and movements but has also been actively contributing to various policy initiatives, including being associated with the WCD and becoming the founder coordinator of a research group called the *Manthan Adhyayan Kendra*, which takes up water and energy challenges in India. Clearly, different world views have shaped and informed the novel studies of Dharmadhikary and Rangachari, borne, in the main, by their contrasting professional commitments and ideological moorings.

Large Dams as Technical Artefacts

Rangachari in a somewhat plainly titled book *Bhakra-Nangal Project: Socio-economic and Environmental Impacts* sets out to evaluate the BNP by taking stock of the project's "positive and negative social, economic and environmental consequences."[11] The effort is neatly lined up like a chartered accountant's balance sheet. On the one hand, the costs: project displacement, waterlogging, salinity, and sedimentation of the reservoir. Juxtaposed to which in an even handed manner are the benefits: irrigation, agricultural productivity, flood mitigation, and hydro-power.[12] The strong, but not stated, assumption is that the BNP can be assessed by a simple tabulation of its measurable impacts. That is, there exists quantifiable "facts" that can convincingly help declare a result through an ex-post project Benefit-Cost (BC) ratio.

To give traction to such a claim, however, requires the equally strong claim that natural substances, though embedded in a plethora of ecological relationships, can nonetheless be meaningfully calculated as discrete units of economic value. That is, an entire world of ecological complexity made up of immense biological variability can be rendered into simple mathematically precise measures and legible economic values. Second, once these economic values are established as costs, they can then be contrasted, almost unequivocally, against another set of economic values such as benefits like irrigation. Thus, ecologies, people or cultures can be transformed into commensurable, substitutable, exchangeable, and equivalent economic values that are open to being repeatedly subtracted and added across time and space.

In other words, as pointed out by critiques of the BC format, nature and people must first suffer a comprehensive loss of quality in order to be then resurrected as plain numbers.[13] It is only through such kinds of conceptual violence involving abstraction and quantification that, for example, forests in a reservoir's submergence zone can be mathematically "compensated" and thereby presumed to have been equalized through an afforestation effort elsewhere. This submerged forest of numbers, therefore, is not treated as a collection of historically arrived biotic and faunal relationships but simply as a given sum of trees. The ledger book on forest cover, consequently, can be made to appear as a simple collation of numbers that can be neatly divided for comprehension –

11 R. Rangachari, *Bhakra-Nangal Project: Socio-Economic and Environmental Impacts* (New Delhi: Oxford University Press, 2006), 7.

12 The Benefit-Cost ratio is a measure of return to investment for every unit of capital invested over the lifecycle of the project. The desired BC ration in India requires that the value of the benefits over the project's lifecycle should exceed the costs of its inputs.

13 For an excellent critique of the neo-classical problem with valuing "non-economic" goods such as environmental relationships and the limitations of the Benefit-Cost-exercise see John Foster, ed., *Valuing Nature: Economics, Ethics and Environment* (London: Routledge, 1997). In particular, see the essays by Robin Grove-White, John O'Neil, and John Foster in the volume.

as a subtraction (trees in the submergence zone) on one side of the balance sheet and as an addition (a plantation of trees) on the other.[14]

Such a BC maneuver also presumes that one can cleanly or credibly transform ecological time into exact units of economic time. That is, all the costs and benefits are accounted for only within the time frame of the dam's estimated lifecycle. Thus, any long term ecological consequences that could follow when the large dam's services (irrigation, hydro-electricity or navigation) terminate will not be treated as part of the immediate calculation. In other words, to assess the performance of a large dam, economic quantification must trump ecological process. The exercise of the "quantifying spirit" that bends natural time to economic time, in fact, becomes crucial to determining how technical efficiency is measured.[15]

Interestingly, Rangachari attempts to sustain his untroubled embrace of the BC format, despite the latter's proven inadequacies. Satyajit Singh, in one of the earliest analyses of large dams impacts in India, concluded that the BC ratio has inevitably proven to be a "tricky" operation and as a style for crunching numbers tended to be open to various kinds of manipulations, notably in the manner in which data and methods could often be generated to show reduced costs, while padding upwards the presumed benefits.[16] The BC ratio's inadequacies in capturing ecological complexity have also been described in a slew of monographs on large dam water projects in India, in particular in the works of Ranjit Dwivedi and Radha D'Souza. Dwivedi, in his exhaustive treatment of the contentious Sardar Sarovar Project (SSP) in India, records how varying outcomes were derived from different BC exercises.[17] He points out, in particular, that the BC ratio

---

14 See the excellent discussion by Ravi Rajan on the emergence of what he describes as modern or continental forestry, which was a mix of Cameralist science and economic reasoning. Traceable as far back as the eighteenth century in Europe, Rajan shows how German and French forestry practices aimed at quantifying forests in order to meet the insatiable demands for timber by the State. Quantification helped makes forests legible to government officials who could set various quotas for extraction. See Ravi Rajan, *Modernizing Nature: Forestry and Imperial Eco-Development 1800–1950* (New York: Oxford University Press, 2006). Also see James C. Scott, *Seeing like a State: How Certain Schemes to Improve the Human Condition have Failed* (New Haven: Yale University Press, 1998), 262–306.

15 See Svante Lindqvist, "Labs in the Woods: The Quantification of Technology During the Late Enlightenment," in *The Quantifying Spirit in the 18th Century*, ed. Tore Frangsmyer, J.L. Heilbron, and Robin E. Rider (Berkeley: University of California Press, 1990), 291–314.

16 Satyajit Singh, *Taming the Waters: The Political Economy of Large Dams in India* (New Delhi: Oxford University Press, 1997), 67–76.

17 The agencies that carried out the BC for the SSP were the Narmada Planning Group (1983); Tata Economic Consultancy Services (1983); World Bank (1985); SSP Narmada Nigam ltd (1989);

ended up being deployed principally to legitimize the project rather than as a method for objective appraisal. The intense social conflicts that subsequently dogged the SSP, according to Dwivedi, were largely brought on by the fact that the project's BC ratio was constantly modified by political concessions, even as developing criterion for meaningfully estimating costs repeatedly eluded the project planners.[18]

Radha D'Souza's study on the interstate disputes on the Krishna river goes a step further in pointing out how attempts to quantify hydraulic data by the Krishna Water Disputes Tribunal (KWDT) were compromised by the fact that there was a genuine absence of reliable time-series measurements on flows in the Krishna river. Critically as well, there were sharply differing spatio-temporal scales in the reading of the river's hydrological behavior: between a geomorphological scale (river runoff and dependable flow), on the one hand, and a limited engineering scale (stream-flow), on the other. Inevitably the selection of the data sets by the KWDT, D'Souza argues, were made as choices borne from political pragmatism rather than from any pretension to scientific judgement.[19] In several ways, these studies overwhelmingly establish that the BC ratio is a type of political arithmetic.[20]

Added to the substantial criticisms discussed above, many of Rangachari's other confidently stated arguments are similarly troubled as well. Most notably in the manner in which he paints the "pre-project scene" of the submergence and the command areas of the BNP, respectively. Undeterred by his own admission that baseline information was not collected at the time of the decision to build the BNP, Rangachari chooses to confidently describe what he perceives to be the "social, cultural, environmental and economic scene that existed both in the catchment and reservoir zone upstream as also the benefited region downstream."[21] The picture he paints is one typical of the standard development narrative that is based on notions about deficits. The downstream zone — comprising what is now South-West Punjab, parts of north-west Haryana, and a small portion of areas in Rajasthan — is sweepingly described as having been, in the none too recent past, landscapes of drought, famine, and peopled by vic-

---

and by the World Bank again in 1990. See Ranjit Dwivedi, *Conflict and Collective Action: The Sardar Sarovar Project in India* (London: Routledge, 2006), 102.

18 Dwivedi, *Conflict and Collective Action*, 99–141.

19 Radha D'Souza, *Interstates Disputes Over Krishna Waters: Law, Science and Imperialism* (Hyderabad: Orient Longman, 2006), 215–235, 433–462.

20 Porter, *Trust in Numbers*, 148–189.

21 Rangachari, *Bhakra-Nangal Project*, 38–55.

tims of recurring flood devastation.[22] In other words, these areas, prior to the BNP, are declared as zones repeatedly wounded by forces of nature and inhabited by populations that were caught in various gradients of naturalized impoverishment.

What is inevitably conveyed in such a superficial and limited description is that the entire region can be defined as one that lacks the messiness of history. Thus, by an almost hop-jump-skip reading of a few nineteenth-century British District Gazetteers and one Famine Commission Report (1860–1861), much of the areas lying within and adjacent to the sprawling *doabs* (flood plains) of the *Sutlej-Beas*, for Rangachari, appear as a mere development deficit, a claim that ignores the manner in which these *doabs* had, across centuries, been harnessed by a range of pastoral groups, subsistence cultivation, cattle rearing, and by thick trading networks that supported many a powerful empire.[23]

Furthermore, critically missing in Rangachari's ahistorical view is the well recorded account of the dramatic transformations that had occurred in the regions through the course of the long nineteenth century: a period in which colonial policies led to the elimination of most cattle rearing "wandering tribes," the relentless conversion of once forested tracts and grasslands into mono-cropped commercial wheat fields through perennial irrigation, the emergence of waterlogging, salinity and malaria, and the oppressive exploitation of settled agriculturalists by colonial revenue strategies. In fact, the transformation of the region's ecology and social worlds was driven, in the main, by colonial attempts to "model the hydraulic environment," through barrages, weirs, and canals. These British initiatives were relentlessly aimed at transforming the Punjab's once variegated social and ecological flood plains into an administratively simplified settled agrarian tract.[24]

Rangachari's elision of the region's colonial imprint, however, should not be treated as a simple omission of detail. Two discursive pretensions are in actuality

---

22 Recent histories have challenged the claim that the downstream zone was famine – prone and a near uninhabitable desert. See David Gilmartin, *Blood and Water: The Indus River Basin in Modern History* (Oakland: University of California Press, 2015) and Daniel Haines, *Rivers Divided: Indus Basin Waters in the Making of India and Pakistan* (New York: Oxford University Press, 2016).

23 Also see Chetan Singh, *Region and Empire: Panjab in the Seventeenth Century* (New Delhi: Oxford University Press, 1991); Indu Agnihotri, "Ecology, Land use and Colonisation: The Canal Colonies of Punjab," *Indian Economic and Social History Review* 33, no. 1 (1996): 37–58; Neeladhari Bhattacharya, "Pastorialist in a Colonial World," in *Nature, Culture, Imperialism: Essays on the Environmental History of South Asia*, ed. David Arnold and Ramachandra Guha (New Delhi: Oxford University Press, 1996), 49–68.

24 Gilmartin, *Blood and Water*, 144–181.

involved in creating such a politics for forgetting. First is the attempt to present the BNP as a technological complex that is to be judged and assessed only by the disinterested expert. The "facts" and "data" are thus not to be distracted by the complications of politics, history, and the play of power. Once purged of such variables involving social power and historical contingency, the problems besetting the BNP can be reduced to being issues of oversight or technical misjudgement. Thus, for example, the multi-layered dilemmas brought on by displacement and rehabilitation are to be sanitised instead as challenges for reforming bad practice rather than as debates over what Pablo Kala describes as "erasure" – the processes whereby subsistence and traditional lifestyles are transformed (erased) and replaced by market-based life worlds.[25] For the sociologist Alf Nilsen, dam induced displacement in post-independent India, however, is conceptually more akin to being a form of "accumulation by dispossession," a notion that he draws from the Marxist geographer David Harvey who aimed to explain how development projects often brought about the unequal distribution of costs and benefits. That is the dispossession of the vulnerable and marginal communities from their subsistence means development projects often resulted in the further concentration of resources amongst "regional, national and global propertied elites."[26] In sum, displacement was not merely a technical or logistical challenge but spoke to messy issues of power and injustice.

Clearly, only by lopping off the deeper political and historical roots of the BNP could the latter be inserted into a narrative about national development. That is, only as a neutral "object of development" could the BNP be located within the singular quest for national productivity, efficiency, economic growth, and thereby inscribed into a spatio-temporal scale for nation-building. The impacts of the BNP are, therefore, tabulated as quantifiable deliverables: a) supply of electric power to the national grid; b) as a statistical increase in total canal irrigation; c) a means for augmenting national agricultural production; and d) a source for adding to the other innumerable intangibles that make up the national economy. In such a script, the impacts of the BNP becomes a truly displaced object without locality or environmental context and can be measured only within an overall balance sheet of nation-making.[27] The Sutlej river, in other words,

25 See Pablo Kala, "In the Spaces of Erasure: Globalisation, Resistance and Narmada River," *Economic and Political Weekly* 36, no. 22 (2001): 1991–2002.

26 Also see Alf Gunvald Nilsen, *Dispossession and Resistance in India: The River and the Rage* (New Delhi: AAKAR Books, 2013), 20.

27 See the celebratory account on dam building in India by Henry C. Hart, *New India Rivers* (Bombay: Orient Longman, 1956). In what was typical of the enthusiasm for large dams in

now truly belongs to the nation and not to a complex fluvial ecosystem nor to the histories of the communities that previously lived by it and alongside it. For nation-building, in other words, people and their ecologies suffer an encompassing loss of place, just as their realities are now increasingly expressed as abstract statistics and within averages. [28]

Having set the study within such apolitical and ahistorical frames, Rangachari then concludes that the BNP has more than matched its expectations. On the question of canal irrigation, we are informed that from the opening of the Nangal works in 1954 till 1984/85, the irrigated zone touched around 3.506 million hectares (Sirhind canal included).[29] The "progressive farmers" in the irrigated tracts, moreover, he surmises, proved to be prompt in managing to adjust their cropping patterns in "tune with profitability and market forces." In the subsequent two chapters, Rangachari goes on to list what he considers to be the manifold gains from increased productivity in wheat and rice, that furthermore amplified the successes of the Green Revolution agricultural strategies in Punjab and Haryana. The inevitable conclusion being that not only did the BNP irrigation network dramatically raise food grain production in India but "yielded significant social and economic benefits without experiencing any unacceptable environmental costs."[30] Added to this story of agrarian success was also the less heralded contribution of hydroelectric power, generated by two power plants at the Bhakra dam. In this estimate, the BNP generated 211 billion kWh (Kilo-Watt Hour) between 1955/56 and 1999/2000 and continues to produce 7000 kWh each year, and lastly, the "incidental benefit" of managing floods,

---

that period, Hart writes his account of river valley development as being integral to the economic biography and political identity of "New India."

28 The tensions between space and place have been vigorously debated by geographers. In his classic on the differences between space and place, the geographer Yi-Fu Tuan broadly suggests that a relationship space is more abstract than place, while the latter is saturated by experience. In such a rendering, it would be critical to understand how a sense of cultural loss might impact displaced communities. See Yi-Fu Tuan, *Space and Place: The Perspective of Experience* (Minneapolis: University of Minnesota Press, 1977). See also the notion of place in Doreen Massey, *For Space* (London: Sage Publications, 2005), 130–142.

29 The figure is quoted from a publication of the Bhakra Beas Management Board, *History of the Bhakra Nangal Project*, 1988. See Rangachari, *Bhakra-Nangal Project*, 89. It is interesting that he should refer to a 1988 BBMB report as the latest information in his book that is published in 2006.

30 Rangachari, *Bhakra-Nangal Project*, 121.

which the BNP reservoir was able to moderate and mitigate in the four decades of its operation.[31]

While Rangachari asserts the above by mainly restating and collating statistically determined quantitative data, he, nonetheless, retains enough caution to alert us at the outset of the book itself that "there has been little systematic collection of relevant data about dam projects in the past" and therefore any "definite conclusions on their performance and impacts are difficult."[32] Hence, he ends with the reminder that there have been, thus far, no "credible" post-project evaluations by any independent professional agency of multi-purpose river valley development projects in India. In effect, data about dams, as Arundhati Roy eloquently observes, may hide more than they reveal, or worse such objective facts do not meaningfully exist.[33]

Are Large Dams Just Politics by Other Means?

Shripad Dharmadhikary, in *Unravelling Bhakra*, anchors his study of the BNP in a particular historical, ecological, and political setting rather than treating the project as a free floating signifier for development.[34] This allows Dharmadhikary to disclose the BNP not merely as a technological complex but, more incisively, as a distinct economic and political moment in post-independent India. The impacts of the BNP are thus essentially treated as fallouts from the larger play of political economy: attempts to industrialize river control; the appropriation of water for assembling forms of social and political domination; and above all else the trying political efforts to transform fluvial flows into national resources.[35] The version of "national development" that the BNP was meant to inaugurate, Dharmadhikary suggests, ended up producing project beneficiaries by creating project victims. Put differently, large dams can be understood as embodying a collection of several win-lose scenarios. And yet, despite arguing that the BNP is a political object, Dharmadhikary remains keen, nonetheless,

---

31 Flood control are not benefits that can be easily claimed. Floods in the Indian subcontinent, in fact, have often been welcomed and treated as being critical to sustaining river health. See Rohan D'Souza, "Event, Process and Pulse: Resituating Floods in Environmental Histories of South Asia," in *Environment and History* 26 (2020): 31–49.

32 D'Souza, "Event, Process and Pulse," 5.

33 Arundhati Roy, *The Cost of Living* (London: Flamingo, Harper Collins, 1999), 18–23.

34 Shripad Dharmadhikary, *Unravelling Bhakra: Assessing the Temple of Resurgent India* (Badwani: Manthan, 2005).

35 This seems to be the tenor of the argument in Singh, *Taming the Waters.*

to underline that large dams are more meaningfully analyzed as technical artefacts.

Dharmadhikary begins with the startling claim that the plans for the BNP arose not from the conventional desire to irrigate semi-arid or drought stricken lands. Instead several festering interstate water disputes between the provinces of Sind and the Punjab in British India actually provide the backdrop. In the post-1947 period these very same provincial skirmishes, in fact, went on to transmute into an international level discord, often referred to as the India-Pakistan conflict over the Indus system.[36] That is, a regional fracas over hydraulic access and rights in the colonial period got transformed in the post-colonial years into a bitter complication over the need to establish the national ownership of the Indus river system. For the newly independent Indian government, commanding the Sutlej as an Indian river meant damming it in order to prevent its flows turning into "wastes" as soon as the waters crossed into Pakistan. At the heart of the project proposal was the aim to create a new Cultivable Command Area (CCA) within Indian territory that would irrigate 2.37 million hectares (mha). This addition, however, Dharmadhikary points out, could be made possible only by cutting off the existing irrigation supplies of 2.21 mha of the CCA of the Sutlej Valley Project that were until then still irrigating lands in Pakistan.[37] In other words, the BNP was essentially about effecting a water transfer, whereby the irrigation benefits in India were going to be matched in almost equal measure by irrigation losses suffered within Pakistan.

As to whether the BNP was decisive in irrigating and powering (through hydroelectricity) the Green Revolution strategy in Punjab and Haryana, *Unravelling Bhakra* argues for severely qualifying such claims. After wading through the often conflicting numbers from government statistical abstracts and publications, there seems to be no "self-evident" case for suggesting that the canal irrigation boost that the BNP ostensibly supplied proved singular in turning Punjab and Haryana into the bread basket of India. Similarly, there are arguments for questioning the other equally enthusiastic claims about the BNP's contribution to hydro-power. In order to lend perspective to the Central Electricity Board's stated data that the BNP produced a total of 6500 MU (Million Units) of power

---

36 Dharmadhikary, *Unravelling Bhakra*, 15–33. Also see Arthur Aloys Michel, *The Indus Rivers: A Study of the Effects of Partition* (New Haven: Yale University Press, 1967), and the recent revisionist study of the Indus Water treaty in Haines, *Rivers Divided.* See also Rohan D'Souza, "Towards an Environmental History of the Indus Water Treaty," in *Ideas, Institutions, Processes: Essays in Memory of Satish Saberwal*, ed. N. Jayaram (Hyderabad: Orient Black Swan, 2014), 157–170.

37 Dharmadhikary, *Unravelling Bhakra*, 24, 29.

a year, Dharmadhikary gives context to this electricity output by linking it to tubewell use in Punjab and Haryana. In 1990/1991, the number of tubewells in use stood at roughly 497,571 for Haryana and 800,000 for Punjab respectively; and upon comparing the electricity requirement for this grand total of 1,297,571 functioning tubewells, the BNP's contribution would be able to meet barely 28 % of the demand.[38] In effect, 72% of all the tubewells in the grain belt would still have to be run either on diesel or with power generated from other sources.

Having thus argued that the BNP cannot be unequivocally celebrated, *Unravelling Bhakra* presents us gripping account of the real costs or hidden debits. On the question of waterlogging and salinization, there is the challenge of making sense of huge uncertainties in the type of existing data, as statistics are compiled at the state level and not at the project level. However, despite the slippery nature of the existing numbers and the fact that the last report of any worth on the subject was compiled and published in 1991 (Government of India Working Group), only tentative figures could be advanced for soils affected by waterlogging, salinity, and alkalinity in the BNP's command area: an approximate of 49.168 thousand hectares for Haryana and about 200 thousand hectares for Punjab. Given this yawning gap in credible data, Dharmadhikary takes up the next best option by making qualitative assessments with field visits to *Badopal*, *Lambakhedi*, and *Lohgarh* villages (Haryana) and *Malout* Town (Punjab). Here the picture that is presented is one of wasted soils, crumbling houses, dead trees, stagnant pools of water, sinking roads, and rising salinity levels in what were previously fairly prosperous zones.

Such undocumented and unacknowledged post-project impacts, Dharmadhikary contends, have simply escaped the statistical record and do forcefully suggest that all may not be right in the way the benefits and costs have been tabulated. In a similar vein, the displacement and rehabilitation of the BNP's project affected remains a story that is yet to be meaningfully told. Officially, the estimate is that 17.876 thousand hectares of land were submerged with approximately 36,000 persons being displaced from 371 villages. On the other hand, the full details of their suffering — forced dispossession, loss of livelihoods, and the sundering of their historical linkages with landscape and identity — Dharmadhikary opines have entirely escaped any systematic survey or careful study. To, consequently, even list the project affected of the BNP as mere costs might be inadequate, if not unjust, in taking stock of the complex and layered emotional and

38 Dharmadhikary, *Unravelling Bhakra*, 123.

economic sufferings that the project displaced might have undergone in the name of development. [39]

On the question of the BNP's contributions to agricultural growth through irrigation, Dharmadhikary provocatively argues that the impacts of the canals were far less spectacular than claimed.[40] Conventional wisdom holds that the BNP made significant contributions towards enabling India's Green Revolution (GR). The GR package was aimed at boosting agricultural output by getting controlled irrigation to supplement a mix of chemical fertilizers, high-yielding seed varieties, mechanization, and the consolidation of land ownership. This GR format, furthermore, was soaked in ideologies of national self-reliance, national development, and nation-building.[41] Whilst, undoubtedly, the output of wheat-paddy did witness a steep rise, for Dharmadhikary, this sudden spurt was not without huge shifts in cropping patterns and social changes. He draws our attention to the following:

> In Punjab, in 1965–66, wheat occupied 39% of the cultivated area, gram 15%, maize 10%, and rice 7%. By 1990–91, wheat area was 44%, gram 1%, maize 2% and rice 27% [...]. In 2002, wheat–rice took up 78% of the total cropped area of Punjab.
>
> In Haryana too, the case is similar, though less acute. In 1966–67, wheat occupied 18% of the total cropped area, gram 26%, bajra [*Pennisetum glaucum*, Pearl Millet] 22%, rice 5%. In 1990–91, this was 36% for wheat, 13% for gram, 12% for bajra, 13% for rice. In 1998–99, wheat and rice accounted for 57% of total cropped area.[42]

The BNP, in Dharmadhikary's analysis, thus, seems to have set in motion a broader agrarian dynamic within the flood plains of Punjab and Haryana that,

---

39 Jean Dreze, Meera Samson, and Satyajit Singh, eds., *The Dam & the Nation: Displacement and Resettlement in the Narmada Valley* (Calcutta: Oxford University Press, 1997).

40 In a recent attempt to revise the accepted understanding of India's Green Revolution, a thesis submitted to the history department at King's college by Kapil Subramanian suggests that the GR was actually brought about by a ground water revolution and not, as popularly claimed, by the introduction of new hybrid seeds. See Kapil Subramanian, "Revisiting the Green Revolution Irrigation and Food Production in Twentieth-Century India" (Ph.D. diss., King's College London, 2015).

41 Two insightful books on the ideological underpinning of the Green Revolution as a techno-science project would be Akhil Gupta, *Postcolonial Developments: Agriculture in the Making of Modern India* (Durham: Duke University Press, 1998), and Jack Ralph Kloppenburg, *First the Seed: The Political Economy of Plant Biotechnology* (Madison: University of Wisconsin Press, 2004[2]). On the origins of the Green Revolution ideology and how it was linked to political attempts to "naturalize" poverty see Eric Ross, *The Malthus Factor: Poverty, Politics and Population in Capitalist Development* (London: Zed Books, 1998), 137–199.

42 Dharmadhikary, *Unravelling Bhakra*, 160.

in essence, comprised the intensification of mono-cropping and the locking of soils into a limited wheat-rice regime.[43] That is, acreage under wheat-rice cropping was made to steadily expand into lands that previously grew a range of mixed crops such as legumes (gram, *Cicer arietinum*) and cereals (bajra, *Pennisetum glaucum*, and maize, *Zea mays*). The dams and barrages as irrigation infrastructures, in effect, ended up ecologically simplifying an otherwise mixed cropping landscape.

Within the curve of the same reasoning, Dharmadhikary goes on to then contest the reigning belief that the BNP was singularly responsible for turning the states of Punjab and Haryana into India's wheat and rice granaries. Or as he puts it, the unquestioning claim that "Punjab = Bhakra (and to a lesser extent Haryana = Bhakra)."[44] His granular study of irrigation data in being specially attentive to aspects such as canal seepage helps him arrive at the conclusion that for the state of Punjab a full 71.8% of its agricultural production actually depends on the "ground water irrigated areas," whilst for Haryana the estimate would be 47.58%.[45] Further, by extrapolating from such calculations, the BNP's canals system as a specific irrigation input, it appears, adds up to or contributes only to a mere 11% for Punjab and about 24% for Haryana of their total agricultural output.[46] For Dharmadhikary, thus, a scrutiny of the available statistics, the official claims, and a considered look at the iconic and mythical status of the BNP strongly suggests that a mere tabulation of the costs and benefits would not meaningfully be able to capture the complexity of the ecological, social, political, and economic impacts.

Dams as "Asset Class"

In reviewing the studies of Rangachari and Dharmadhikary, this essay might appear to be merely fleshing out how a technocrat and an activist have respectively differed over the large dam question in India. While the technocrat concentrates on evaluating the technical performance of the project, the activist, in contrast, situates the project within the larger complications of political economy. It is not

43 For an excellent review of the new revisionist writings on the Green Revolution in India see Glenn Davis Stone, "Commentary: New histories of the Indian Green Revolution," *The Geographical Journal* 185, no. 2 (2019): 243–250. Also see Richa Kumar, "India's Green Revolution and Beyond," *Economic and Political Weekly*, 54, no. 34 (2019): 41–48.

44 Dharmadhikary, *Unravelling Bhakra*, 229.

45 Dharmadhikary, *Unravelling Bhakra*, 119.

46 Dharmadhikary, *Unravelling Bhakra*, 125.

hard to conclude that such distinct frameworks can easily result in a situation where the contending parties might be speaking across rather than to each other. What, however, makes these studies novel is their efforts at setting the conceptual grounds for a post project evaluation of the BNP within the overall context of the WCD exercise, which, as indicated earlier, sought to break the deadlock between the pro-dam and anti-dam groupings. Though Rangachari and Dharmadhikary do mostly stick to their respective scripts, as technocrat and activist respectively, they, nonetheless, also credibly make the case for scrutinizing large dams in terms of their already realized outcomes.

The clinching persuasion of the BNP, for Rangachari, lay in the project's ability to deliver on a huge number of unstated indirect and incidental benefits such as the purported immunity from famines, poverty alleviation, and industrial development. Dharmadhikary, in contrast, flags several types of mismatches between the project's stated claims and what has been delivered. In particular, arguing that it was ground water extraction rather than surface water through the canal network that actually enabled and spurred irrigation in the BNP's command areas. Though the studies retain a sharp distinction between the technical artefact and the political object in their analyses, they both do imply, inadvertently or otherwise, that a meaningful dialogue over the BNP and large dams in general is possible if we can somehow meaningfully measure, count, and debate the benefits and costs. Put differently, Rangachari and Dharmadhikary are migrating the large dam debate in India from the previous anti-versus-pro dam framework to the WCD template that sought to distinguish between the good dam and the bad dam.

On the other hand, if a common conceptual ground does indeed exist between the activist and the technocrat, how should the political speak to the technical? In this regard, Sanjeev Khagram helpfully weighs in by exploring the links and implications between dams and democracy in India. In the initial years, according to him, the ruling dispensation in India energetically pursued and heroically constructed large dam projects as part of a "top-down, state-led, economic-growth focused and technocratic development vision."[47] Popular anti-dams struggles, however, soon broke out and by the 1980s "practically every big dam across India was facing some sort of organized resistance."[48] From the latter half of the 1990s, the muscular opposition to large dams, interestingly enough, steadily began waning and showed signs of what Khagram describes as arising

---

47 Sanjeev Khagram, *Dams and Development: Transnational Struggles for Water and Power* (New Delhi: Oxford University Press, 2005, 2004[1]), 33.
48 Khagram, *Dams and Development*, 34.

from three steadily consolidating trends: a) better organization and mobilization by pro-dam actors; b) the deepening of the neo-liberal economic policies of privatization and liberalization in the Indian water sector; and c) the mobilization of marginalized groups such as tribal, lower castes, and subsistence peasants by Hindu fundamentalist religious movements and growing political repression.[49]

Popular agitations and resistance to large dams in India, in fact, continued to decline throughout the opening decades of the twenty first century, even as a number of inter-basin water transfers, irrigation and hydroelectric projects kept on being planned and even executed. According to the sociologist Amita Baviskar, this steady weakening in the otherwise robust popular challenge to large dams was largely a result of a sustained shift in tactics. Many of these erstwhile critics and campaigners, it is pointed out, tended to abandon calls for popular mobilization and agitations by opting instead to battle it out in courts, government committees and by getting involved in techno-managerial disputes. That is, for Baviskar, in India, there emerged a perceptible mood shift in which the technical domain seems to have trumped the field of mass politics and thereby turned the challenge against large dams into mostly becoming a scrimmage of sorts between experts.[50]

Oddly enough, despite the evident weakening of popular movements, dam induced social conflict and political tension are hardwired into the infrastructure of the large dam.[51] As aptly surmised by the historian Daniel Klingensmith, the sources for disquiet and potential resistance against large dams remains latent within how the engineered transfer of water from flowing rivers has been effected:

> Both proponents and critics of dams would acknowledge that dams necessarily create changes in uses of, and access to, rivers. This inevitably means a transfer of power over rivers as resources: away from local control and customary law, and to bureaucracies and state regulation, away from small agricultural producers and from users of common lands and to large producers and to owners of privatized property.[52]

Though the WCD report of 2000 made clear that building a "good dam" was incumbent on meaningfully addressing an exhaustive list of social and technical

---

49 Khagram, *Dams and Development*, 63.

50 Amita Baviskar, "Nation's Body, River's Pulse: Narratives of Anti-Dam Politics in India," *Thesis Eleven* 150, no. 1 (2019), 26 – 41.

51 Marcus Nusser, "Technological Hydroscapes in Asia: The Large Dams Debates Reconsidered," in *Large Dams in Asia: Contested Environments Between Technological Hydroscapes and Social Resistance*, ed. Marcus Nusser (Heidelberg: Springer, 2014), 1 – 14.

52 Klingensmith, *'One Valley and a Thousand'*, 13.

standards, this did little to dampen the spirits of governments and the dam building industry. If anything, close on the heels of the WCD report there followed the world over a renewed burst of interest in and funding for large dam construction. In part, a fresh quest for producing non-fossil fuel energy drove governments to address climate change mitigation through hydroelectric projects.[53] Accordingly, in one considered estimate, by 2014, a total of 3,700 hydropower dams with a capacity of more than one megawatt (MW) had either been planned (83%) or were actually already under construction (17%), with a large chunk of these projects being located in China, India, and Brazil. The aim was to rapidly step up global hydropower electricity capacity from 980 Gigawatts (GW) in 2011 to about 1,700 GW within the next 10 to 20 years.[54] While roughly 75% of these dams were listed under the category of small and medium (generating between 1 and 100 MW), the largest slice of producing up to 93% of hydroelectric power was to be generated by 847 mammoth-sized large dams, each of which could be expected to produce more than 100 MW. It should also be noted that of the 955 hydropower dams built after 2001, 81% of these projects were located in South America (427), closely followed by Asia (342). Most observers of the dam building industry, in fact, see a robust future for hydropower development in the emerging economies of Southeast Asia, South America, and Africa.[55] In sum, despite all the caution and contrition of the WCD process, it appears that the twenty-first century will witness another fresh bout of damming.

In a landmark paper, social scientists Rhodante Ahlers, Margreet Zwarteveen, and Karen Bakker point to a significant conceptual departure within the large dam story by linking the recent enthusiasm for dam building to the emergence of a fresh set of calculations, forces, and measurements.[56] The first burst of large dam construction that occurred in the twentieth century, they underline, was chiefly driven by nation states, who aimed to achieve national economic development and undertook to build dams as public projects. Dams in this phase, for the authors, could be metaphorically likened to a "Trojan

53 Manju Menon and Kanchi Kohli, *Large Dams for Hydropower in Northeast India: A Dossier. South Asia Network on Dams, Rivers and People* (New Delhi: Kalpavriksh, 2005).
54 Christiane Zarfl et al., "A Global Boom in Hydropower Dam Construction," *Aquatic Sciences* 77 (2015): 161–170.
55 Peilei Fana et al., "Recently Constructed Hydropower Dams were Associated with Reduced Economic Production, Population, and Greenness in Nearby Areas," *PNAS* 119, no. 8 (2022): 1–11.
56 Rhodante Ahlers et al., "Large Dam Development: From Trojan Horse to Pandora's Box," in *The Oxford Handbook of Megaproject Management*, ed. Bent Flyvbjerg (Oxford: Oxford University Press, 2018), 1–25.

horse" – "embodying far more than instruments for water storage."[57] That is, the dams internalized the imperatives of the nation-state such as geo-politics, the political reordering of landscapes, monumental engineering, and the efforts in several cases for extending capitalist relations of production. In effect, the large dam of the twentieth century proved to be the "tangible material embodiment of political economic relations."[58]

Dam construction in the twenty-first century, on the other hand, for Rhodante et al., is marked by a defining role for private financial flows in infrastructural development, in which the latter is principally configured as an "asset class." The term asset class, as explained by Nicholas Hildyard, refers to the process of turning infrastructure into a financial platform: whereby private equity firms, banks, various types of financiers, and investors acquire stakes in the infrastructural project through loans, credits, and debt instruments.[59] Consequently, the complicated financial architecture of the project not only makes establishing the actual ownership of the dam obscure but, critically as well, it gets even harder to pin down responsibility. Rhodante et al., in fact, throw into sharp relief the example of the *Nam Theun 2* dam in Laos to highlight how the latter as an asset class created by a public-private consortium requires that the financial agreements and documents relating to the project be kept confidential in accordance with international and national law. Not only were critical details such as the dam's operating costs, debt liabilities, and water management priorities thus not subject to public scrutiny but, astoundingly as well, the consortium involved in building the dam was under absolutely no obligation whatsoever to share information with the public.[60] In effect, for Rhodante et al. the twenty-first century large dam as an asset class is best captured in the metaphor of the "Pandora's Box" – hidden complications and obscure internal arrangements.[61]

Conclusion

Clearly, frameworks to debate and discuss the modern large dam have been evolving over the years. The studies of Rangachari and Dharmadhikary, as I suggest in this essay, were striking efforts to reconsider how the impacts and contri-

57 Ahlers et al., "Large Dam Development," 9.
58 Ahlers et al., "Large Dam Development," 9.
59 Nicholas Hildyard, *More than Bricks and Mortar: Infrastructure as an Asset Class: A Critical Look at Private Equity Infrastructure Funds* (Manchester: Corner House Publications, 2012).
60 Ahlers et al., "Large Dam Development," 12.
61 Ahlers et al., "Large Dam Development," 11–14.

butions of large dams could be meaningfully assessed. Though their differing standpoints, as technocrat and activists respectively, focused on a post-project evaluation of actual outcomes of India's famed Bhakra-Nangal Project, their studies, at heart, aimed at engaging with the World Commission on Dams process. In short, instead of getting locked into the previous dead-end and increasingly circular arguments between the pro-versus-anti dam reasoning, Rangachari and Dharmadhikary sought to find conceptual grounds to evolve the notion of the good dam.

What, nonetheless, remains central and defining to their analysis of the BNP is what Rhodante et al. would metaphorically consider as a "Trojan Horse" — referring to the large dam of the twentieth century that embodied the political and economic relations of the nation state. While challenges against these dams did frequently erupt, especially following the brutal displacement of mostly subsistence and marginal communities, the twentieth-century dam could nonetheless be pried open for public scrutiny with its claims debated and often enough subject to democratic resistance. The internal arrangements of the Trojan Horse, in other words, could be revealed and resisted precisely because it fell into the realm of the nation making public project or the public good. On the other hand, the subsequent twenty-first-century dam or what Rhodante et al. refer to as being evocative of the Pandora's Box, however, not only severely limits access to public scrutiny but radically obscures aspects of ownership and responsibility. Put differently, the large dam of the twenty-first century, by being principally assembled as a financial platform, unlike a public good, can dodge and evade public accountability.

Given that another frenetic round of dam building has begun, especially in the continents of Asia and Africa, the twenty-first-century dam will not only further intensify ongoing debates over what constitutes a good dam but, critically as well, will increasingly foreground issues of financial transparency, public scrutiny, and democratic decision making.[62] At the heart of the issue, however, will remain the big and central question: can large dams be built through market efficiencies without meaningfully enabling public accountability?

62 For essays indicative of growing anxieties and dangers from large dam construction without regulatory oversight, see Kelly D. Alley et al., "Visualising Hydropower Across the Himalayas: Mapping in a Time of Regulatory Decline," *Himalaya, the Journal of the Association of Nepal and Himalayan Studies* 34, no. 2 (2014): 52–66. Also see Douglas P. Hill, "Transboundary Water Resources and Uneven Development: Crises In and Beyond Contemporary India," *South Asia: Journal of South Asian Studies* 36, no. 2 (2013): 243–257.

III Forum: Alternative Development Indices (ed. Iris Borowy and Corinna R. Unger)

Herman Daly

A Note on the Historical Origins of ISEW-GPI

The Index of Sustainable Economic Welfare (ISEW), which later evolved into the Genuine Progress Indicator (GPI), was first presented as an appendix to *For the Common Good* (1989).[1] It grew out of the dissatisfaction that many had long felt with the GNP, because the latter was designed to measure economic activity, not welfare, although it was frequently considered "the best measure of welfare that we have." Furthermore, even to the limited extent that it did measure welfare, there was nothing sustainable about the measure in that its growth required depletion of natural resources beyond renewable capacity.

In his classic *Economics of Welfare*, A.C. Pigou divided total welfare into economic welfare and non-economic welfare, thus:

Total Welfare = Economic Welfare + Non-Economic Welfare

The reason for Pigou's distinction was that economic welfare can meaningfully be measured by money, while non-economic welfare cannot meaningfully be measured by money.

However, to be numerically summed the two terms would require some common unit of measure. To add or subtract the two terms, either non-economic welfare must be shrunk and bent to fit the measuring rod of money, or economic welfare must be stretched into conformity with a more general unit of non-economic welfare, say "social utility." To escape this problem, as Abramowitz put it, echoing Pigou: "Economists have relied, however, on a practical judgment, namely, that a change in economic welfare implies a change in total welfare in the same direction if not in the same degree."[2]

If they move in the same direction, then economic welfare by itself is a "good enough" indicator of change in total welfare. This was more or less true in the empty world, but ceased to be true as the world became full and the economy pressed against containing ecosystem limits. The gain in economic welfare

1 Herman Daly and John Cobb, *For The Common Good: Redirecting the Economy Toward Community, the Environment, and a Sustainable Future* (Boston: Beacon Press, 1994^2, 1989^1).

2 Moses Abramovitz, "Economic Growth and its Discontents," in *Economics and Human Welfare: Essays in Honour of Tibor Scitovsky*, ed. Michael J. Boskin (New York: Academic Press, 1979), 3–22.

https://doi.org/10.1515/9783110730234-011

from growth can now easily be more than offset by a loss of non-economic welfare from natural ecosystem services provoked by the extra depletion and pollution of nature required by increased production, or by a deterioration in the moral quality of society induced by the widespread use of a meretricious new "good," or a dangerous new technology. In other words, reductions in economic welfare in an increasingly full world result from the increasing production of unmeasured "illth" as a joint product with measured wealth. Increases in illth must be measured and subtracted from increases in wealth. It is a matter of common sense that growth in the economy can become uneconomic in an inclusive welfare sense, but to show this precisely requires a common unit of measure.

In *For the Common Good* John Cobb and I followed mainly the non-monetary strategy of reasoning in terms of social utility, conceiving of *Homo economicus* as person-in-community rather than atomistic individual. We showed the shortcomings of GDP, and made the theoretical case that GDP growth could, and probably has, become uneconomic in the sense that it causes a loss of non-economic welfare that is greater at the margin than the gain in economic welfare (at least for rich countries). We were satisfied with the case we had made, and initially did not want to try to make the same case in monetary terms because the measuring rod of money is treacherous, with market prices reflecting only marginal utility (exchange values); they do not measure total utility, much less the welfare experienced by the person-in-community as opposed to atomistic individuals.

However, John's son, Clifford Cobb, a very helpful critic, argued that even so we should also attempt a money measure of welfare simply by adding a few neglected costs and benefits that could be expressed in money, and rearranging existing GNP sub-accounts to separate those that measured beneficial activity from those that measured regrettable or defensive activity made necessary by other production. We also made a correction for the increasing inequality in distribution (an extra dollar to the rich signified less welfare than an extra dollar to the poor, so we weighted it less). The net sum from these, and a few other reasonable adjustments, would then be a better (at least less arbitrary) monetary measure of total welfare than GNP. Since GNP was never intended as a measure of welfare, it was not hard to make a better measure, even if still far from perfect. We could then correlate our ISEW with real GNP and see how they tracked. It turned out that they were closely correlated up until around 1980 and then diverged significantly with GNP continuing to rise while ISEW became constant or slightly declining. We considered the result significant, and rather conservative in that the major component of both time series was the same, namely Personal Consumption. There was thus an autocorrelation bias making it statistically difficult for the two series to diverge. Yet they did diverge. Furthermore we had made no correction for the diminishing marginal utility of total income as it grew. We only corrected for marginal utility differences in distribution between rich and poor classes, not for differences over time resulting from growth of total income of both classes.

We were encouraged in our efforts by the fact that Nordhaus and Tobin had earlier made a similar effort.[3] They devised an index, Measured Economic Welfare (MEW), and had correlated their MEW with GNP and found a significant positive correlation over an extended time period. They used that to conclude that GNP was a "good enough" measure of welfare, and therefore MEW was not needed. However, Clifford divided their time series (1925–1965) in half and showed that in the more recent and more relevant half (1947–1965) the correlation was much lower. So GNP was becoming less correlated to MEW over time. And, in addition, we felt that our ISEW was a better index of welfare than Nordhaus-Tobin's MEW and, contrary to their conclusion, indicated that GNP had become a perverse index of total welfare, in more recent years.

In sum, we decided that the monetary measure of the ISEW gave a supplementary *a fortiori* argument to our non-monetary arguments in chapters 3 and 7. So we added an Appendix developing the monetary ISEW. Economists like monetary numerical reasoning better than conceptual-dialectical reasoning. Consequently the Appendix attracted more attention than the related chapters 3 and 7 in the text, even though both reached the same conclusion.

Subsequently John and Clifford encouraged further development of the ISEW in a very exemplary manner. They identified a list of national accounts experts who would likely be critical of the ISEW, offered them an honorarium to write a critique, published their critiques, and revised the ISEW accordingly, or else explained why not.[4] This led to the revised ISEW in the second edition of *For the Common Good*, which later evolved into the GPI and other variants.

A friendly critic astutely pointed out the fundamental inconsistency underlying chapter 3's reliance on non-monetary measures and the Appendix's reliance on monetary measures.[5] Our arguments in the text were based on the concept of "strong sustainability," i.e., the recognition that natural and manmade capital are complements not substitutes, and the one in short supply is the limiting factor. The limiting factor has changed from manmade capital to remaining

---

3 William Nordhaus and James Tobin, "Is Growth Obsolete?," in *Economic Growth*, pub. National Bureau of Economic Research (New York: Columbia University Press, 1972), 509–564.

4 Clifford W. Cobb and John B. Cobb, Jr., *The Green National Product: An Alternative to Gross National Product to Measure Wellbeing* (Lanham: University Press of America, 1994).

5 See Herman E. Daly and John B. Cobb, "The 'Debunking' Interpretation and the Person-in-Community Paradox: Comment on Rafael Ziegler," *Environmental Values* 16, no. 3 (2007): 287–288.

natural resources and services which are closely tied to non-economic as well as economic welfare. The phenomenon of complementarity and the resulting limitationality of natural resources and services was captured in dialectical reasoning of chapters 3 and 7. The ISEW, however, by necessity of monetary measure as a common denominator, implicitly assumed substitutability and consequently "weak sustainability." Without complementarity there can be no limiting factor, so monetary measures, on which the ISEW was necessarily based, are blind to the more limiting condition of strong sustainability. The role of money as a fungible common denominator means that a dollar's worth of natural resources is indifferently substitutable for a dollar's worth of capital or labor in production, which is weak sustainability, not strong sustainability.

In Pigou's terms, adding economic and non-economic welfare with the measuring rod of money can more easily increase total welfare if manmade and natural capital are considered substitutes. But if they are complements, then natural capital can be a limiting factor and a loss of welfare (both economic and non-economic) resulting from its depletion can easily reduce total welfare.

In addition to the strong sustainability difference not captured by the monetary measure was the basic difference in assumptions about *Homo economicus*, the one who actually experiences the welfare being discussed and measured. Welfare is not a thing but an experience. Therefore one must know something about the subject which experiences welfare, namely humans. In chapters 3 and 7 we defined *Homo economicus* as the person-in-community rather than the atomistic individual of neoclassical economics. The person-in-community is constituted by relationships with the rest of the community, and unlike the independent atomistic individual assumed by neoclassical economics, his welfare is influenced by the welfare of others with whom relationships form his very identity. The person-in-community's welfare is not reducible to the money value of what he individually consumes. This important reality is missed by the market-based measuring rod of money.

In sum we considered our conceptual arguments to be more basic and more critical of GNP, while the numerical accounting corrections of the Appendix were weaker since they necessarily assumed weak sustainability and the neoclassical atomistic individual. Nevertheless, the numerical argument in the Appendix was more convincing to economists because it relied on their own numerical accounting methods to reach the same basic conclusion as chapters 3 and 7. In other words, the strong sustainability and person-in-community assumptions gave a more forceful critique of GNP. But the weak sustainability and atomistic individual assumptions of the ISEW allowed us to, in a sense, beat the neoclassical growth economists at their own game.

Efforts to develop improved indices of welfare and of sustainability continue. However, GNP (or the now favored variant, GDP, Gross Domestic Product) continues to dominate both thought and policy of economists and governments. Although GNP/GDP is not a measure of welfare, it is a pretty good index of the volume of resource flow from depletion to pollution – that is to say the entropic metabolic throughput which the economy imposes on the ecosystem. It measures the physical cost of maintenance of the stock of wealth that is the direct source welfare. If we could maintain the same stock of wealth with a lower throughput we would be better off, not worse off. As Kenneth Boulding said, GNP should be relabeled GNC – "Gross National *Cost*". Maybe a good strategy for the future would be to keep "GNC" as an index of cost, and to start over again on an independent index of welfare. This would allow a more direct comparison of costs and benefits of physical throughput growth.

Hans Diefenbacher

The Origins of the National Welfare Index (NWI)

Since the mid-1980s at the latest, there has been a discussion in Germany among economists who do not belong to the neoclassical mainstream on the question of the extent to which the primary objective of economics, namely to achieve unlimited growth in principle, should be relativised. Initially, I had participated in this discussion from a theoretical-historical perspective that resulted in a special issue of a journal that examined the relationship between economics and ecology in several different approaches.[1] An important reason for this appeared to us that the system of national accounts with GNP as the central unit could provide a completely wrong benchmark.[2] That is why I found it highly interesting when John B. Cobb, Jr., visited me in Heidelberg on the occasion of a trip to Germany and introduced me to his work *For the Common Good*, which he had just published together with Herman Daly, especially to its appendix on the newly developed Index for Sustainable Economic Welfare (ISEW).[3] Shortly after this visit, the idea of transferring the statistical concept of the ISEW to Germany with a calculation of a time series since the beginning of the Federal Republic of Germany came up, which I realized in the following years – however, with a considerable limitation, because a back-calculation for the whole of Germany failed: Despite great efforts, I did not succeed in determining a reliable time series for several components of the ISEW for the territory of the former German Democratic Republic.[4] The result of these first efforts of a transmission have been published in German and in English.[5]

---

1 Hans Diefenbacher, "Natur und ökonomische Theorie," *Universitas* 41, no. 486 (1986): 1101–1109.

2 See, for example, the contributions of Hans G. Nutzinger, "Das Konzept des qualitativen Wachstums und die Schwierigkeiten seiner Umsetzung," *Universitas* 41, no. 486 (1986): 1136–1148; Christian Leipert, "Ist 'humaner Wohlstand' möglich?," *Universitas* 41, no. 486 (1986): 1121–1135.

3 Herman E. Daly and Jr. John B. Jobb, *For the Common Good: Redirecting the Economy toward Community, the Environment, and a Sustainable Future* (Boston: Beacon Press, 1989). The annex contains the Index of Sustainable Economic Welfare: 401–457.

4 On the problems of comparing growth and production indices in state socialist and capitalist countries see Rolf Wagenführ, *Der internationale wirtschafts- und sozialstatistische Vergleich* (Freiburg: Haufe, 1959); Frank Haller, *Sozialistische Akkumulations- und Wachstumstheorie* (Berlin: Duncker und Humblot, 1974).

https://doi.org/10.1515/9783110730234-012

At the time, the publication was well received by the scientific community, the media, and politicians.[6] The reactions from science ranged from cautious praise and approval of the fact that, with the present calculation, the possibility of an alternative welfare calculation had been proven to be feasible in principle, to sharp criticism: with an appropriate and not at all unrealistic monetarization of the negative external effects in the ecology sector, the overall result in the ISEW could well have turned negative – and even the pure possibility of negative welfare appeared to the critics to be completely absurd.

Politically, however, this work supported the position of the Green Party, which had already demanded a rapid replacement of the conventional calculation of GDP by an "eco-social product" a few years earlier. Their initiative resulted in political pressure, which in 1990 led to the establishment of the Scientific Advisory Council on Environmental-Economic Accounting at the Federal Ministry for the Environment, Nature Conservation and Nuclear Safety (BMU), which provided very good theoretical and conceptual support for the development of environmental-economic accounting at the Federal Statistical Office, for example through its clear systematisation of environmental costs; however, in its fourth and final statement in 2002, the Council argued definitively that there should not be an official eco-social product in the future.[7] The intention of the Federal Government in office in 1990, headed by Minister for the Environment Klaus Töpfer, to modify the traditional national accounts in such a way that the burdens on the environment resulting from economic activities would be adequately taken into account, as well as corresponding measures for the protection of the environment, was described as "potentially extremely impressive," "but not as easy to put into practice as the originators of the ideas had obviously imagined."[8]

But the consensus of this negative attitude did not last very long, even though it has become the cantus firmus of the Federal Statistical Office since

5 Hans Diefenbacher, *Der 'Index of Sustainable Economic Welfare': Eine Fallstudie für die Bundesrepublik Deutschland, 1950–1992* (Heidelberg: FEST, 1993); Hans Diefenbacher, "A Case Study of the Federal Republic of Germany," in *The National Green Product: A Proposed Index for Sustainable Economic Welfare*, ed. Clifford W. Cobb and John B. Cobb, Jr. (Lanham: University Press of America, 1994), 215–246.

6 A cross-section of the media response to the NWI in general can be found at https://www.fest-heidelberg.de/fne-themenfeld-wohlfahrtsindizes/, accessed May 24, 2022.

7 Beirat Umweltökonomische Gesamtrechnungen beim Bundesministerium für Umwelt, Naturschutz und Reaktorsicherheit, ed., *Umweltökonomische Gesamtrechnungen: Vierte und abschließende Stellungnahme zu den Umsetzungskonzepten des Statistischen Bundesamtes* (Wiesbaden: Statistisches Bundesamt, 2002), 35–37.

8 Beirat Umweltökonomische Gesamtrechnungen, *Umweltökonomische Gesamtrechnungen*, 18.

this publication. As early as November 2007, the European Union, together with the European Parliament and with the cooperation of the Club of Rome, the OECD, and the WWF, organized an international conference under the heading "Beyond GDP" with the aim of sifting through the existing and working out new suitable indicators for measuring prosperity.[9] In Germany, slightly earlier that and in the same year, 2007, the Federal Environment Agency funded a project entitled "Expert Dialogues on the Further Development of the National Sustainability Strategy." In the framework of this project two such dialogues on the topic of growth and welfare measurement took place. These expert dialogues led to a workshop at the Federal Ministry for the Environment in 2009 on the topic of the National Welfare Index, which discussed a first set of components for such an index developed by Roland Zieschank of the Environmental Policy Research Centre at the Free University of Berlin (FU) and by the author of the present paper.[10] These activities were certainly strengthened by the fact that the French President Nicholas Sarkozy set up a "Commission sur la mesure des performances économique et du progrès social" under the leadership of Joseph Stiglitz, Amarty Sen, and Jean Paul Fitoussi, which on the one hand was to work out improvements in measuring the performance of the economy and on the other hand was to discuss the definition and measurement of social progress in general; the final report was published in 2009 and contained a catalogue of topics for further work, which intersected to a large degree with the first set of components for the National Welfare Index (NWI).[11] Thus, the discussion on the NWI had proven to be connectable to the international discussion; dissatisfaction with the existing system seemed to produce similar solutions across borders. However, a German-French attempt to create an indicator-based synthesis in 2010 had again "only" produced a system of indicators without any fundamental criticism of the use of GDP; among other things, improvements were proposed in

---

9 What has remained is at least a website that continuously documents current publications and has been updated at least until May 2022, accessed May 25, 2022, https://ec.europa.eu/environment/beyond_gdp/index_en.html.

10 Hans Diefenbacher and Roland Zieschank, *Wohlfahrtsmessung in Deutschland: Ein Vorschlag für einen nationalen Wohlfahrtsindex* (Dessau: Umweltbundesamt, 2019). Accessed May 24, 2022, https://www.umweltbundesamt.de/sites/default/files/medien/461/publikationen/3902.pdf.

11 Commission sur la mésure des performances économiques et du progrès social, "Rapport" (Paris, 2009). Accessed May 24, 2022, https://base.socioeco.org/docs/rapport_francais.pdf; see also Joseph Stiglitz and Amartya Sen, "Note Problematique de Depart des Travaux de la Commission sur des Alternatives au PBI," (Paris: CMPEPS, 2008). Accessed May 24, 2022, https://base.socioeco.org/docs/com_stiglitz_300291317_1_.pdf.

the consideration of services within the framework of a satellite system for household production.[12]

The first set of components of the NWI was still based on the elements of the Index for Sustainable Welfare (ISEW) and its further development into the Genuine Progress Indicator (GPI), whereby components that were not included in the ISEW/GPI were initially examined and calculated: net new debt and public spending on ecological transformation. In the end, both were not included in the basic variant of the NWI for conceptual reasons. Two other components were shortlisted, but then dropped, mainly due to a lack of data availability at that time: the costs of anthropogenic natural disasters and the costs of the loss of species. On the other hand, two core variables of the ISEW were taken out in a first revision of the NWI, as they brought the NWI too much into the field of short-term highly volatile and purely economically caused changes: the net changes in the value of fixed assets and the changes in the capital account. Methodologically, the index differed above all in that it did not contain any cumulative components and thus only showed flows for a specific year.

The authors have always understood the NWI as an open system that has to be receptive to good further suggestions regarding new components or procedural changes.[13] Such suggestions have been made in particular at the level of the federal states for some of which we have calculated the Regional Welfare Index (RWI) in recent years. Among other things, a change in the calculation method of the component "income distribution" from the Gini index to the Atkinson index and the inclusion of a new component, "costs of involuntary unemployment," was examined.[14] Both proposals were ultimately not realized. In the larger method revision from the NWI 1.0 to the NWI 2.0, on the other hand, the costs of the use of nuclear energy were newly included in the components of the NWI, since their problems were completely disregarded in the traditional national accounting systems.[15] The use of nuclear power differs significantly from the use of other

12 Sachverständigenrat zur Begutachtung der gesamtwirtschaftlichen Entwicklung/Conseil d'Analyse économique, ed., *Wirtschaftsleistung, Lebensqualität und Nachhaltigkeit: Ein umfassendes Indikatorensystem* (Wiesbaden: Selbstverlag, 2011), 47. Accessed May 24, 2022, https://www.sachverstaendigenrat-wirtschaft.de/fileadmin/dateiablage/Expertisen/2010/ex10_de.pdf.

13 Dipl. Verw. Wiss. Roland Zieschank (FU), Prof. Dr. Hans Diefenbacher (FEST/University of Heidelberg), Dorothee Rodenhäuser, M.A. (FEST), Dr. Benjamin Held (FEST).

14 See Anthony B. Atkinson, "On the Measurement of Inequality," *Journal of Economic Theory* 2, no. 3 (1970): 244–263; for more details see also, Frank Alan Cowell, "Measurement of Inequality," in *Handbook of Income Distribution, vol. 1*, ed. Anthony B. Atkinson and François Bourguignon (Amsterdam: Kluwer, 2000), 87–166.

15 Hans Diefenbacher et al., *Aktualisierung und methodische Überarbeitung des Nationalen Wohlfahrtsindex 2.0 für Deutschland 1991 bis 2012* (Dessau: Umweltbundesamt, 2016), accessed

energy sources due to some special features, e.g., the generation of radioactive waste and the danger of a nuclear accident, as seen in Fukushima and Chernobyl. The costs to be taken into account in the NWI therefore include the costs of the search for a final storage site, the disposal of radioactive waste, the dismantling and decommissioning of nuclear power plants, as well as costs that would be incurred by liability insurance against the "greatest accident to be assumed" (GAU). The next version – NWI 3.0 – was published just at the beginning of this year. It contains new components and comprehensive improvements of the methodology of the calculation of different old components that cannot be described here due to the lack of space.[16]

Over the years, attention for the NWI and its federal state variants – the regional welfare index (RWI) – initially increased significantly and then remained at a fairly good level, but did not increase any further. At the national level, the authors have managed to publish the NWI every year, in recent years with the help of the Hans Böckler Foundation, which is close to the trade unions, and in cooperation with the Institute for Macroeconomics and Business Cycle Research (IMK) in Düsseldorf.[17] It is likely that the NWI currently is the only alternative to GDP in Europe that is presented annually. For a while, it seemed as if it might be possible to place the NWI at least in an official annual indicator report – the "Environmental Data" of Germany's Federal Environment Agency (UBA). In the 2017 edition, the NWI appears as the final chart of a more comprehensive collection of data, as a kind of summary of developments in Germany.[18] From 2019 onwards, however, the presentation of the "Environmental Data" was changed and the NWI disappeared from this official data collection.[19] In other official documents, for example most recently in the dialogue version of the German

May 25, 2022, https://www.umweltbundesamt.de/sites/default/files/medien/378/publikationen/texte_29_2016_aktualisierung_und_methodische_ueberarbeitung_des_nationalen_wohlfahrtsind.pdf.

16 For more details, see Benjamin Held, Dorothee Rodenhäuser, and Hans Diefenbacher, *NWI 3.0: Methodenbericht Nationaler Wohlfahrtsindex 3.0* (Düsseldorf: Hans-Böckler-Stiftung, 2022), accessed May 25, 2022, https://www.boeckler.de/de/faust-detail.htm?sync_id=HBS-008250.

17 See the latest report: Benjamin Held, Dorothee Rodenhäuser, and Hans Diefenbacher, "NWI 2021: Rückgang der Wohlfahrt in der Corona-Pandemie," *IMK Policy Brief* 115 (2022), accessed May 25, 2022, https://www.imk-boeckler.de/fpdf/HBS-008226/p_imk_pb_115_2022.pdf

18 Umweltbundesamt, ed., *Daten zur Umwelt 2017: Indikatorenbericht* (Dessau: Umweltbundesamt, 2017), 140–141, accessed May 25, 2022, https://www.umweltbundesamt.de/sites/default/files/medien/376/publikationen/daten_zur_umwelt_2017_indikatorenbericht.pdf.

19 See Umweltbundesamt, "Umweltzustand und Trends," accessed May 25, 2022, https://www.umweltbundesamt.de/daten/umweltzustand-trends.

Federal Government's National Sustainability Strategy 2020/2021, reference is made to the existence of the NWI, but it is not explicitly used.[20]

It has been possible in several cases to calculate the RWI on the basis of an assignment by the respective federal state; but here, too, it must be stated clearly that in no case has it been possible to establish the RWI as part of the official reporting of a federal state. In some German federal states it has at least been possible to repeat the RWI calculation once, but at the present time, in no federal state is there any interest in taking note of the RWI periodically, for example annually or every two or four years, maybe with the exception of Brandenburg. Often it is the case that the immediate usability of the results for practical work determine acceptance or criticism of the NWI/RWI: It is politically quite clear that if the commission for the calculation was given by a state chancellery or a ministry, there is the hope and also the expectation that the result of the index would not be too negative and thus support government policy at least in an indirect way. Conversely, actors who count themselves as part of the opposition are interested in seeing their existing criticism of "inaction" or "wrong" government policies confirmed. This refers not only to the overall result, but also specifically to individual components that can be associated with a certain design of the respective policy, for example in the field of mobility or generally energy and climate policy. There was a case where the governing parties saw themselves supported by the index and used it for political advertising for a certain time; in another federal state, the opposition lost all interest in "their" RWI, since the state had quite presentable results in a whole series of components compared to other federal states.

Negotiations were initiated with a number of other federal states with the aim of calculating a first time series and, in the best case, to periodically update the current values. During the discussions it became clear that there is hardly any basic knowledge about the construction of GDP and of alternative indices, but there is a vague feeling of dissatisfaction and a certain familiarity with the fact that criticism of GDP as a welfare measure has spread.

There is a committee of the departments of the statistical offices of the federal states that are entrusted with environmental-economic accounting.[21] Its

---

20 See Bundesregierung, *Deutsche Nachhaltigkeitsstrategie Weiterentwicklung 2021: Dialogfassung* (Berlin: Bundesregierung, 2020), 184, accessed May 23, 2022, https://www.bundesregierung.de/resource/blob/998006/1793018/73d3189a28be9f3043c7736d3e1de4df/dns2021-dialogfassung-data.pdf?download=1.

21 The body is called Umweltökonomische Gesamtrechnungen der Länder; it annually produces its own indicator report. For the most recent report see Umweltökonomische Gesamtrechnung der Länder, ed., *Indikatorenbericht* (Düsseldorf: Information und Technik Nordrhein-West-

work is of great importance because in the Federal Republic of Germany statistics are first and foremost a responsibility of the federal states. Districts and independent cities have standardized delivery obligations towards the federal state, just as the federal states have delivery obligations towards the federal office of statistics (Statistisches Bundesamt). In principle, the work continues between the member states of the European Union and Eurostat, which is why the introduction of a statistical innovation can only be realized in a procedure coordinated among the various levels.

The working group at the level of the federal states has dealt intensively with the NWI at one of its half-year meetings, but could not agree on a common procedure, and finally did not "adopt" the regional NWI. In this respect, the opportunity to standardize the regional variant of the NWI was not taken, and its introduction in the federal states remains dependent on the interest of individuals and the respective constellation in supplementing welfare reporting. The decision-making process often drags on for a long time; in some federal states, the introduction of the RWI or of other alternatives have probably failed for good.

Finally, a special feature is the activity of the Health and Environment Department of the City of Munich. A working group of this office had already considered the transferability of the NWI to the city of Munich in 2009 and commissioned FEST to conduct a feasibility study. This work was the first in which an application of the NWI to a smaller unit of accounting than a nation was examined. In two meetings between the working group and the author of the study, the data situation and especially the sometimes problematic delimitations for smaller territorial units were discussed. For example, the energy consumption of electricity is attributed to the location of the power plant, which does not correspond to the location of energy consumption in all cases. In the end, the research report on Munich draws a rather sobering balance, which at the time was mainly due to the reliability of the poor data situation: Above all, the auxiliary procedures for making projections corresponding to a number of components through correlating substitute variables such as the share of the population or the share of Munich's GDP in the respective total values for Germany were not always satisfactory. In this way, the result came up with such a cumulative margin of uncertainty that in the end it was decided not to publish the time series of the NWI for Munich.[22] Now, however, in the winter of 2020/2021,

falen, 2020), accessed May 25, 2022, https://www.statistikportal.de/sites/default/files/2020-06/ugrdl_graf_2020_0.pdf.

22 Hans Diefenbacher, *Möglichkeiten und Grenzen regionaler Wohlfahrtsmessung: Eine Studie am Beispiel der Stadt München* (Heidelberg: Unpublished manuscript, 2010).

it was possible to start a new attempt together with the city of Munich, which will, in all likelihood, be completed successfully in the coming summer.

Overall, a partly optimistic, partly pessimistic résumé can be drawn. The theoretical concept of the NWI as a new welfare measure is not yet fully established; there are new theoretical debates that must be taken into account whenever a new welfare measure is considered.[23] Domestic and foreign effects of components need to be better delineated, and immediate effects of components on welfare need to be separated from developments that will be relevant only in the future. The monetarization of important components can only be carried out on the basis of normative decisions: these are essential questions that will continue to accompany the discussion. Data availability, on the other hand, has improved significantly in recent years. It has been shown that it is possible to work continuously with the NWI and its regional variants, and that the relationship between the development of GDP and NWI is very different in different phases. This allows for a more substantial and, above all, empirically enriched discussion on the relationship between growth and welfare, and many political discussions on the concept of prosperity and welfare in one of the materially particularly rich countries of the world are stimulated here with a new perspective. Progress in changing societal reporting systems, however, takes an extremely long time. Above all, however, there is resistance in the practice of statistical implementation. “The toils of the mountains,” wrote Bertolt Brecht in 1949 in his poem “Perception,” “lie behind us. Ahead of us lie the travails of the plains.”

23 See for example Jonas Van der Slycken and Brent Bleys, “A Conceptional Exploration and Critical Inquiry Into the Theoretical Foundation(s) of Economic Welfare Measures,” *Ecological Economics* 176 (2020): 1–10.

Karma Ura

GNH-Led Development in Bhutan

This short account deals with how GNH came about and describes the challenges of implementing it.[1] Happiness was not a sudden inception in the mind of the Fourth King of Bhutan, His Majesty Jigme Singye Wangchuck. In important ways, the idea is rooted Vajrayana Buddhism that prevails in Bhutan and its long-term attention to the psychology of happiness and the training of desirable mental processes such as attention, will, feelings, sensations, intentions, desires, and mind-body practices.[2] In addition to such bodily and subjective concerns, certain sutras like *Anana Sutta* deal with the main causes of joys of a householder that include enjoyment of wealth and being at the same time free from household debt.[3] Generally, Buddha's teaching is about happiness as the basic preference of sentient beings, individually and collectively. Consequently, happiness as the goal of governments and leadership occurs in indigenous sources of Bhutan and of Buddhist Himalayas.[4]

This basic preference for happiness and its broad sets of "satisfiers" are charted schematically in the nine domains of the Gross National Happiness index (GNH). Unlike in neoclassical economic theory, the GNI does not see human beings exclusively as excellent consumers abounding in omniscient knowledges about market clearing prices, unbeatable quality, and most efficient suppliers of goods and services to optimize his or her satisfaction.[5] Human beings' happiness draws on communities, families, and significant others, and

---

1 Drawn loosely from my "GNH Index" lecture delivered at the Sheldonian Theatre, University of Oxford on January 8, 2019.

2 For a discussion on Buddhism and contemporary psychotherapy, see Gay Watson, *The Resonance of Emptiness a Buddhist Inspiration for Contemporary Psychotherapy* (Delhi: Motital Banarasidass, 1998).

3 According to the *Anana Sutta*, the four blisses and joys of a householder are described as the joy of ownership, the joy of making use of or enjoying wealth, the joy of debtlessness, and the joy of blamelessness in terms of bodily, verbal, and mental actions. See Bhikkhu Thanissaro, trans., *Anana Sutta: Debtless*, 1998, accessed May 25, 2022, http://www.accesstoinsight.org/tipitaka/an/an06/an06.045.than.html.

4 Gongsa Mipham Wangpo, *Discourse on the Legal Decree of Precious Palden Drukpa, Victorious in All Directions*, trans. Karma Ura and Jigme Thinley (Thimphu: Centre for Bhutan & GNH Studies, 2020).

5 Aaron Ahuvia and Elif Izberk-Bilgin, "Well-being in Consumer Societies," in *The Oxford Handbook of Happiness*, ed. Ilona Boniwell, Susan A. David, and Amanda Conley Ayers (Oxford: Oxford University Press, 2013), 483–497.

https://doi.org/10.1515/9783110730234-013

the process of contributing and being contributed by them is a deep part of happiness.[6]

The concept of GNI evolved slowly and gradually. For about three decades, till 2006, the government of Bhutan under the GNH founder, the Fourth King of Bhutan, framed policies that were broadly and intuitively consistent with it. In 2002, the king launched a constitution-drafting process for Bhutan leading to a multi-party democracy and directly elected government through universal franchise in 2008. The constitution included a provision obliging the state policies, among others, to pursue conditions for GNH.

As the stage was being set up for democratically elected governments that could change every five years, it was believed that GNH indicators could be helpful to seek adherence of the politicians and bureaucrats to long-term GNH goals. In late 2006, the fourth King abdicated in favor of the Fifth King, His Revered Majesty Jigme Khesar, who then directed the government to initiate an index for GNH in 2007. During the following year, the concept of the nine domains of GNH was adopted after much deliberation.[7] To itemize, the nine domains are: psychological well-being, community vitality, time use, ecological resilience and diversity, cultural diversity and resilience, good governance, education, health, and living.[8] Though they are listed separately, there is profound interdependence and non-linear relationship between and among them, and none exist in isolation of the other. Yet it is necessary to qualify that causal understanding in relationships between so many important variables are needed for programming than we have knowledge at present. We do not fully know the substitution rate between and within the nine domains. How much in one domain can be given up in favor of another to obtain the same level of well-being? That was a question that arose during discussion on the weighting of domains. However, each domain is equally weighted in the GNH composite index because each domain is important in its own right.

6 They list social conditions rather than material consumption, processes rather than outcomes, wider negative effects of unemployment beyond income loss for the unemployed as non-material parts of well-being. Bruno S. Frey and Alois Stutzer, "Economics and the Study of Individual Happiness," in *The Oxford Handbook of Happiness*, ed. Boniwell, David, and Ayers, 431–447.

7 GNH takes center stage. In fact, the command to create a GNH index was also received through the then Secretary to HM the King, Dronyer Dasho Ugyen Dorji, as well as Lyonpo Kinzang Dorji, interim Prime Minister of Bhutan.

8 For a complete conceptual overview and policy interventions in each domain, see Centre for Bhutan Studies & GNH Research (CBS & GNHR), *A Compass Towards a Just and Harmonious Society: 2015 GNH Survey Report* (Thimphu: Centre for Bhutan Studies & GNH Research, 2016).

Nevertheless, each domain is not given equal policy consideration. Although people agree broadly to the idea that each domain is important in and of itself, the allocation of official budget as means to happiness and well-being is still underdeveloped. The budget allocation is still skewed towards physical and social infrastructure such as health, education, roads, culture, environment, agriculture, and energy sectors. There is as yet no explicit allocation for psychological well-being, community vitality or balanced time use. Fiscal design in still wanting in this respect, and more will be said on this later.

The evidence-based application of GNH started in 2007. In 2006 and 2007 a GNH pilot survey was carried out. Based on this pilot survey we decided on a panoply of indicators that covered a wide range of material and non-material variables that would be estimated by collecting data through national surveys. Since then, the Centre of Bhutan in GNH studies, which is charged officially with GNH metrics, has conducted national GNH surveys in 2010 and 2015. The 2021 survey is underway. In each survey 8,000 randomly sampled households were interviewed. All Bhutanese citizens of 15 years of age and above are eligible to be interviewed. Each face-to-face interview comprises about two hours of intense questions and conversations based on a structured questionnaire. Some questions are standard, similar to those also asked in Europe and North America. For others conceptual, cultural, and linguistic differences between English and Dzongkha have emerged in our survey, making us wonder about their validity in Bhutan.

Let me cite one example of the dangers of mistranslation from the 2017 national census. Severe psychological distress is felt by 3% of the Bhutanese.[9] As a distinct item, one indicator of social isolation of an individual is loneliness. Our interest in finding out the prevalence of social isolation led to inserting a simple question in 2017 national census asking whether people felt lonely or not. The result was unusable because we found a mistranslation and misinterpretation of the word loneliness which did not exist in Dzongkha, which, while in itself was thought-provoking, had derailed our efforts.[10]

9 CBS & GNHR, *A Compass*, 84.

10 Later we found out that these two major languages of Bhutan – Dzongkha and Tshangla – do not have an equivalent word. The nearest word in Dzongkha to loneliness is "tonghaha" (Wylie stong har har) which literally means feeling a sense of emptiness. The next closest word in Dzongkha seems to be "bag mi chag" (wylie bag mi chags), which literally means "not getting habituated" to the place. A recently published dictionary of Dzongkha coined a new phrase, or neologism, for loneliness rather incorrectly, as "cig pur skyo wa" (Wylie gcigpu skyoba), which literally means "unhappy alone".

Overall, the experience with the application a quantitative understanding to GNH based on periodic surveys and data analyses is around a decade old. The surveys are unfortunately not longitudinal. Tracking the same set of 8,000 respondents above 15 years would generate probably better understanding, yet tracking 1,000 out of 8,000 can be more feasible. This has been done for the 2021 national GNH survey.

The survey process is complex. The data for GNH indicators come in many shapes, such as Likert scale, Likert type scale, quantitative, dichotomous, and Cantril ladder. The GNH survey questionnaire consists of 135 questions, excluding 18 demographic questions.[11] The 135 questions elicit 642 answers or 642 variables. To give a breakup of the variables that the questions yield, there are 51 Likert scale variables with neutrality in the middle; 53 Likert type variables without such symmetry, 19 Cantril ladder responses option variables, 133 dichotomous variables, 33 multiple choice variables, 343 open-ended quantitative variables, and 10 open-ended qualitative variables. Most of the Likert scale variables questions have a five-point Likert type scale, such as satisfied, very satisfied, with "neutral neither satisfied not dissatisfied" in the middle, and dissatisfied or very dissatisfied on the other end.

The last two successive surveys resulted in many indicators that measure the changes in GNH among many demographic groups across the country. The mass of variables or data from the survey are processed into 33 indicators, with roughly four indicators for each domain of the nine domains of GNH. Each of the 33 indicators is a crunched number, to speak in terms of average, made from eight variables, after weighting the variables.[12] We switched to the Alkire-Foster method of aggregation in 2008.[13] One of the distinctive advantages of this aggregation method is that it allows for aggregation over a wide range of data types that can be organized into a hierarchy of indicators.

The fundamental problem any weighting raises is a very difficult one, because buried in the question of weights is the interrelated questions of preferences, choices, outcomes, and values.[14] But we can also think of equally weighted domains as a simple set of necessary goods that would increase the probability of achievement of the conditions of happiness. In this way weights are intuitive,

11 For GNH questionnaire, see CB&GNHS, *A Compass*, 305–340.

12 Karma Ura et al., *An Extensive Analysis of GNH Index* (Thimphu: Centre for Bhutan Studies, 2012).

13 Sabine Alkire and James Foster, "Understandings and Misunderstandings of Multidimensional Poverty Measurement," *The Journal of Economic Inequality* 9 (2011): 289–314; see also CBS & GNHR, *A Compass*, 57–58.

14 Amartya Sen, *Rationality and Freedom* (New Delhi: Oxford University Press, 2003), 65–118.

and focus attentions on key intended outcomes. Weighting and aggregation have facilitated the construction of the GNH index while also drawing some complaints of inaccessibility by officials and media in Bhutan. But one can apply the same criticism about incomprehensibility to GDP and its growth rate accepted among economists. It is accepted because it is taken for granted by the people and it is taken for granted because it has been active for long enough, until it becomes a societal artefact. In contrast, the GNH index is regarded well by certain global think tanks and academics.

Public policies increasingly require measurable evidence even in Bhutan and this is where the GNH index comes in. Originally, the aims behind GNH index were to (1) guide plans by benchmarking to indicators, (2) frame the allocation of the budget, (3) track changes of GNH over time, (4) compare Bhutan's performance with other nations by producing certain comparable statistics on life satisfaction, (5) life-domain satisfactions, General Health Questions, healthy days most of which are also integrated into GNH index. The aim of generating such internationally comparable data is to provide these data to other international users, and on a needs basis other variables.

It was crucial to receive the support of the highest leadership. With his usual foresight and vision, it was easy for his enlightened leadership to actively support the new metrics. However, as any realist knows, detailed implementation involves a wide range of actors. In the case of Bhutan, the two most important actors are the bureaucracy and to a lesser degree the private business sector. It is perhaps accurate to characterize the sprawling bureaucracy as the most pervasive and dominating actor in Bhutan.

As the GNH quantitative framework was introduced, one section of the bureaucracy was skeptical about it and argued that GNH should not be reduced to a set of numbers. Instead, they argued that GNH should remain an inspiration and an ideal. Others argued that for it to guide policies and programs, it must acquire some precision. People clarify their vision by specifying attainable targets. Such targets could also help citizens to judge actual performance, whether of the government or, where relevant, of the people themselves. The debate continues. Not all sections of the bureaucracy have come around to understanding and applying GNH in their organizations to assess their programs either before or after their implementations, even though a methodology to do so has been prepared. This remains a challenge that can only be resolved through widespread training and outreach, and explicit regulations.

From the beginning, GNH has been constructed as a contrast to GDP, especially in the media. Calculations of the Bhutanese GDP began in 1983 for the first time and it was projected backwards to 1980. The Bhutanese per capita income is estimated to have reached close to $3,262, equivalent to $11,230 at PPP, in 2019.

By far more resources and manpower are allocated to the collection and analysis of data for GDP than GNH in Bhutan. And there are also predicaments in the minds of many officials about the primacy between GDP and GNH when it comes to major decisions.

GDP, along with a host of its subsidiary indicators, is the most widely used indicator world-wide. It is and should be a measurement of the size of the economy. But it has become more than that. It changes the behavior of the government and people in that they perceive it, rightly or wrongly, as equivalent to their welfare. The illusion of maximum GDP per capita as maximum welfare persists, and that changes the behavior of governments towards it.

The ambivalent relationship between GNH and GDP has not been clarified completely in one section of the Bhutanese bureaucracy. The main body in charge of social economic planning in Bhutan is the Gross National Happiness Commission, as renamed by His Majesty the King. It was earlier known as the Planning Commission. Its new name indicates its purpose: to integrate all policies, programs, and projects towards GNH. In recent years, however, the Ministry of Finance, has emerged as the alternative pole advocating GDP and related metrics, relegating GNH in a subtle way. The debate on the primacy between GDP and GNH is partly between the Gross National Happiness Commission on one side and the Ministry of Finance on the other.

Nevertheless, both domestically and internationally, the GNH is making steady progress. Inspired by the Bhutanese resolution to the General Assembly in June 2011, recommending that governments make happiness and well-being a focus of public policy, the United Nations has since declared March 20 to be the World Happiness Day, now marked each year by a fresh edition of the World Happiness Report. The first of these reports was prepared for the UN High Level Expert Meeting in April 2012. The World Happiness Reports uses data from the Gallup World Poll collected in a comparable way from more than 150 countries.[15] The country rankings are based on the life evaluations, which have been shown to better capture international differences in life circumstances, and to be themselves supported by high levels of positive effects. But it must be noted that there are huge differences in what the World Happiness Report and what the GNH measure as happiness.

15 Worried about the possible unrepresentativeness and in-authenticity, both the national newspaper, Kuensel, and the Prime Minister of Bhutan in his State of Nation's address on GNH in 2016, alerted the citizens and asked them to report if they knew of Gallup survey; none has come forward to this day. Our office wrote to Gallup in 2016 but they did not share their data, although they said they carried out survey by email and telephone.

In Bhutan, at present, there are five technically specific ways in which GNH indicators are being applied in the administration of the country:

Firstly, the GNH index and some of domain indicators and sub-indicators are directly used as a benchmark in the Five-Year Plan on which to make further progress. At the overall national level, the Five-Year Plan is guided by national targets and key results. In the current plan, 17 baselines or targets are drawn from GNH indicators such as sufficiency levels in mental health, safety, community vitality, skills, political participation, fundamental rights, subjective well-being, values, assets, income, housing, etc.

Thereby, the composite GNH index is used as an overall national baseline. Between 2010 and 2015, the performance of health, education, culture, living standard, environment, time use, and good governance improved, and hence, overall, the GNH index improved. However, the index number improved only marginally: it was 0.743 in 2010 and it rose to 0.756 in 2015. The five-year difference is only 0.013, which suggests a percentage growth rate of 1.7 % in five years or 0.35 % per year. Thus, its decimal movements are not entirely capable of grabbing headlines and public attention. This is because not all things improve if we measure most things that matter, and they offset the gains made in other areas. The slow rate of change is a consequence of 277 variables, some of which fall back during broader movement forward. Meanwhile, the GDP gives dramatic percentage changes.

Secondly, the GNH index is also used as weighted criterion in the allocation of the budget among the local governments, composed of 20 districts, four urban municipalities at the level of middle tier of administration, and 205 counties or gewogs at the lowest tier in the vertical organization of the country.[16] Among these local governments' weights of GNH index is 10 % for gewogs and 15 % for municipalities and districts.

Thirdly, policies in the central government are formulated by subjecting them to vetting with GNH policy screening tools, which consist of 22 criteria drawn from the GNH and implemented according to a well-defined process since 2008, revised further in 2015.[17] So far, 15 out of 22 draft policies have been approved, with a majority getting modified to some degree by the process of policy screening.

16 Gross National Happiness Commission, *Draft 12 Five Year Plan* (Thimphu: Royal Government of Bhutan, 2018).

17 See Cabinet Secretariat, "Protocol for Policy Formulation," March 15, 2015, unpublished.

Fourthly, the GNH index has been used to evaluate a large rural horticultural project after it was implemented.[18] The project's aim was to grow 40 different varieties of fruits and vegetables over 2,166 acres benefitting 64 households. The impact study used the Propensity Score Matching method to evaluate the impact of the project on beneficiaries versus non-beneficiaries on all nine domains of GNH. This method of evaluation is very promising and might get diffused over time.

There is a fifth instance where a GNH application is under way. A GNH certification for business has been designed as an assessment framework for business corporations. After initial formulations and tests, its application will start on a wider scale in the future. Several state enterprises and leading private companies have undergone GNH certification for business in 2020. A few foreign companies abroad have applied for GNH certification though the outbreak of the Covid-19 pandemic has led to the postponement of assessment.

Furthermore, the national law institute of Bhutan is also grappling for the first time with a novel question: what consequences are there in the legal principles if happiness is its main premise, and what else can they do in the administration of justice if happiness is its cornerstone.

In addition, there is a variety of dispersed applications of GNH which are difficult to survey, such as its presence as a discourse in media and political campaigns, as a subject in academia and in schools, as courses of mindfulness in the civil service and public enterprises, as an evaluation tool in some projects, as a way to stimulate awareness of key aspects of society in such areas as community action, and so forth. In other words, GNH is vying for its space in a dynamic society where several ideas are at play, explicitly or discretely.

18 Jigme Phuntsho, *Fruits of Happiness: How Horticulture Enhance GNH in Mongar* (Thimphu: Centre for Bhutan Studies, 2017).

Saamah Abdallah

The Happy Planet Index

This contribution, on the Happy Planet Index (HPI), has been written for a yearbook on global development. And yet the creators of the HPI – including Nic Marks, whose brainchild it was, and myself – are not scholars of development. The main purpose of the HPI was not to inform development in lower-income countries but to question development in higher-income countries. Nevertheless, we have always recognized its relevance for understandings of development across the world, and the global interest in the HPI demonstrates that we are not alone. We are happy to be able to contribute to the debate on what makes "good" development.

This article will provide a short history of the HPI, outlining the intentions of its creators, considering its impact, and outlining our future plans. Although it has attracted widespread interest from important actors, the index has not been officially implemented by any country as a measure of development or progress. But that was never the goal. Rather we sought to contribute to a change in the narrative about what counts as progress. We believe that the HPI has been successful in doing so.

Origins

In the optimistic early years of the twenty-first century, the world seemed to be on a trajectory of steady growth and globalisation.[1] Per capita GDP globally had been increasing at about 3% per year. By 2008, it would reach twice the value it had been in 1993.[2] International trade was increasing at an even faster rate.[3] Since 1994, more than half the world's population has lived in democracies.[4] Francis Fukuyama's *End of History* may have attracted ridicule, but to some ex-

1 "OECD Economic Outlook,Volume 2006, Issue 1," OECD 2006, accessed May 19, 2022, https://doi.org/10.1787/eco_outlook-v2006-1-en.

2 "World Bank Open Data," accessed April 13, 2021, https://data.worldbank.org/.

3 Giovanni Federico and Antonio Tena-Junguito, "A Tale of Two Globalizations: Gains from Trade and Openness 1800 – 2010," *Working Papers in Economic History* (Madrid: Universidad Carlos III de Madrid, 2016), accessed May 19, 2022, https://e-archivo.uc3m.es/bitstream/handle/10016/22354/wh1602.pdf.

4 Max Roser, "Democracy," *Our World in Data*, March 15, 2013, accessed May 19, 2022, https://ourworldindata.org/democracy.

https://doi.org/10.1515/9783110730234-014

tent it still reflected the sense of steady global progress, democratisation and liberalisation.

But, of course, those interested in environmental issues were not so optimistic. CO_2 emissions were rising almost as fast as GDP,[5] and the threat of climate change already loomed large.

The need to highlight the environmental (and social) costs of economic growth had led in 1989 in the USA to Herman Daly and John Cobb creating a new index – the Genuine Progress Index, originally called the Index of Sustainable Economic Welfare.[6] The index, which is also described in this volume in the contribution by Herman Daly, starts with a measure of economic production within a country, and then adjusts this value for various environmental and social costs of the economy (e.g., air pollution or car accidents) and some social benefits (e.g., household labor). The New Economics Foundation, including Nic Marks, worked with Tim Jackson at the University of Surrey to adopt the index and calculate a UK version in 1994.[7]

Whilst the UK index did seem to strike a chord in the public,[8] Marks had several concerns about it. The calculations behind the ISEW were complex and involved many assumptions (e.g., how does one value the loss of natural habitats, or what cost should be put on time spent commuting?).[9] More fundamentally, whilst the ISEW recognizes the importance of environmental and social impacts, it still starts from the assumption that more economic consumption is, all else being equal, a good thing. In other words, it is ultimately rooted in standard economic preference satisfaction theory and says nothing about people's actual feelings or experiences with their lives.[10]

5 "Supplement Data of Global Carbon Budget 2020 (Version 1.0)," Global Carbon Project, accessed April 13, 2021, https://www.icos-cp.eu/science-and-impact/global-carbon-budget/2020.

6 Herman E. Daly and John B. Cobb, *For the Common Good: Redirecting the Economy toward Community, the Environment, and a Sustainable Future* (Boston: Beacon Press, 1989).

7 T. Jackson and N. Marks, "Measuring Sustainable Economic Welfare – A Pilot Index: 1950–1990," Stockholm Environment Institute, Sweden, January 1, 1994, accessed May 19, 2022, https://www.osti.gov/etdeweb/biblio/7177041.

8 Robin Young, "Was 1976 the Best Year of Your Life?," *The Times*, March 17, 2004, accessed May 19, 2022, https://www.thetimes.co.uk/article/was-1976-the-best-year-of-your-life-jzx06htmz25.

9 Saamah Abdallah et al., *Regional Index of Sustainable Economic Well-Being Development Project – Final Report*' (London: New Economics Foundation, 2010).

10 Paul Dolan, Tessa Peasgood, and Mathew White, "Final report for Defra: Review of research on the influences on personal well-being and application to policy making", August 2006, accessed May 19, 2022, http://randd.defra.gov.uk/Document.aspx?Document=SD12005_4017_FRP.pdf.

Meanwhile, economists had begun to take interest in the work of positive psychologists such as Ed Diener and Marty Seligman,[11] and the idea that subjective measures of wellbeing, instead of economic measures, could be used to assess the overall welfare of a nation. Books such as Richard Layard's *Happiness: Lessons from a New Science* were early bestsellers in the new field of happiness economics.[12] And one of the key lessons from subjective wellbeing was that economic growth did not seem to be leading to happier people – the so-called *Easterlin Paradox*. The now familiar graph showing rising GDP alongside flatlining subjective wellbeing had been first produced by Richard Easterlin for the USA back in 1974,[13] but replicated in more recent years and in more countries.[14] In the UK, the Prime Minister's Strategy Unit produced an analytical paper looking at evidence on the determinants of life satisfaction that even included a replication of the Easterlin Paradox for the UK.[15]

The Index

It was the fusion of happiness economics with environmental concerns embodied in the ISEW that inspired Marks to create the HPI. The HPI models human society as having one key input (environmental resources) and one key output (human wellbeing).[16] It proposes that a society's (or country's) goal should be to achieve the highest level of human wellbeing with the lowest consumption of environmental resources. This goal can be understood as an efficiency goal – human wellbeing divided by environmental resource use. This reflects the IUCN's (The World Conservation Union) call for a metric capable of measuring "the production of human well-being [...] per unit of extraction from or im-

11 Ed Diener and Martin Seligman, "Case for a National Well-Being Index," *Science and Spirit* 17, no. 2 (2006): 36–38.
12 Richard Layard, *Happiness: Lessons from a New Science* (London: Penguin Press, 2005).
13 Richard A. Easterlin, "Does Economic Growth Improve the Human Lot? Some Empirical Evidence," in *Nations and Households in Economic Growth: Essays in Honor of Moses Abramovitz*, ed. Paul A. David and Melvin W. Reder (London: Academic Press, 1974), 89–125.
14 Layard, *Happiness*; R. A. Easterlin et al., "The Happiness-Income Paradox Revisited," *Proceedings of the National Academy of Sciences* 107, no. 52 (2010): 22463–22468.
15 Nick Donovan, David Halpern, and Richard Sargeant, *Life Satisfaction: The State of Knowledge and Implications for Government* (London: Prime Minister's Strategy Unit, 2002).
16 Nic Marks et al., *The (Un)Happy Planet Index: An Index of Human Well-Being and Environmental Impact* (London: New Economics Foundation, 2006).

position upon nature,"[17] and thereby holds the inherent tension between human wellbeing and planetary sustainability.

The HPI argues that everything that happens in between, in particular economic growth, is purely a means to an end, and not necessarily the best means. As such, whilst it is important to measure economic growth and other features of the economy, they should not be understood as measures of progress or good as in and of themselves.

The HPI uses the ecological footprint, developed by Matthis Wackernagel and William Rees in the 1990s, as its measure of environmental resource use.[18] The ecological footprint combines several environmental impacts, including CO_2 emissions, but also food production and forest-based goods, into a single metric. Meanwhile human wellbeing is measured using happy life years, a metric developed by Ruut Veenhoven,[19] which adjusts life expectancy at birth using data on average reported wellbeing (initially measured using life satisfaction) within a country. We expected that the integration of an established measure like life expectancy, which is of course also included in the UN's Human Development Index, would be uncontroversial, but actually some purist happiness economists disagreed with its inclusion, because it meant that a long but unhappy life was treated as equivalent to a shorter happier one.

The HPI is, with some statistical adjustments, happy life years divided by ecological footprint.

Despite many headlines to the contrary,[20] of course the index does not focus on the "happiest country on the planet." People in Costa Rica and Mexico (the top two countries in the latest edition of the HPI)[21] do not necessarily have a better quality of life than those in wealthier countries such as the USA or Sweden. But the index does indicate that the Costa Rican economy (or society) is more efficient at "converting" environmental resources into human wellbeing. In other words, even if Costa Rica's average life expectancy and average reported

---

17 William Mark Adams, "The Future of Sustainability: Re-Thinking Environment and Development in the Twenty-First Century," *IUCN Renowned Thinkers Meeting*, 2006, accessed May 19, 2022, https://portals.iucn.org/library/node/12635.

18 William E. Ress and Mathis Wackernagel, "Ecological Footprints and Appropriated Carrying Capacity: Measuring the Natural Capital Requirements of the Human Economy," *Focus* 6, no. 1 (1996): 45–60.

19 Ruut Veenhoven, "Happy Life-Expectancy," *Social Indicators Research* 39, no. 1 (1996): 1–58.

20 See, for example, Anna Hodgekiss, "Revealed, the Happiest Countries in the World," *Mail Online*, November 20, 2014, accessed May 19, 2022, https://www.dailymail.co.uk/health/article-2842403/Revealed-happiest-countries-world-contented-life-head-Costa-Rica-Vietnam-Norway-UK-fares-better-Spain-Australia.html.

21 "Happy Planet Index," accessed April 21, 2021, http://happyplanetindex.org.

wellbeing are a little bit lower than in Sweden, Sweden's ecological footprint is 2.6 times larger. In a simplistic sense, given the environmental dangers we face, it would be better for humanity if Sweden transformed to be more like Costa Rica than if Costa Rica were to transform to Sweden. From a development perspective, the argument is that developing countries should look more towards Costa Rica as a model of development than Sweden. Indeed, given the finite resources of the planet, it is currently impossible that the whole world could be like Sweden – we would need more than four planets worth of resources to achieve that.

Impact

The first HPI was published in July 2006, with subsequent editions in 2009, 2012 and 2016. Financial support came from Friends of the Earth and the AIM Foundation.

The HPI achieved widespread recognition as soon as it was launched. The first report was downloaded and read in at least 185 countries, and the survey that was included on the first website was completed by 100,000 respondents. The second report achieved two million page views within the first two years of its launch, again with worldwide reach (visits from 221 countries or territories).

Media coverage was extensive both in the UK (BBC World TV, Sky News, BBC Radio 4, the *Daily Mail*, the *Guardian*, and the *Financial Times*, just to mention a few) and worldwide. In 2009, the HPI featured on the front page of the *New Scientist* magazine.[22] A forthcoming study comparing media coverage of alternative indicators of progress within the UK found 227 articles about the Happy Planet Index between 2006 and 2018, with 49 articles appearing in the first year of its launch.[23] This indicates greater media coverage than similar initiatives such as the Social Progress Index, OECD Better Life Index and Genuine Progress Indicator. Another study found that, of 24 different alternative indictors, the HPI had the most diverse press coverage (i.e., was reported in the greatest variety of publications).[24]

---

22 "Issue 2725," *New Scientist*, September 12, 2009, accessed May 19, 2022, https://www.newscientist.com/issue/2725/.

23 Fabio Battaglia, personal communication with the author, February 2019.

24 Stephen Morse, "Measuring the Success of Sustainable Development Indices in Terms of Reporting by the Global Press," *Social Indicators Research: An International and Interdisciplinary Journal for Quality-of-Life Measurement* 125, no. 2 (2016): 359–375.

The HPI's intended audience was not academic, but dozens of academic papers have also referenced it, and it has been presented in several academic conferences.

The HPI has never been officially implemented by any national government but that was never its creators' objective. The New Economics Foundation's position on what should genuinely replace GDP was elaborated on several years later, with the recommendation of five headline indicators.[25]

The HPI's goals were manifold and evolved over the years, but can be summarized as follows:

1. highlight the inadequacies of using GDP as a measure of progress;
2. promote the use of subjective wellbeing indicators in policy;
3. show how current development models are incompatible with staying within environmental limits;
4. stress the message that good lives need not cost the Earth.

In terms of the first two goals, the Index can be seen as part of a movement that has been somewhat successful. Since 2006, critiques of GDP have become more widespread and subjective wellbeing data is now widely collected, not least in the UK, where the ONS's Annual Population Survey is one of the largest official surveys in the world regularly including questions on subjective wellbeing. Direct causal effects are of course difficult to determine, but the HPI was quickly noticed by actors that have been important in this movement, including the ONS, the OECD, the European Commission, and the UK Conservative Party. It is understood that David Cameron considered the HPI when he announced that the UK would develop its own wellbeing index.[26]

The HPI and other work conducted by the New Economics Foundation also inspired actors around the world to collect alternative measures of progress, from regional governments (e.g., Trentino-Alto Adige in Italy and Caerphilly in Wales) to national governments (e.g., Vanuatu and Ecuador).

Last but not least, the HPI was referenced in the ninth edition of the *Lonely Planet* for Costa Rica!

---

25 Karen Jeffrey and Juliet Michaelson, *Five Headline Indicators of National Success: A Clearer Picture of How the UK Is Performing* (London: New Economics Foundation, 2015).

26 Tomáš Hák et al., "Review Report on Beyond GDP Indicators: Categorisation, Intensions and Impacts. Final Version", October 2012, accessed May 19, 2022, https://base.socioeco.org/docs/_wp-content_uploads_2012_12_d1.1_brainpool_review_report_beyond-gdp_indicators.pdf.

Tensions and Challenges

The HPI is simpler than most alternative measures of progress but that does not mean that there were no tensions or challenges to address in its creation. For the first edition in 2006, the main data source for subjective wellbeing data was the World Values Survey, but that only covered 64 countries.[27] I had to use some quite "heroic" techniques to estimate comparable wellbeing scores for the remaining countries, either from other data sources which used other questions, or simply using a regression model, which is ultimately a publication in its own right.[28] We were very relieved in 2009 when we were able to use real data for most countries, thanks to the Gallup World Poll. But even then, compromises had to be made. The World Poll's main wellbeing question is Cantil's so-called "ladder-of-life" scale. Although it does correlate with our preferred life satisfaction scale, it tends to relatively favor wealthier countries,[29] which slightly diluted our main narrative that wealth does not bring happiness.

Another important debate which we wrangled with for the first edition was whether we should produce rankings. I and my colleague Sam Thompson, who had at the time just completed a PhD, were sceptical of the robustness of creating a ranking. As well as an overall score, the HPI is also based on a "traffic-light" system which uses thresholds to identify whether countries are doing well on each of the three components. We wanted this traffic-light system to be given equal exposure in the report. However, our colleagues in Communications, for example Ruth Potts, were adamant that a ranking was necessary to attract media attention. She was right – and we certainly did not need to repeat that debate for the second edition!

But perhaps a more fundamental debate has been the tension between the positive and negative narratives embodied in the HPI. We wanted to highlight that good lives do not have to cost the Earth, and that sustainable wellbeing is within reach if only we look at other models. But the reality is that no country on the planet has ever achieved a green traffic light on all three components. Whilst Costa Rica has ranked highest in the last three editions, its ecological footprint has always been a little larger than what is sustainable. That is why the first report was called the (un)Happy Planet Index. This critical tone might

---

27 Marks et al., "The (Un)Happy Planet Index."

28 Saamah Abdallah, Sam Thompson, and Nic Marks, "Estimating Worldwide Life Satisfaction," *Ecological Economics* 65, no. 1 (2008): 35–47.

29 Christian Bjørnskov, "How Comparable Are the Gallup World Poll Life Satisfaction Data?," *Journal of Happiness Studies* 11, no. 1 (2010): 41–60.

have been appropriate in 2006, when the mainstream narrative was so positive. But with the financial crisis of 2008, growing nationalism, and the Covid-19 pandemic, it is perhaps not the most effective communication tool.

The Future

In some ways, the HPI has already achieved its objectives. Subjective wellbeing data is now regularly collected by official bodies in most wealthy countries, and several others (e.g., New Zealand, Italy, Wales and Colombia, to name a few) have integrated alternative indicators into policy-making processes. However, whilst more people may be aware of environmental limits than 15 years ago, and dealing with climate change is definitely higher up political agendas,[30] there is still some way to go to promote the idea that good lives do not need cost the Earth. Indeed the climate agenda now is often dominated by very scary and demotivating predictions of the catastrophes to come, with very little by way of a positive image of how our lives could still be better if we transform our lifestyles now.

None of the people who created the HPI are still at the New Economics Foundation. However, working with the Wellbeing Economy Alliance, we published an update in October 2021, which allowed us to track change over time in the 15 years leading up to the Covid-19 pandemic.[31] The HPI again revealed interesting patterns. Whilst some countries and regions, including Africa and Western Europe, have enjoyed gains in HPI over the years, others, such as India, have seen big falls. Meanwhile the multiple impacts of the pandemic have led to different outcomes in different regions: the huge death rate in Brazil lead to a decline in HPI, whereas in much of Western Europe and North America the massive decrease in ecological footprint surprisingly led to scores rising. The pandemic has shaken up people's values and demonstrated that progress cannot be assumed to be linear. We believe that it is a good time to highlight that there is an alternative view of how our economies should develop.

---

30 Cary Funk et al., "Science and Scientists Held in High Esteem Across Global Publics," *Pew Research Centre*, September 29, 2020, accessed May 19, 2022, https://www.pewresearch.org/science/2020/09/29/science-and-scientists-held-in-high-esteem-across-global-publics/.
31 "Happy Planet Index," accessed June 28, 2022, https://happyplanetindex.org/.

Nick Cullather

Commentary: The New Epicureans

It may be up to each generation to invent a happiness index of its own. Since the turn of the twentieth century, at irregular intervals and for different reasons, social scientists and government planners have tried to design a yardstick of human satisfaction. The ordeals of achieving an agreed-upon standard are as numerous as its practical advantages. As a guide for planning and a point of comparison, it would establish the state as the arbiter and trustee of the personal wellbeing of all citizens, something monarchies, dictatorships, and democracies have always claimed to be.

It would also provide a counterpoint to measures of economic growth, which since the 1930s have been a surrogate gauge of governmental performance. In a 1968 speech, Robert Kennedy cataloged the dissatisfactions of using GNP (gross national product) or GDP (gross domestic product) as a barometer of social health. These aggregates of income, trade, goods, and services included "air pollution and cigarettes advertising, and ambulances to clear our highways of carnage [...] special locks for our doors and the jails for the people who break them [...] nuclear warheads and armored cars for the police to fight the riots in our cities."[1] He might have added the things it did not count: the labor of childrearing and caring for family members, the cost of racial exclusion, and the unequal distribution of the benefits of growth.

Global inequality and climate change add fresh urgency to the search for an alternate calculus, and an emerging field of "happiness studies" furnishes ingredients for new statistical models. Each of the authors in this section were involved directly or indirectly in developing a happiness index. Saamah Abdallah co-authored with Nic Marks and Nicola Steuer a Happy Planet Index (HPI). Karma Ura invented and maintains Bhutan's Gross National Happiness index (GNI). German economist and environmental reformer Hans Diefenbacher is one of the originators of Germany's National Welfare Index (NWI), and Herman Daly, an American economist in the tradition of Henry George, conceived the Index of Sustainable Economic Welfare (ISEW), which inspired both the HPI and the NWI, as well as ISEW's successor, the Genuine Progress Indicator (GPI).

While they are in dialogue with one another, they disregard (whether by accident or design it is hard to tell) the long history of happiness indexing. Going

---

1 Stephen J. Macekura, *The Mismeasure of Progress: Economic Growth and its Critics* (Chicago: University of Chicago Press, 2020), 84.

https://doi.org/10.1515/9783110730234-015

back a full century, social scientists, corporations, and governments have tried to produce a comprehensive indicator of well-being, not always but regularly and often referred to as a Happiness Index. Booms in happiness indexing run counter-cyclically to the global economy, that is, both innovation and interest in alternative measures of life quality tend to peak at times of global uncertainty and financial collapse. The period just after World War One, the Depression years of the 1930s, the immediate postwar period of the late 1940s, the early 1970s, and the 1990s each produced a distinct outpouring of new happiness indexes. The practice fell into disuse in the go-go 1950s and 1960s only to pick up again in the 1970s as gas lines formed and the Bretton Woods system crumbled. It is therefore unsurprising that the period since the 2008 financial crisis, years overshadowed by climate change and pandemic, have been a golden age for happiness indexers.

Kennedy explained the need for a new measure as a reaction against the problems of national incomes accounting, but a happiness index was invented a couple of centuries before Simon Kuznets first calculated GNP. In 1776, as Britain's North American empire disintegrated, Jeremy Bentham outlined a "felicific calculus" as a simple guide for government.[2] The aspiration for a standard metric of life quality arises from a more fundamental questioning of the growth narrative coupled with doubt about the capacity of democracy or liberal institutions to apportion resources fairly and efficiently. The happiness index represents an ideal of governmental and economic rationality, replacing tough political choices and feuding economic ideologies with an antiseptic, technical procedure.

The advantages of such a system are many. Voters would have a neutral gauge by which to assess the achievements of politicians and programs, independent of party or personality. For banks and corporations, an index would provide a steady set of targets without the capriciousness of markets or stock prices. There is no shortage of reasons for governments, scientists, and businesses to return, again and again, to this project; the problem appears to lie, not in making an index, but rather making one that lasts.

Constructing a composite index requires one to decide, first, what ingredients – housing, job satisfaction, health, friendships, food, absence of warfare, personal freedoms, etc. – constitute a fulfilling life, and then second, to establish ratios by which these measurable ingredients may be weighted against one another. Do a few square meters of floor space make up for a loss of 500 calories a

2 Mitchell C. Wesley, "Bentham's Felicific Calculus," *Political Science Quarterly* 33, no. 2 (1918): 161–183.

day in diet? It is through these choices, necessary to constructing a complex model, that the biases and ideologies infecting the larger society come into the index itself. It may have been crucial to the acceptance of Bhutan's Index that Ura chose not to introduce weights, but as he acknowledges, the index is incomplete without them.

The exercise is also prone to the logical fallacy of reification, the assumption that because an abstraction has a name that it is therefore a concrete object that may be measured and compared. The European Social Survey, for instance, measures such things as vitality, "positive emotion," and resilience.[3] Even seemingly parallel units, years of education for example, hide unknowable differences. Reasonable people may disagree about what to measure and how to count it, but whatever is decided will represent a compromise that is unique to its time and place. Consequently, happiness indexes have a short shelf-life. They present a fading statistical snapshot, not of the material conditions or physical comforts of the populace, but of the fears and yearnings of a moment.

The indicators discussed here provide a case in point. None measure "happiness" as a conscious state. Rather, they aggregate measures that the modeler views as essential to happiness. In the case of the HPI and the ISEW, it is a balance between "goods," such as life expectancy and income distribution, and sustainability "bads," such as energy depletion and climate effects. The NWI, according to the *Umweltbundesamt*, "is the sum of 20 monetarily assessed components, the most important of which is real consumption expenditure weighted by the distribution of income."[4] It has a German, middle-class feel, balancing moderate consumption against debit variables such as crime and traffic accidents.[5] Bhutan's indexable values include the preservation of Mahayana Buddhism. Variables and the weights change over time and from country to country. And individual economists love to mix in new formulas based on the newest techniques.[6] The result is a Babel of numbers. To try to juxtapose them would be akin to comparing cantatas and K-Pop.

---

3 Eric Harrison and Saamah Abdallah, *Looking Through the Wellbeing Kaleidescope: Results from the European Social Survey* (London: New Economics Foundation, 2016), 4.

4 Umweltbundesamt, "Indicator: National Welfare Index," accessed May 25, 2022, https://www.umweltbundesamt.de/en/data/environmental-indicators/indicator-national-welfare-index#at-a-glance.

5 "Beyond GDP: Economists Search for New Definition of Well-Being," *Der Spiegel*, September 22, 2009, 11.

6 Tadhg O'Mahony, Paula Escardó-Serra, and Javier Dufour, "Revisiting ISEW Valuation Approaches: The Case of Spain Including the Costs of Energy Depletion and of Climate Change," *Ecological Economics* 144 (2018): 292–303.

The modern happiness index (HI) had its origins, as so many twentieth-century ideas did, in Vienna, where "the world was often coming to an end, usually to wine-garden songs."[7] From the 1920s until they were driven into exile or murdered, the "Vienna Circle" of logical positivist philosophers would meet at Café Landtmann, a few tables away from Freud, to invent rules for applying reason to social problems. A vocal member of the group was Otto Neurath, best known today for devising the style of "infographics" that adorn newspapers and magazines, a device for introducing complex economic concepts to illiterate audiences. In the "Red Vienna" period from 1918 to 1934, Neurath was both advocate and overseer of comprehensive systems of technocratic planning, but his first foray into applied social science was an attempt to develop an alternative to money.

The abolition of money had been a staple of utopian fiction since Thomas More, but in 1918 Lenin's Soviet regime in Russia and the short-lived Bavarian Soviet Republic began to discuss how it might be achieved in practice. Neurath saw this as a moment of possibility. In an address in Munich in April 1919, he assured ad hoc governing councils that "happiness as the effect of social institutions may be treated quite scientifically. Precisely the utopias of the coming years should help to promote the development of a comprehensive doctrine of happiness." On the streets outside Red Army units battled with counterrevolutionaries, milk and flour had vanished from markets, and the city was locked in a general strike.[8] Neurath, however, was buoyant. Settling on the correct measuring formulas would be no more difficult than making budgetary choices, and it would lead to the introduction of new kinds of social statistics. Economic liberalism was a kind of quantitative censorship, limiting the number and variety of statistics considered valid. Frederick Winslow Taylor's influential time-and-motion studies, for instance, only measured exertions that benefited the employer. A reverse Taylorization could ensure maximization of pleasure. A truly socialist state agenda would open the way for a Central Economic Office to conduct surveys of all aspects of the public's psychological and physical *Lebensstimmung*, or quality of life.[9]

---

7 Frederic Morton, *A Nervous Splendor: Vienna 1888–1889* (New York: Penguin, 1979), 60.

8 Allan Mitchell, *Revolution in Bavaria, 1918–1919* (Princeton: Princeton University Press, 1965), 323–324.

9 Otto Neurath, "Through War Economy to Economy in Kind," in *Empiricism and Sociology*, ed. Marie Neurath and Robert Cohen (Dordrecht: Reidel, 1973), 123–157; Otto Neurath, "Inventory of the Standard of Living," in Otto Neurath, *Economic Writings: Selections 1904–1945*, ed. Thomas E. Uebel and Robert S. Cohen (Dordrecht: Springer, 2004), 513–526, 515.

Within days of this presentation, *Freikorps* surrounded Munich and the leaders of the Bavarian Soviet surrendered and went to the gallows, but Neurath returned to Vienna and continued pushing for a data-driven "modern social Epicureanism."[10] He was not alone in seeking statistical tools to crack open the mysteries of economy and society. In 1920, the International Labour Office (ILO) standardized techniques for measuring standard of living based on diet, housing, wages, and prices.[11] But Neurath was more optimistic about how much a statistician could learn about the true state of things. Over the next ten years, he carried on a debate with Ludwig von Mises and Friedrich von Hayek, forebearers of neoliberalism, about how much of the economy could be made visible. For Mises and Hayek the number and variety of human interactions would forever defy categorization. The state should not try to manage what it could not see.[12] Neurath agreed that calculations based on money alone were incomplete, but that rational panning was still possible. The solution to the inadequacy of statistics was more and better statistics.[13]

This faith in the quantitative arts is what unites happiness indexers across the decades. When Diefenbacher dismisses the "negative attitude" of ministry officials who doubt that environmental costs could be systematically measured, we see again through the eyes of Otto Neurath. Were Neurath alive, he might gently chastise Daly for setting such a low bar for ISEW. The end goal of the Epicurean statistician is not to improve upon bourgeois indicators (even Mises and Hayek would find GDP a weak read), but to approach "complete knowledge."[14] Planning will become scientific and rational once the gap between reality and quantitative representation is finally narrowed. Anything short of that was what the Vienna Circle would call metaphysics.

Following its countercyclical pattern, the Depression revived the global appetite for information on social wellness. One of Herbert Hoover's first actions following the stock market crash was to establish a national commission to compile "a body of systematic facts about social problems, hitherto inaccessible, that will be of fundamental and permanent value."[15] The Mitchell survey studied vi-

---

10 Otto Neurath, "Economic Plan and Calculation in Kind: On the Socialist Order of Life and the Human Beings of the Future," in Neurath, *Economic Writings*, 405–465, 415.

11 Macekura, *The Mismeasure of Progress*, 21.

12 Quinn Slobodian, *Globalists: The End of Empire and the Birth of Neoliberalism* (Cambridge: Harvard, 2018), 86.

13 Thomas E. Uebel, "Introduction: Neurath's Economics in Critical Context," in Neurath, *Economic Writings*, 1–108, 8.

14 Neurath, "Economic Plan and Calculation in Kind," 417.

15 "Survey of Social Problems Planned," *Baltimore Sun*, December 20, 1929, 6.

tality, family life, leisure activities, changes in work, mortality, and a list of other variables in which unemployment was conspicuously absent. Wesley Clair Mitchell, an economist at Columbia, was aided by his student, Simon Kuznets, in making these massive compendia. The Rockefeller Foundation funded it, along with the influential Middletown studies designed by Helen and Robert Lynd. In 1937, Britain launched its ambitious Mass Observation of everyday life, with thousands of volunteers answering questionnaires and keeping diaries. Launched with reformist goals, these data-gathering initiatives were soon converted into marketing tools. Middletown became a manual for advertisers. In the United States, the leading happiness researcher was Dr. Henry C. Link, who pioneered sampling techniques at the Gallup organization and went on to advise Lord & Taylor and Gimbel's department stores before joining a business consultancy, the Psychological Corporation, as head of marketing and social research.[16] Constructed with growing sophistication, happiness surveys were used to manage wage expectations, develop campaigns, and sell the public on the doctrine of free enterprise.[17]

"At each point in the history of happiness measurement, from the Enlightenment through the present, hopes for a different social and economic world flicker into view," William Davies observes. "This emancipatory spirit flips swiftly into a conservative one, once the same body of evidence is used as a basis to judge the behavior and mentality of people, rather than the structure of power."[18] This pattern continued into the 1990s, which began with a bold and surprisingly durable experiment in life-quality measurement, the United Nations Human Development Index. Designed by Mahbub ul Haq, a director of Pakistan's Plan Commission and a high-ranking World Bank official who pushed the institution toward a poverty-reduction agenda, the HDI was the product of a reformist group within the development community that included OXFAM and economics Nobelist Amartya Sen. The formula for "human development" was expressly intended to challenge the dominant neoliberal paradigm as well as what the group saw as half-measures – such as sustainable development and social capital – that represented a compromise between market fundamentalism and human needs.

The HDI of 1990 was a composite index that included just three indicators, infant mortality, purchasing power, and literacy, equally-weighted to make a sin-

16 William Allen White, "The Way to Happiness," *New York Herald Tribune*, March 14, 1937, SM3.

17 Alfred R. Zipser, Jr., "Wants Public Sold on Free Enterprise," *New York Times*, October 2, 1946, 43.

18 William Davies, *The Happiness Industry* (London: Verso, 2015), 251.

gle number. It was not intended to be more sophisticated than GDP. Instead, Haq felt, it needed to be "equally vulgar" to "displace GDP per capita from its preeminence."[19] The press still refers to the HDI as a happiness index, with a typically acerbic headline in *The Economist* proclaiming "Joy to the World," but Sen insisted that what it really measured was capability, a term more precisely focused on substantive opportunities and capacity to engage in processes.[20] Human capabilities measured the power and the freedom to exercise human rights.

The UN's Human Development Reports launched a movement and provided the quantitative underpinning for the Millennium Development Goals and the Sustainable Development Goals. It generated real international pressure to raise (or to appear to raise) levels of basic education, nutrition, and health.[21] Inevitably, the formula began to be tinkered with as constituents questioned the weighting and added indicators such as per capita CO2 emissions, a gender inequality index, and indexes for sanitation and housing. Changes in formula made the index less useful for tracking progress over time, but it also contained the potential to mask the familiar, historical conservative shift. The UN Development Program adapted its rhetoric, defining human development almost entirely in terms of education and health, and Sen worried about the "accommodating gestures coming out of the citadels of economic growth," but Desmond McNeill of the University Oslo finds that the HDI has been surprisingly resilient over the years in retaining its critical edge.[22]

This is a harder claim to make for national indexes. Since 2011, when David Cameron's Tory government announced a happiness index for Britain, China and Germany have each published national indexes. Created by government and for government, none of these have sounded a strong note of dissent against economic orthodoxy. Among these, Bhutan's Gross National Happiness Index stands out as both the oldest (c. 1972) and the most celebrated. In 2011, the UN General Assembly passed a resolution urging all nations to follow Bhutan's example.[23] A key feature is its purportedly direct impact on policy. For the first

---

19 Mary S. Morgan and Maria Bach, "Measuring Development from the UN's Perspective," *History of Political Economy* 50 (2018): 193–210, 199.

20 "Joy to the World," *The Economist*, December 20, 2018, 112; Amartya Sen, "Human Rights and Capabilities," *Journal of Human Development* 6, no. 2 (2005): 151–166.

21 Dhanmanjiri Sathe, "The 'Corruption' of the Human Development Index," *Economic and Political Weekly* 47, no. 17 (2012): 18–20.

22 Desmond McNeill, "Human Development: The Power of the Idea," *Journal of Human Development* 8, no. 1 (2007): 5–22.

23 United Nations, General Assembly, "Res. 65/309. Happiness: Towards a Holistic Approach to Development," July 19, 2011.

three decades, according to Ura, the monarchy "framed policies that were broadly and intuitively consistent with it." The happiness policy was in force in 1990, during the regime's violent suppression of pro-democracy demonstrations and the equally violent expulsion of 135,000 ethnic minorities.[24] After 2008, when the king declared Bhutan a democracy and ordered an election, happiness became the principal feature in Bhutan's international branding. A few critics, according to *The Economist*, grumbled that "GNH provides ideological cover for repressive and racist policies," but that did not prevent Thimphu from becoming a regular pilgrimage site for happiness researchers.[25]

The relationship between national and international happiness indexes is difficult to pin down, but Bhutan demonstrates that having a national happiness policy does not guarantee a high place in international happiness rankings. Bhutan stands at fifty-sixth among 140 countries in the Happy Planet Index and one hundred and twenty-ninth of 189 in the HDI. Parsing the many global indexes is also a bewildering task. There are a few constants – Norway invariably ranks near the top – but on the Happy Planet Index Costa Rica and Mexico are each among the top scorers, the most efficient, according to Saamah Abdallah, "at 'converting' environmental resources into human wellbeing." They stand at the top of other charts too. In OECD data, Costa Rica and Mexico rank first and third respectively in income inequality; one and ten in the ratio of people living below the poverty line. Mexico ranks number one in housing overcrowding.[26] The HDI places both countries squarely in the middle tier. Luxembourg lingers just above Chad at the bottom of the HPI despite landing in the top 25 in the HDI.[27] It is hard to know what the Grand Duke ought to make of that.

The contradiction and churn endemic to the indexing process may actually be its greatest contribution. The Neurathian impulse to scrap the current social indicators and devise new formulas may foster statistical innovation as well as a sincere questioning of how government performance should be assessed. In this dialectic, the HDI is the new baseline but it could use improvement. Like Bhutan's and many of the current batch of HIs, it fails to measure personal freedoms or power relations on the assumption that capabilities flow from physical and environmental conditions. It is important to remember, however, that simply im-

24 "Bloodshed in Bhutan," *Times of India*, September 27, 1990, 12; "Bhutan Army Guns Down 327 People," *Times of India*, September 28, 1990, 13.

25 "The Pursuit of Happiness," *The Economist*, December 18, 2004, 117–121.

26 OECD ed., *Income inequality (indicator)*, 2021, accessed September 2, 2021, https://data.oecd.org/inequality/income-inequality.htm.

27 Happy Planet Index, accessed September 2, 2021, http://happyplanetindex.org; Human Development Data Centre, accessed September 4, 2021, http://hdr.undp.org/en/data.

proving an index brings it no closer to acceptance. After all, the most influential barometers in any field – think of the calorie, Dow Jones average, Neilsen ratings, SAT scores, etc. – endure precisely because they are gross oversimplifications. Were this to happen to happiness, it might be a loss. Some things are too important to become statistics.

List of contributors

Saamah Abdallah is a freelance researcher on wellbeing and an Associate at the Centre for Thriving Places. He is currently completing a PhD in Communication Science at the University of Erfurt.

Iris Borowy is Distinguished Professor of History at Shanghai University.

Frederick Cooper is Professor Emeritus of History at New York University.

Nick Cullather is Professor of History and International Studies at Indiana University.

Herman Daly is Emeritus Professor at the University of Maryland School of Public Policy, formerly Senior Economist in the Environmental Department of the World Bank, and prior to that Alumni Professor of Economics at Louisiana State University.

Hans Diefenbacher is Associate Professor of Economics at the Alfred-Weber-Institute of the University of Heidelberg.

Rohan D'Souza is Professor at the Graduate School of Asian and African Area Studies, Kyoto University.

Nicholas Ferns is Research Fellow in the School of Philosophical, Historical and International Studies at Monash University.

Dena Freeman is Distinguished Professor of Global Studies at the College of Liberal Arts of Shanghai University.

Eric Helleiner is Professor and University Research Chair in the Department of Political Science and Balsillie School of International Affairs at the University of Waterloo.

Artemy M. Kalinovsky is Professor of Russian, Soviet, and Post-Soviet Studies at the Departments of History and Political Science at Temple University.

Verena Kröss holds a PhD in History from Jacobs University Bremen and works as a policy advisor on International Finances, Business, and Human Rights at the NGO World Economy, Ecology and Development (WEED e.V.) in Berlin.

Jack Loveridge is Research Associate at the Center for Research on Globalization, Peace, and Democratic Governance (GLODEM) at Koç University.

Stephen Macekura is Associate Professor of International Studies in the Hamilton-Lugar School of Global and International Studies of Indiana University.

https://doi.org/10.1515/9783110730234-016

Ruth Rempel is Associate Professor of International Development Studies at Menno Simons College, a college of Canadian Mennonite University.

Corinna R. Unger is Professor of Global and Colonial History (19th and 20th centuries) at the Department of History of the European University Institute.

Karma Ura is Head of Royal Government of Bhutan's policy think tank, The Centre of Bhutan & GNH Studies.

Margherita Zanasi is Professor of Chinese History in the Department of History of Louisiana State University.

www.ingramcontent.com/pod-product-compliance
Ingram Content Group UK Ltd.
Pitfield, Milton Keynes, MK11 3LW, UK
UKHW022226051026
15624UKWH00002B/378

9 783110 735161